Satur...
an...
Preside...

Saturday Night Live and the 1976 Presidential Election

A New Voice Enters Campaign Politics

WILLIAM T. HORNER *and*
M. HEATHER CARVER

McFarland & Company, Inc., Publishers
Jefferson, North Carolina

ISBN (print) 978-1-4766-7184-0
ISBN (ebook) 978-1-4766-3059-5

LIBRARY OF CONGRESS CATALOGUING DATA ARE AVAILABLE

BRITISH LIBRARY CATALOGUING DATA ARE AVAILABLE

Front cover: (center) Chevy Chase in the 1970s (Photofest);
(bottom) photograph of the White House by J. T. Sorrell (iStock)

Manufactured in the United States of America

*McFarland & Company, Inc., Publishers
Box 611, Jefferson, North Carolina 28640
www.mcfarlandpub.com*

For our daughters, Tricia and Ellie, who give meaning
and purpose to everything else.
We love you, ladies.

To the late, great Tom Davis, whose kind
response to a letter and time generously given
to interviews made this book possible.

Acknowledgments

We would like to thank the following individuals for their willingness to be interviewed: Tom Davis, Ron Nessen, Lorne Michaels, Kenan Thompson, Jerry Rafshoon, Pat Caddell, Bob Orben, Gary Weis, Julian Bond, Garrett Morris, Dan Aykroyd, and President Jimmy Carter.

We also thank Jackson County, Missouri, legislator Scott Burnett, who helped us make inroads with people in the Carter Administration. Without his early assistance, this project might not have gotten off the ground.

We extend special gratitude to Gary Kass, whose encouragement and editorial prowess helped shape this into a book people want to read.

Thanks to Mike Hendricks for his invaluable assistance in helping us with the indexing of this book.

Finally, we would like to acknowledge the University of Missouri, where we have researched and taught for the last seventeen years. It is a privilege to work at Mizzou.

Table of Contents

Preface: "I'm Gerald Ford and You're Not."

*Saturday Night must stay a live show. I've fought for that,
to keep it theater, a pure communication between
writers, players, and audience.*—Lorne Michaels[1]

When *NBC's Saturday Night* premiered in 1975, the United States was led by Gerald R. Ford, who had not been elected president.[2] Nor had he been elected vice president. He was appointed to the vice presidency and assumed the presidency when Richard Nixon was forced to resign from office in shame. As *Saturday Night* (which soon became *Saturday Night Live* and, to many, *SNL*), the show's creative team had two presidents to skewer, one because he was a crook, the other because maybe, just maybe, he wasn't smart enough to be president. And then it was time for a presidential election and the team at *SNL* had yet another politician to target, an unknown southern governor who seemed like maybe, just maybe, he was too good to be true. All of this in the first season of a television show that has now been on for over forty seasons. *SNL* has never been all about politics, but it has always commented on the politics of the day.

As Day and Thompson assert, "Michaels conceptualized *SNL* as revolutionary not because it would break new satiric ground but because of this 'pure communication'—the presentation of authentic selves, unfiltered and uncensored."[3] The fall of 1975 was ripe for a new twist on comedy with a collective audience looking for irreverent humor about society, pop culture, and politics. Thus, *SNL* was born. On Saturday nights that fall, viewers across the country got to tune in to live theater. The viewers were not in the studio audience, but they still shared a relationship with events unfolding there, as exciting as any improvisational theater experience: What would happen? How would the live drama play out?

In its premiere episode on October 11, 1975, George Carlin was the

1

guest host, Janis Ian and Billy Preston were the musical guests, and Gilda Radner, Laraine Newman, Jane Curtin, Garrett Morris, John Belushi, Chevy Chase, and the Canadian-born Dan Aykroyd comprised the original cast, the "Not Ready for Prime-Time Players." Lorne Michaels, one of the driving forces behind the creation of *Saturday Night*, a Canadian who has produced *SNL* for nearly all of its forty seasons, said of his vision for the show:

> My background was comedy, and the music was of equal importance to me because it was of enormous influence on my generation. So, I wanted short films, I wanted politics, and so it was the mix and then the proportions—I knew what all the ingredients were, I didn't quite have the recipe, you know, until somewhere in the middle of the first season, but I knew what the mix was, the things I was interested in. And I think that I, and the people I brought into it, we were all part of that time, and an hour before the show, we'd come from the audience, and I think we knew there were a lot of people like us out there.[4]

Remaining on the air for four decades and entertaining what is now three generations of Americans, *SNL* has been a mirror of the country's culture and politics, in both its sketches and its "Weekend Update" segment, which has always been one of the show's most popular segments. Michaels spoke of the anti-authoritarian voice of the show, particularly with regard to politics, when it began:

> I think it's a lot to do with me and I don't mean that in a kind of vain way, I mean it in the sense that when we began, when I started, it was, I am a product of the times I came of age in. The show came on the air right after Watergate. A couple of years earlier the Smothers Brothers had been thrown off television for challenging authority. But, you know, all the established order had been overturned. The war and Watergate and the recession of the early '70s, everything was being questioned. And distrust of authority was just in the air.

As Michaels notes, the anti-establishment focus of *SNL* was very much a foundational part of the show. From the ancient Greek plays to William Shakespeare's works to musicals on Broadway, theater has always had an inherent political nature, but it is not always overtly political. The very essence of comedy is the fool as a trickster. In its sketches, *SNL* has taken on the role of the trickster, the instigator, and the not-so-innocent bystander of the American political scene. Michaels continues,

> And I'm trying to be profound here—there is something really established in the American DNA in the American character, that is frozen in adolescence and whether it's Huck Finn or Holden Caulfield, it's the always questioning of authority, and a kind of defiance and standing up to it. And it's about the only time in your life that it sort of just comes with the territory—screenwriter Michael O'Donoghue used to say that sophomoric was a liberal code for funny—and, you know, if we

were being dismissed as adolescent, well, that was not a thing we took as a big thing. Because it's always the adolescent that stands up and says "The guy is lying," or "He's an asshole." So, I think that the show was born in that time and those are the things that I was interested in.[5]

One of *SNL*'s strengths is that its production team has remained attentive to creating American political theater. Through long sketch improvisational comedy, it parodies, satirizes, and makes fun of much more than politics and politicians. The fact that the show has never been dominated by any one particular type of comedy or subject explains why it has survived for more than seven hundred original episodes, countless specials, dozens of spin-off movies, and the successful post–*SNL* careers of many of its actors and writers. This diversity makes its occasional political impact more powerful. At times, *SNL* has not only portrayed political issues, but it has become just as much a part of the conversation from TV studio to the center stage of American politics, whether it is presidential campaigns, its treatment of the Clinton-Lewinsky scandal, or the actions of a wide array of political personalities, from Al Sharpton to Angela Merkel.

1

SNL, Live Theater and Politics

To change the course of human events.—Lorne Michaels, when asked what power and influence *SNL* has[1]

Lorne Michaels was joking—to a degree—when he said *SNL* alters the course of human events, however he clearly feels that the show plays a significant role in American politics. He spoke specifically of the elections of 2000 and 2008. He did not suggest that *SNL* actually changed the outcome of these elections, but he definitely felt the show was part of the national conversation about them. Michaels said:

> We are a comedy show. I don't take it that seriously. I think we're a voice in there and, in some instances, we're like a safety valve. You know, like you can blow off steam. But every now and then we have an effect. I think we affected the 2000 debates—the Gore-Bush debates. I think certainly in—with John McCain coming on the show himself the weekend before the election—Saturday before the Tuesday—and working with Tina [Fey] as Sarah Palin—that was a fairly huge thing.[2]

Michaels is continuing a paradigm of theater that can be traced back to the ancient Greeks—creating comedy to reflect the politics of the day and influence the future politics of civilization.

Sometimes, it is the way *SNL* has presented politicians that the American people remember more than the way the politicians presented themselves. During the 2000 presidential campaign, two indelible impressions were created by Darrell Hammond, as Al Gore, and by Will Ferrell, as George W. Bush, in three debate sketches that aired on *SNL* on consecutive weekends in October. In the first of these sketches, Gore glances around impatiently and speaks ponderously of putting Social Security and Medicare in a "lock box," while George Bush sums up an inarticulate performance by telling Jim Lehrer that the one word which best justifies his candidacy is "strategery."

Speaking of these two impressions, Michaels said, "You know, 'strate-gery' seems to sum up a view of George Bush that made him more human, I think. I think people knew people like George Bush. They didn't, so much, [know] people like Al Gore. He seems like the kid in class you didn't like so much."[3] These characterizations of political figures create meaning for audiences. Whether seen as positive or negative, the actors are creating a different perspective about how politicians think and behave. In theater, playwrights must create characters that the audience finds human—*SNL* tries to take the personas of political figures often seen as super-heroes and reveal ways that they are actually "human."

In 2008, *SNL*'s team dove head first into the election with its take on press favoritism toward Barack Obama; the decision to have a non–African American actor, Fred Armisen, play Obama; the indelible portrayal of Vice Presidential candidate Sarah Palin by Tina Fey; and the appearances of Obama, Hillary Clinton, Palin, and John McCain on the program at various times during the election cycle. The sketch, "A Special Message from Senator John McCain and Governor Sarah Palin," which aired on November 1, the Saturday before the election, featured both the senator and his wife, Cindy, side by side with the fake Sarah Palin, played by Tina Fey, hawking campaign souvenirs on QVC.

Asked whether he thought McCain's appearance on the show hurt or helped the senator's campaign, Michaels said, "I think at that point probably the election might have been lost, but I thought this is the only country in the world where that could have happened. So, I think that we are hopefully just part of the debate."[4] Michaels is simultaneously celebrating American patriotism and *SNL*'s presence as a site of political discussion.

SNL has been part of the debate since its very first season, when Gerald Ford, Jimmy Carter, and more than a dozen other candidates were battling it out for the White House. McCain appeared on *SNL* in 2008 with an actress parodying his running mate because over three decades earlier Ron Nessen and Gerald Ford made it possible to even conceive of politicians engaging in such behavior. As Doris Graber notes in *Laughing Matters*, social scientists will always disagree with each other if shows such as *SNL* have the power to affect election returns, but shows like *SNL* have an impact regardless of what quantitative analysis shows. Graber asks, "When *Saturday Night Live* actors parody presidential debates or inaugural addresses, do viewers gain fresh insights into the pivotal issues of the campaign or do they learn to view politics as little more than silly verbal sparring? The answer to these questions is 'all of the above.'"[5] Shows such as *SNL* influence the national conversation, they influence the behavior of politicians, and they create lasting impressions of those politicians. Unfortunately, the tools that political scientists might rely on to answer questions about the influence of a show like *SNL*, such as the National Election Survey or the General Social Survey, didn't ask questions about *SNL* and the campaign in 1976.

When *SNL* premiered, its first season and a half coincided with the presidential election of 1976, and politics was a frequent source of material. Ford certainly understood the power of political humor, as the frequent victim of it in a variety of venues, including the popular new show *SNL*. Ford said, "There are two ways to become an authority on humor. The first way is to be one of the perpetrators. You know them: comedians, satirists, cartoonists, and impersonators. The second way to gain such credentials is to be the victim of their merciless talents. As such a victim, I take a backseat to no one as far as humor is concerned."[6]

On *SNL*, Ford was portrayed by Chevy Chase as a bumbling, inarticulate, if lovable, fool. Michaels said, "I think Chevy's Gerald Ford was, you know, oddly benign."[7] But he acknowledged the lasting—and false—impression Chase's impression of Ford left, saying, "I think the bumbling really probably wasn't there, because Ford was an athlete, but because he tripped and that coincided with when we were first on the air, it just kind of stuck. You know, that he was well-intentioned, but kind of bumbling."[8] Carter, on the other hand, was portrayed as just a little slick, a know-it-all, a guy who was maybe earnest to a fault. But on balance, between two clearly imperfect candidates, would you rather be the guy who's a little slick, maybe a little sneaky, or the guy who's too dumb to be president?

Ford and his press secretary, Ron Nessen, tried, in the midst of a hard-fought primary campaign for the Republican presidential nomination, on one SNL episode in April of 1976, to take control of the jokes when Nessen appeared as the weekly guest host. The episode began the way nearly every single one has begun for forty years, with a "cold open," a sketch that airs before the credits. This episode started with an uncomfortable-looking President Ford in a taped segment, uttering the famous opening line:

> FORD: Live from New York, it's *Saturday Night*!
> (*The opening credits montage follows; President Ford reappears.*)
> FORD: Ladies and gentlemen, the press secretary to the president of the United States.

Following Ford's historic appearance, Nessen, a balding, middle-aged, former journalist, walked onstage to the polite applause of the audience and began his monologue: Nessen then told the audience that doing a show such as *SNL* wasn't very different from the press briefings he held each day at the White House, implying they were just as comedy-filled.

This was the first time a politician appeared on *SNL*, alongside the same comics who were taking comedic potshots at the administration. Thus began a tradition that reaches new heights every time American presidential election cycles begin anew, as politicians actively seek the show's attention and audience. Perhaps the move to become part of the drama through live television was an attempt to become more of a director than an actor, more a writer than an audience member, or, perhaps, an attempt to simply be relevant.

Decades later, during the 2008 campaign, *Washington Post* media and politics columnist Howard Kurtz remarked on *SNL*'s ability to shape people's impressions of politicians, writing, "Now we already knew that 'SNL' could shape public perceptions of a candidate.... Back in 2000, Darrell Hammond's take on a sighing, eye-rolling Al Gore stung so badly that Gore's own handlers made him watch a tape to see how he was coming off in the debates."[9] Eight years later, with the 2016 campaign, the *SNL* portrayal of Donald Trump took several turns from an applauded celebrity, to a buffoon, to a loathsome elected official. Trump and Hillary Clinton each appeared on *SNL* alongside cast members portraying them.

During the 2016 campaign, there were twelve contenders for the Republican nomination when the Iowa Caucus was held and the primary season began, including the eventual nominee, Donald Trump. On the Democratic side, there were three, including Hillary Clinton, Bernie Sanders, and Martin O'Malley. During the primaries, Hillary Clinton, Bernie Sanders, and Donald Trump all made appearances on *SNL*. And, in terms of parody, two candidates in particular got a great deal of *SNL*'s attention: Donald Trump and Bernie Sanders. Both were portrayed during most of the campaign by actors who were not regular members of the cast. Early in the season, the job of impersonating Donald Trump fell to cast member Taran Killam, but on December 19, former *SNL* regular Darrell Hammond, who left the show as a cast member and returned as the show's announcer after the death of Don Pardo, took over the job of impersonating Trump. The job of impersonating Bernie Sanders fell to a doppelgänger who was almost as uncanny in his ability to impersonate Sanders as Tina Fey was in mimicking Sarah Palin: writer/comedian Larry David. Also during the season, Jay Pharoah played Ben Carson as a strange, vaguely threatening man; Taran Killam switched from Trump to Ted Cruz when Hammond began impersonating Trump.

As ever, the real politicians were drawn to the show, wanting to be part of the fun it was having at their expense. The role of Hillary Clinton was played by series regular Kate McKinnon, and the two appeared together in a sketch which aired in the first episode of the season, on October 3, 2015, as they sat at a bar and talked about the campaign, with Bill Clinton, portrayed by Darrell Hammond, coming along at the end. But the major contribution of a real politician, though he had never run for office before, was made by Donald Trump, who hosted the show on November 7, 2015. In the same show, Larry David again appeared as Bernie Sanders, Darrell Hammond played Trump as the real Trump delivered the opening monologue.

The most remarkable moment of the evening came when Trump's daughter, Ivanka, appeared in a sketch with Trump entitled "White House 2018." In an Oval Office meeting, Trump discusses various of his campaign promises coming true: He is informed by "Secretary Omarosa," played by Sasheer Zamata, that Putin has gotten out of the Ukraine and that Trump made Putin cry; the war in Syria is over and ISIS has been wiped out; the president of Mexico, Enrique Pena Nieto, played by Beck Bennett (who regularly appears as Vladimir Putin), walks into the Oval Office to present Trump with a $20 billion check to pay for the border wall; he's told there's an emergency problem—American people are just sick of winning; his daughter, Ivanka, enters as the secretary of the interior, and announces a plan to cover the Washington Monument with gold mirrored glass. Trump finishes with an inspirational speech in which he says these accomplishments are just the beginning, that he told the writers to keep things modest, and that there is nowhere to go but up. His wife, "First Lady Melania," played by Cecily Strong, interrupts to tell people to dream of Melania as the first lady. While the sketch has several moments where the jokes fell flat with the audience, the sketch resonates differently after the election and Trump's inauguration as president, as much of what they tried to play for laughs (including the idea of Trump at the helm) is now taking place in the "real" world.

Much of what appears on *SNL* is a parody of what happened in the week prior to the broadcast, but this sketch from Trump's episode is far from the first time that things the *SNL* crew parodied on screen have come true. This began in the very first season of the show and has continued through to the most recent episodes.

Since Trump won the presidency, the show has become one of the most outspoken outlets for criticism of the administration. Even before Trump took the oath of office, the show had taken a decidedly different take on Trump than it had the previous year. Arguably, the forty-first season of *SNL,* in 2015–2016, was an aid to the Trump campaign. It certainly didn't hurt him. Since winning and taking office, *SNL* has offered some of its most scathing criticism of a U.S. president ever. This began by once again switching the actors who portray Trump, replacing Hammond with the seemingly perennial guest host, Alec Baldwin. The show also featured incendiary commentary about the relationship between Trump and Putin, played by Beck Bennett; Trump advisor Steve Bannon parodied as the Grim Reaper; a truly unsettling series of portrayals of Trump aide Kelly Anne Conway by Kate McKinnon; and a rollicking, angry portrayal of White House Press Secretary Sean Spicer by Melissa McCarthy. Unsubstantiated rumors suggested that President Trump was so troubled by the notion of a woman portraying a man in his administration he considered firing Spicer. But, again, it is far from the first time the show has shown favor to a candidate during the primary season, only to turn on him when he becomes president. This is particularly evident in some of the truly harsh commentary episodes of the show hosted by Julian Bond and Ralph Nader made about Jimmy Carter after Carter was treated with a friendly, though not completely uncritical, tone during the campaign.

From the beginning, *SNL* made itself relevant in both the news media's and the public's discussion of politics in a way that remains true in the 21st century. The program's first cast and group of writers created a legacy of commenting on current events, including politics, which endures today. Following a model established in 1975 and 1976, *SNL* continues to skewer politics and politicians and, on multiple occasions, has prompted politicians to appear on *SNL* to try to either be part of the theatrical scene or take advantage of jokes at their opponents' expense. Prior to the appearance of Ron Nessen and his boss on *SNL,* other politicians appeared on television comedy shows to try and bolster their images, or to show they were really just regular guys, or both. The most notable of these was Richard Nixon, who played the piano for Jack Paar and incredulously asked America, "Sock it to *me?*" on *Laugh-In.* But when Ford appeared on *SNL,* it ushered in a new era of politicians mixing it up with popular culture and established the new show as a cool and hip platform for politicians to try and prove how fun-loving, regular, and how in-on-the-joke they really are. Over the years, "doing" *SNL* has become something many politicians feel they have no choice but to do. And with figures such as Donald Trump, those appearances bolstered his profile while raising the show's ratings.

Since Nessen and Ford broke the ground, the list of political figures who have appeared on *SNL* includes: Ralph Nader, George McGovern,

Jesse Jackson, George Herbert Walker Bush, George W. Bush (who introduced a prime time all-politics episode), Al Gore, Hillary Clinton, Sarah Palin, Barack Obama, and Donald Trump. When politicians appear in person on *SNL*, they are doing so for a variety of reasons: promoting themselves; trying to reclaim control of their images; showing that they can take a joke, as Ford did; demonstrating that they are just regular people, as Gore has done frequently; or to confront the jokesters who have been making fun of them, as New York Governor David Paterson did. Politicians want a chance to "play" themselves because the *SNL* gang is more than willing to play them for laughs. Many political figures have been portrayed and parodied by the actors of *SNL* over the years, and politicians seem to believe that appearing themselves gives them a chance to take some control over how they are portrayed. But theater is not a genre that holds control as a vital tool. The very essence of theater is that while the plays, the sketches, the scenes are written, there is no accounting for what will happen in the *liveness* of the event. Even the meticulous Lorne Michaels's work on the show goes up before a live audience and control over the final product is simply impossible. Some politicians have been such staples for impersonation on *SNL* over its four decades that they have been portrayed by multiple cast members in succeeding generations of the cast.

Over the course of its forty-year run, *SNL* has become an institution parodying American culture *and* politics, offering observations about current events that often encapsulate the national "conversation." This was especially true when *SNL* was the only program of its kind, in a media environment of three broadcast networks and little else when it debuted in 1975, but it remains true today, when its sketches are immediately disseminated on the Internet in bite-sized, focused chunks. Not only did the show entertain and influence in the moment, but the Nixon, Ford, and Carter of *SNL* have endured; many people, young, middle-aged, and old, are familiar with Chase's impersonation of Ford and are able to recall Chase, as Ford, falling over a podium, or from the top a ladder as he did in a December 20, 1975, sketch, "Christmas Eve at the White House." As the audience watched in anticipation, Ford climbed a ladder, mumbling to himself about putting the last ornament on the tree. As he reached, struggling to hang the ornament, he loses his balance and crashes to the ground. Smiling, Chase looked into the camera and said the show's famous opening line: "Live from New York, it's *Saturday Night!*"

In the sketch, all of the elements of the picture of Ford that Chase wanted to draw were there: incompetence, clumsiness, and a sense that the country was being run by a man who was not effective enough to do something as mundane as topping a Christmas tree. The memory of Chase's impression of Ford isn't limited to the Baby Boomers who came of age watching the show in its infancy. It is Chase's Ford that today's college students know and respond to in lectures about politics and the media. Chase's characterization is the one that multiple generations of Americans think of when they are asked about Gerald Ford.

In the mid–1970s, Michaels wanted *SNL* to be a TV show for a generation which disclaimed TV, which meant that for many viewers, its take on the news might be the only news they saw. Today we see this continue on *SNL* and myriad other programs, such as *The Daily Show*; more heavily steeped in news format than theatrical form, these shows are very popular. Now at the Brookings Institution as journalist-in-residence, Nessen commented how Americans, especially younger Americans, learn about politics. He sees the roots of this change in the earlier *SNL* seasons. Nessen said that the lines between news and entertainment are blurred in today's society. In his work with the Pew Research Center for the People and the Press, surveys showed the lines getting even more blurred. For example, in one survey, Pew asked people where they got at least some of the information they used to decide who to vote for in the next election. Nessen spoke of the shows which blend news and entertainment, late-night talk shows and other similar programming, including *SNL*. He said of these shows: "Now my background is news and I was at NBC for 12 years and I like some of these programs but they're not news, they're entertainment. But this line is getting blurred. I think *Saturday Night Live* is a prime example of that."

Nessen asserted that the changes have concerned him for a long time. He related his experience as a board member for the Peabody Awards for outstanding radio and television, explaining that the former host of *The Daily Show*, Jon Stewart, won Peabody awards for election coverage in 2000 and 2004 because his "coverage" was better than any others the committee could find. He said, "The criterion for Peabody is excellence, it's the only criterion and we couldn't find anybody. We gave a Peabody to Jon Stewart both years, 2000 and 2004. I think a lot of people were troubled by it but I think that's a real concern and I think some of that started in that period of time."[10]

Nessen accurately cited the Pew data. The researchers at the Pew Research Center for the People and the Press have documented the influence on young people of the kind of infotainment Jon Stewart, Stephen Colbert, Samantha Bee and others have offered for several years. Bob

Orben, who was Ford's head speechwriter, made this observation about the viewing habits of today's youth: "Kids today don't read and they're getting a huge amount of their information from television, meaning Jon Stewart, Colbert, Maher, that sort of show, and they're getting, theoretically, their facts on what's going on from these shows because Stewart has to set up what he's talking about. It's not a good way to learn current events or to get a judgment on what's going on."[11] Of course, such televised (and now Internet-based) infotainment was also part of *SNL* and shows which preceded it, such as *The Smothers Brothers Comedy Hour* and *Rowan and Martin's Laugh-In*, along with many other predecessors from the 1950s and 1960s.

People who worked in entertainment television in the 1970s understood the impact their industry had on the American people. In 1971, the president of the CBS Broadcast Group, Richard Jencks, said, "I am not one who thinks the only virtuous thing we do is news. It is possible more minds have been moved by entertainment. What is the effect of the large numbers of black faces on television entertainments?" Jencks continued, "Should we do more news, and less entertainment? That's hard to say."[12] Jencks understood the impact of entertainment television on people's political perceptions, as did Nessen and Chase. Was Barack Obama helped in winning the presidency by "President David Palmer," portrayed by the African American actor Dennis Haysbert on the Fox show *24*, who broke the color barrier first? Such questions are relevant and important to ask and their answers need to be considered seriously by scholars of popular culture, media and politics. In 1975 and 1976, *SNL* helped forge a link between entertainment and politics.

Traditionally, live theater was defined in a very straightforward way, with performers and audiences being present in the same location together. Performance theorist Philip Auslander notes that "over time, we have come to use 'live' to describe performance situations that do not meet those basic conditions." He goes on to explain that with broadcasting technology, "We began to speak of 'live broadcasts.'" Auslander's theory, therefore, expands the "classic" liveness of physical co-presence to include the "temporal simultaneity of production and reception." An *SNL* performance offers both a live audience experiencing the comedic sketches in the moment and a television viewing audience experiencing the show as it occurs on Saturday night. The sense of connection to others that Auslander demonstrates occurs in various forms of a social and internet liveness which are all at work in *SNL*. For "the experience of liveness is not limited to specific performer-audience interactivities but to a sense of always being connected to other people, of continuous, technologically mediated co-presence with others known and unknown."[13]

Through television, the 1976 campaign brought drama even more into politics by delivering a "faster" message. Political cartoons, another means of lampooning politicians, couldn't reach as many audience members as quickly as an episode of *SNL*. The survival of *SNL* in today's market, saturated with instant media and image, is a testament to its strong foundation in theater. *SNL* can compete because it is different than other comedy forms. The combination of forces that has kept the show as long-form sketch comedy, regularly performed live on Saturday night, has made the show a forty-year part of the American political dialogue. *SNL*'s direct influence on perception of a candidate's ability to lead the country, resulting in a vote cast at the polls, is not measurable. But the various vectors of ways in which *SNL* has influenced how politics are discussed in households, at school, and at work, have undoubtedly been in play for the past four decades. In this book, we explore the beginnings of *SNL*'s political role with the 1976 campaign, through an in-depth examination of the show, based on interviews, archival material, scholarly and journalistic publications.

As Graber writes in *Laughing Matters*, several studies in the book "report the widely believed assertion that President Ford's clumsiness in *SNL* skits contributed to his loss of the 1976 election."[14] Why does this matter to the politics of today? Perhaps it is because, as Graber continues, "Satirical reports about Senator Hillary Clinton may diminish her chances for becoming a viable contender for the presidency."[15] To contextualize the cultural relevance of *SNL* and politics, we begin the examination of the first season of *SNL* and its impact on Campaign '76.

2

Ford's Image Problem
Began Before *SNL*

I clearly remember attending the 1975 Gridiron Dinner in Washington.... After an evening of hilarious and very pointed humor, I made these remarks: "I've learned how much of a lifesaving medicine a little laughter is for presidents. So if a fine evening of fun and friendship like this is good for presidents, it must also be good for America. The Gridiron Club nurtures this great national asset. And I'm very glad we can all poke gentle jokes at ourselves and one another just this way—singeing without really burning—and I hope it will always stay that way. Americans are a very diverse people, living together in many different styles and many different places. We are united more by the way we look at things than by the traditional ties of blood or belief or battles long forgotten. And when we are able to look at the brighter side of our troubles, and the lighter side of our struggles, and see the smile that lies just below the surface of our neighbor's face, I think we Americans are at our very best."

It wasn't always easy to believe completely in such grand remarks. Even that evening my words had been preceded by skits that included lines like: "Big Jerry's in the study hall walking up and down and chewing gum like crazy." Sitting there with a smile on your face while this sort of thing is being said isn't easy. But the truth is, you can't have humor only when you want it or how you want it.—Gerald Ford[1]

Network television's influence in 1976 is difficult for today's generation to fathom. As Geoffrey Baym notes, "The domination of broadcast network television has been fractured by twenty-four-hour cable, which itself has become complicated by digital, on-demand, and web-based content ... the number of media sources has increased infinitely, while the number of people paying attention to any one of them has shrunk correspondingly."[2]

To contextualize the scene before *SNL* made its entrance on the American stage, Ford's position in the 1976 presidential election bears examination. The 1976 presidential election began with a fierce battle for the

Republican nomination, the outcome of which was uncertain until the national convention in Kansas City, when the unelected incumbent President Gerald Ford finally wrested the nomination from his vigorous challenger, Ronald Reagan. On the Democratic side, the nomination was won by a previously little-known former governor of Georgia, Jimmy Carter, who beat out a field of more than a dozen candidates.

With a national campaign that really began in 1972, when he lobbied for the vice-presidential nomination on McGovern's ticket, Carter used a marginal victory (he got more votes than anyone else, but only had 28 percent of the delegates and finished second to "uncommitted") in the first-in-the-nation Iowa caucus to build momentum for a string of victories in primary elections and party caucuses. Carter's Iowa victory, covered by the news media as a major upset, allowed him to take the country by storm and fairly quickly gather enough delegates to win the nomination from a field that included such well-known candidates as Senator Henry "Scoop" Jackson, Representative Mo Udall, and unannounced, but everpresent figures like Senators Ted Kennedy and Hubert Humphrey.

Ford became president in the midst of America's greatest political crisis of the 20th century, Watergate—the investigation of election wrongdoing by President Richard Nixon and many members of his administration. Not only was Ford never elected president, he was never even elected vice president. Ford was only in position to become president in August of 1974 because he was appointed to the post by Nixon after Spiro Agnew was forced to resign from office in a tax evasion scandal. When Ford took over the presidency, outside of Washington, D.C., he was still largely unknown to all but the constituents of his Grand Rapids, Michigan, congressional district.

Still, Ford was welcomed to the White House by a nation that was happy to see Nixon go. At his inauguration, Ford uttered some of the most famous words in American politics in a speech written by his longtime advisor, Bob Hartmann.

> I believe that truth is the glue that holds government together, not only our government but civilization itself. That bond, though strained, is unbroken at home and abroad. My fellow Americans, our long national nightmare is over. Our Constitution works. Our great Republic is a government of laws and not of men.[3]

Ford disagreed with Hartmann about the national nightmare line, but the trusted advisor prevailed upon the new president to use it, convincing him that drawing such a stark line was necessary if the American people were to accept his leadership.[4] Bob Orben, who became Ford's head speechwriter, said that Hartmann "fought to keep it in because Ford was concerned about, well, he had been a friend of Nixon's for many years and thought it was too harsh and Hartmann, according to his book, said he would quit if it was taken out."[5] And, for a brief time Hartmann was proven right. The American public accepted Ford as a breath of fresh air, a welcome change from the dark days of Richard Nixon.

Ford was unassuming and friendly, qualities that often go a long way in the United States. As historian John Greene writes, "For the first month both press and public fawned over the new president. Entertained by such scenes as a pajama-clad president on the front stoop of his Alexandria, Virginia, home retrieving the morning newspaper and waving to the press, America took no time at all in bestowing upon Ford the ultimate accolade from Middle America: he was christened a regular guy."[6] Ford abandoned many of Nixon's more imperious and standoffish habits, making many changes that were well-received, including such small things as calling the family's quarters in the White House "the residence," instead of the "executive mansion."

The honeymoon was short, however. Ford's image problems began in earnest when, one month into his presidency, on Sunday, September 8, 1974, he pardoned Richard Nixon. Pardoning Nixon was something Ford earlier said he wouldn't do when he spoke about it hypothetically during his confirmation hearings in the Senate to become vice president. Pardoning Nixon was also something that Jerald terHorst said Ford would not do when terHorst gave his first press briefing as Ford's presidential press secretary. As historian Barry Werth describes, "terHorst told the press he'd just been advised that Nixon hadn't issued any pardons, to himself, or anyone else. A reporter followed up by asking if Ford would consider issuing a pardon himself. Ford had been asked the same question ten months earlier ... answering, 'I don't think the American people would stand for it.' Without checking, terHorst said Ford still opposed granting Nixon immunity from prosecution. 'He is not in favor of immunity?' the reporter asked again. 'I can assure you of that,' terHorst repeated."[7]

When Ford pardoned Nixon, Ford, terHorst, and others around Ford were seen by many in the press and the public as liars who were conspirators in Nixon's culture of corruption. One of the most damaging parts of the fallout was the resignation of terHorst. As *Time* reported, "Of course, nothing would be easy now, and the furor promises to be intense. terHorst's swift resignation was a symptom of what may lie ahead. Said terHorst: 'I couldn't in good conscience support the President's decision, even though I knew he took the action in good conscience.' Republicans who had delightedly looked forward to the deflation of Watergate as a major issue in November, now dejectedly faced the prospect of defending to the voters Ford's grant of a pardon."[8] Werth wrote, "Ever since Ford had introduced terHorst, his first appointee as president, to the press corps as 'one of yours,' the press, Mary McGrory wrote, 'has lost its head for Jerry Ford.' Now, nearly all reporters took terHorst's side in his protest against Ford's decision. 'I resigned,' he told them, 'because I just couldn't remain part of an act that I felt was ethically wrong.' For all Ford's discussion of God and conscience, the press concluded that terHorst's act of conscience trumped the president's."[9]

As terHorst wrote, "With one short message, he erased the national euphoria that had attended his first thirty days in the White House. The public mood was already black on Monday September 9.... Now the same doubts, skepticism, and ugly rumors that had paralyzed the country during the depths of the Watergate scandal had returned to haunt Ford."[10]

In an effort to put an end to speculation about his motives in pardoning Nixon, Ford did something no President since George Washington had done: he went to Capitol Hill and testified before a congressional committee, the Subcommittee on Criminal Justice of the Committee on the Judiciary. Facing the panel, he said that he had pardoned Nixon to change the national focus. He said, "I wanted to do all I could to shift our attentions from the pursuit of a fallen President to the pursuit of the urgent needs of a rising nation."[11]

Ford wrote in his autobiography, "I was convinced that my appearance had accomplished its objective. 'I hope that I have at least cleared the air,' I said, 'so that most Americans will understand what was done and why it was done. And again, I trust that all of us can get back to the job of trying to solve our problems both at home and abroad.'"[12] That desire, however, was overly optimistic, and lingering anger and suspicion about Watergate and the Nixon pardon dogged Ford throughout his presidency and tainted his election campaign in 1976.

The pardon came as a terrible shock to most Americans who had no warning it was coming. It also did terrible political damage to Ford and the Republican Party, which lost forty-eight seats in the House of Representatives and four seats in the Senate in the 1974 midterm elections, making it very difficult for Ford to be a policy leader as president. His presidential strategy became a strategy of "no," as he vetoed sixty-six bills in his two-and-a-half years as president. In the early stages of the 1976 campaign, Ford trailed Carter—or virtually any Democrat, for that matter—by twenty to thirty points in polls. Ford claimed early in his presidency that he had no intention of running for the office in 1976 and his pardon of Richard Nixon, despite his seemingly heartfelt claim that the pardon was a necessary part of national healing, contributed to Ford's extreme disadvantage when he eventually decided to seek the presidency in his own right.

Ford became a target of all kinds of criticism—sometimes couched in politics and sometimes couched in more personal terms—deserved and undeserved. Not the least of this criticism came couched in laughter from a new television show that hit the airwaves on October 11, 1975. SNL found an easy target in the thirty-eighth president. As a leader, Ford was virtually unknown to most of the nation one day, and the vice president of the United States the next. A few months later, Ford was the president and a month after that, he was the man who pardoned one of the most hated men in America at the time. His public image was almost always a problem for Ford.

Not only did Ford have to contend with suspicions about his motives for pardoning Nixon, he also had to deal with an almost immediate impression, voiced by his political opponents and exacerbated by the news media, by Johnny Carson on *The Tonight Show*, and by a few unfortunate stumbles captured on camera, that he was a nice, but clumsy and not particularly bright, fellow. It was an image that greatly frustrated Ford's supporters, aides, and closest advisors. One aide, speaking without attribution, said, "What can we do? Can we tell Johnny Carson to stop telling jokes about how dumb the President is? Can we call up Herblock [the *Washington Post*'s political cartoonist] and complain about his caricatures of the President?"[13]

As the previous quote about his Gridiron experience reveals, Ford was, according to many reports at the time, not affected by the jokes and questions in the same way as his aides. One aide, speaking off the record, said, "It just rolls off his back. He doesn't get uptight."[14] Another anonymous aide said, "He is aware of this perception, but he is much calmer about it than I am. He is a pro. He has been around a long time, and his attitude now is that he just has a job to do and he is going to do it."[15] A third official, also speaking off the record, said, "When I was upset, he just said to me: 'Just develop a thicker skin.' He has a very high level of confidence in himself. The reason for it is that he has been one of life's winners. He has proved his physical and mental worth to himself. He has proved his political worth—he has never been a political loser. He has been a successful father and husband. He has done well in whatever he has tried. I have never seen or sensed in him a moment of self-doubt. He is a problem-solver, not an ideologue."[16] However, as the reporter who compiled these quotes observed, "There is a consensus among political experts that if Mr. Ford is to be elected he must overcome a widening public suspicion that he is an amiable, vacillating, accident-prone bungler who is sitting in the Oval Office until a real President can be elected."[17]

From where did Americans get this "widening public suspicion" about Ford? They got it from the coverage he received in the media, both news and entertainment. Just as the print media of the Gilded Age shaped an inaccurate image of presidents like William McKinley, who was wrongly depicted as a puppet controlled by Mark Hanna, the increasingly visual news media of the mid–1970s affected the lens through which many Americans saw Gerald Ford.[18] The media are the way in which we interpret politics. The technology they use has changed over time, but the impact and influence of the news media has, if anything, only accelerated by new technology.

Gerald Ford and the Media—A Rough Ride

Ford's troubles with the media began long before *SNL* hit the airwaves. The show's lampooning of Ford commenced with its first episode, when Chevy Chase told several jokes about Ford on "Weekend Update" that played to a theme that would be emphasized on an almost weekly basis—that Ford was clumsy and not smart enough to be president, but it didn't invent that theme. While *SNL* certainly magnified and reinforced an image of Ford that made many Americans question whether he was competent enough to be president, that impression originated with the comments of other politicians and the reporting by journalists who covered the thirty-eighth president. Like other Americans, the cast and crew of *SNL* followed—and built on—a picture of Ford that was delivered to them by the news media. As a generation of young journalists who gained their first experience covering Vietnam, the Pentagon Papers, and Watergate turned their guns on Ford, he almost didn't stand a chance. When the almost always negative news coverage was compounded by a comedian doing a wildly popular impression of him on the nation's television sensation, *Saturday Night*, he *really* didn't stand a chance. If *SNL* had an impact on the election of 1976, it did so by building comedy from the bountiful raw material provided by journalists.

When *SNL*'s writers and actors came along and paid attention to what some of the journalists were saying and writing about Ford, they found ample material. One columnist, Nicholas von Hoffman of the *Washington Post*, once compared Ford to the ultimate 1970s fad, the Pet Rock, in a column. In his column, von Hoffman was critiquing Ford for what von Hoffman characterized as a deliberately deceptive stand on abortion—saying he supported an anti-abortion amendment while "allowing" Betty Ford to speak often of her support for abortion. In his second-to-last paragraph, von Hoffman wrote this scathing sentence: "Or, we can give the Fords the benefit of the doubt and say they have not meant to find a new way to fool the electorate. Then we're left with the same old Jerry, whom they have to dress in suits with a vest and pose next to the Great Seal of the Republic to remind people he's something more than America's pet rock."[19] Comparing Ford to the rock was a harsh condemnation. The comparison made its way right into a joke on *SNL's* "Weekend Update" by Jane Curtin: "*Washington Post* newsman Nicholas von Hoffman this week referred to President Ford as 'America's Pet Rock.' Ford responded by writing an angry note, wrapping it around his head, and throwing himself through von Hoffman's window."[20]

One of Ford's most outspoken critics was Richard Reeves, part of a new class of journalists-as-celebrities, ushered into existence by the enormous attention the *Washington Post* reporters Bob Woodward and Carl Bernstein received for their coverage of Watergate. Reeves made his reputation as a political correspondent for the *New York Times*, and then continued his career writing for magazines like *Esquire*, and *New York*, which is where much of his work critical of Gerald Ford was published. Reeves also authored a bestselling book about Ford, *A Ford, Not a Lincoln*, which was published in October of 1975, six months after Ford first voiced his intention to run for his own term as president and the same time *SNL* premiered.

The insult in the title of Reeves's book is obvious but, unfortunately for Ford, was made all the worse by the fact that they were his own words. When Ford took the oath of office to become Vice President on December 6, 1973, he said, "I am a Ford, not a Lincoln. My addresses will never be as eloquent as Mr. Lincoln's. But I will do my very best to equal his brevity and his plain speaking."[21] At the time, the speech, once again written by Hartmann, was well-received by many. It struck a self-deprecating, humble note that played well, especially given the arrogant, controversial and corrupt vice president he was replacing, Spiro Agnew. Reeves, however, felt differently. He said, "As best I can remember I considered the phrase trite, too clever by half."

While Ford was president, Reeves was one of his most outspoken critics. The issue of *New York* that contained the Reeves article "Jerry Ford and His Flying Circus: A Presidential Diary" had a clown with a WIN button (a much-maligned part of Ford's Whip Inflation Now campaign) on the front cover and a doctored photo of Ford disembarking from Air Force One wearing clown make-up and a Bozo wig. In almost every venue, Ford was forced to deal with both reporting and jokes about his averageness, his apparent clumsiness, and a lack of the level of intelligence we expect from our presidents.

Like many of his colleagues, Reeves was also tremendously critical of Ford's decision to pardon Richard Nixon. Reeves wrote, "On television that Sunday afternoon, September 8, Gerald Ford's taped image said he was granting the pardon 'to heal the wounds throughout the United States.' On those terms, the decision was a monumental misjudgment, an act of extraordinary political stupidity. What he had done was to reopen the wounds of Watergate; he had destroyed his own capability to reunite the nation. Mistrust bound us together again and the viciousness of the past two years resurfaced."[22]

Reeves was a major participant in the creation of two of the major media narratives about Ford. Reeves discussed the impact of the two narratives he offered—Ford as affable dope and Ford as somehow complicit in the Nixon scandal—acknowledging that he had helped popularize the image of Ford as dumb, while suggesting that the corruption narrative was far bigger than just his reporting. Reeves said, "I think the affable dope had something to do with our stuff, the Nixon pardon created far more of a firestorm than a single writer ever could."[23]

Sometimes journalists have the chance to reflect on their earlier work and reassess what they reported. According to Ford's head presidential speechwriter Bob Orben, Richard Reeves was one such journalist. Orben spoke of his anger with Reeves when Ford was in office. Orben said, "I was very unhappy about Richard Reeves. About seven, eight years ago there was a resurgence of remorse on the part of many people who have criticized Ford and I was at an event where Reeves did essentially a public apology of his criticism of Ford at the time. And this was true of many journalists, and with good reason. I won't go into a defense of Ford, but I think in time historians will realize what an important job Ford did at that point and how he was precisely the right person at the time."[24]

In the late 1990s, Reeves began to publicly rethink some of his most negative assessments of President Ford. In an interview on National Public Radio on the occasion of Ford's death in 2006, Reeves explained his change of heart:

I reassess it with great pain, but I was lucky enough, I thought, that Ford lived long enough that I could have the chance to think about it and also talk to him about it and apologize to him about it. The thing I focused on was that I had asked him why he pardoned Nixon and he said something to me then. He said America couldn't be governed if Nixon was being dragged from courtroom to courtroom, which he certainly would have been had he not been pardoned. And if that were the case, a president could not gain the attention of the country. I laughed at that. I think a lot of people did. Since then, having lived through say, O.J. Simpson and Monica Lewinsky and—I realized that Ford was right. And I mentioned that briefly once in a television interview. And the secretary to the editor of *American Heritage* gave me a call and said, 'Would you write a piece for us'? I wrote a piece which they put on their cover called "I'm Sorry, Mr. President." Ford wrote to me, called me and we communicated back and forth over the years. And he said in public well, he thought I had always been fair. I'm not sure I was."[25]

In his *American Heritage* essay, Reeves suggested that Ford's legacy was bigger than a collection of impressions or incidents. He wrote:

The day-to-day politics and stumbling fade in memory, as it should, though poor Jerry Ford has had to live with endless reruns of the comedian Chevy Chase imitating his clumsiness week after week on *Saturday Night Live.* Presidents are not paid by the hour. The job is essentially to react, and we pay for their judgment—a word Ford routinely mispronounced as "judge-a-ment." In retrospect Ford's judgment turned out to be better than his pronunciation. His big job, as defined in a transition plan written by a group of young Nixon staffers working without the knowledge or permission of either Nixon or Ford, was simply: "Restoration of the confidence and trust of the American people in their political leadership, institution and processes." On balance he did that, producing more trust than confidence—or at least he checked or slowed the slide toward today's foul public cynicism. To do so, Ford decided he had to pardon Nixon.... I mean that Ford understood (or guessed at, it doesn't matter which) something that I now realize was true. He told me something in 1974, or not too much later, that I can only paraphrase because I did not take it seriously enough, that it would have been impossible to govern the country if there had been open charges against Nixon..."[26]

Reeves, with perspective and maturity, came to see errors in his characterization of Ford. He also seemed to understand the damage his coverage (and that of his colleagues) did to Ford, along with the significant help of *SNL*.

In his autobiography, Ford wrote, "As President, I'd come to appreciate just how much the White House press corps is an institution in itself. Our professional relationship had been adversarial—which was fitting and proper—but on a personal level that relationship had been friendly and warm. This is not to say that I didn't get angry at some columnists—Tom Wicker and Anthony Lewis of the New York *Times*, Richard Reeves of *New York* magazine—when they sat in their ivory towers and wrote poppycock about me. They *did* upset me from time to time. My negativity about them, however, didn't carry over to the regulars on the White House beat."[27]

The combination of negative coverage by prominent journalists, like Reeves, and the rough treatment Ford received from popular entertainers made it difficult, if not impossible, for the president and his administration to project a positive image. Ford had an uphill climb trying to counteract his negative public image. Reeves said of the combination of negative press and comedians on Gerald Ford's reputation, "I think it had quite a bit of attention and influence. The pictures and *Saturday Night Live*, I'm sure, had more impact on the public. But I had influence on my peers."[28] And influence on his peers meant that he helped spur more negative reporting of Ford, and more negative reporting of Ford made its way onto *SNL*.

In response to a question about his motives for criticizing Ford as he did in 1975, Reeves said, "I did not hope to influence the election; I don't think that thought ever entered my mind. I was young and it was more about me than about him."[29] In his book *What the People Know*, Reeves argues that one of the problems with the news media in the 21st century is that reporters have become too much a part of the story. That kind of reporter involvement in their own stories—driven by reporters' desires to be involved in their own stories—arguably dates back to the fame achieved by Woodward and Bernstein. In *A Ford, Not a Lincoln*, Reeves wrote, "It is not that the press has no power; it has a great deal. But it is not an institution consciously and consistently dedicated to accumulating the exercise of control over other institutions or other people's lives. It is, in fact, diverse, cantankerous, rarely consistent and often unconscious about the power it has, not unlike a bunch of kids throwing firecrackers around the Metropolitan Museum of Art."[30]

However, what the press reports has an impact and if what they report is slanted, or inaccurate, it can have an enduring impact on the history that is written later. For many Americans, Ford will always be a bumbling, dull-witted, and possibly corrupt politician. In other words, they will see him as the man Reeves saw him as in 1975, not as the more honorable man Reeves came to see.

Like Reeves, Chevy Chase also came to feel bad about the way he had treated Gerald Ford and went on to become friends with Ford and his family. In 1976, in an interview in *Time,* Chase said derisively of the president, "Ford is so inept that the quickest laugh is the cheapest laugh, and the cheapest is the physical joke."[31] In a 1988 *Playboy* interview, Chase seemed a little remorseful about how he treated Ford, although he also refused to back away from it completely. He said, "I'll never forgive myself for some of the things I said about him on *Saturday Night Live*…. It was really just comedy, easy cheap-shot comedy. Having met the man and gotten to know him and his family somewhat, I regret some of it, because it's kind of embarrassing to see him now. He's very sweet, almost grandfatherly. On the other hand, I loved doing it and would probably do it again." As he aged, and after Ford died, Chase continued to express some regret over how he treated Ford, in large part because he got to know Ford as a person.[32] In a recent biography of Chase, written with his cooperation, it is reported that Chase felt sad and a little guilty about how he had treated Ford onscreen. He said, "I valued our friendship and the gentle and kind qualities both the President and Mrs. Ford had. And Jayni and I will always know how lucky we are to have known 'Jerry and Betty.'"[33] Although Ford felt that the negative treatment on *SNL* hurt him, he was gracious, even magnanimous, about it later, inviting Chase to appear at a conference on political humor at the Ford Presidential Library.

In his book *Humor and the Presidency*, Gerald Ford wrote of both the personal insult he felt regarding the jokes and his willingness to let that bitterness go as part of the territory of being President:

> I must be truthful and admit that the comic representations of me by Chevy Chase and others were sometimes hard for me and my family to take. Though it was essential to grin and bear it, it could and did hurt. If you'll forgive me some immodesty, I thought myself to be a fair athlete…. With that in mind, I would then watch Chevy Chase come crashing down a staircase as Jerry Ford. Now I ask you—was I being treated fairly? The question is clearly rhetorical. And the answer has nothing to do with fairness. The portrayal of me as an oafish ex-jock made for good copy. It was also funny. Maybe not to me, but as much as I might have disliked it, some people were laughing. At the very least, even if no one else was going to laugh, you can be sure the Democrats would![34]

Regardless of how bad Reeves or Chase may have felt in 2006 when Ford died, or how magnanimous Ford felt in his post-presidential years, the truth is that, in 1975, comedians across the nation told jokes about Ford similar to those Chase was telling, and news media outlets across the country expressed sentiments similar to those of Reeves, though not always with his ferocity.

An article published in *Time* was ostensibly about the image problem Ford suffered from—as a dull bumbler—and it contained some sentences that seemed sympathetic to the President's plight, such as: "Moreover, the President could conceivably begin to win sympathy for his inadvertent clumsiness, especially if the jokes grow too cruel, as they are on the verge of doing."[35] However, despite occasional lines that leaned toward sympathy, there was no effort in the article to dispute Ford's clumsiness, only to take advantage of the public's perception of it. This somewhat sympathetic sentence came only toward the end of a story that devoted its first several paragraphs to cheerfully burnishing Ford's poor image, beginning with: "Gerald Ford left Washington last week in his distinctive way. After a convivial evening at the White House, he wished guests 'a merry Christmas and a merry—uh—a happy New Year.' Then, as he was walking toward his helicopter, his legs got tangled up in his dogs' leashes. A day later, he was waiting on the ski-lift line at Vail, Colo., when one of the chairs swung around and almost knocked him over. Two days later, he took a spill on the slopes. Many skiers do the same, of course, but Ford's spill was duly recorded by cameras and splashed across TV screens and front pages."[36]

The article then devoted several paragraphs to reprinting the jokes of comedians from Las Vegas to *SNL*, and ended with this passage: "Nonetheless, the ridicule factor is fast becoming yet another worry for Ford's strategists. Jim Squires, Washington bureau chief for the *Chicago Tribune*, makes the point that Ford is in trouble because his physical and verbal blunders coincide with 'a series of political and policy blunders that leave no doubt they're all being pulled off by the same guy.' Frets an influential Republican politician on the fast-circulating Ford jokes: 'I think they are hurting him. No one wants an image as a buffoon, least of all a President.'"[37] It should be noted that rather than quoting the strategists purported to be worried about Ford, the passage includes a quote from a reporter and an unattributed quote from a "Republican politician." With reporting such as this, how could "Ford strategists" do anything *but* worry?

If Reeves was among the most mean-spirited critics of Ford, the president's reputation as friendly but not too bright was frequently emphasized by others in the press. Ford's second press secretary, Ron Nessen, wrote that reporters questioned Ford's intelligence, often to his face, from the beginning of his time in the White House. Nessen wrote:

> In Ford's first TV interview as president, Harry Reasoner of ABC told him a major public criticism was that "you have not got the magnitude of the grasp of the presidency.... Can you grow in this job, sir?" Ford patiently recited his educational background and his twenty-five years of experience in Congress.... In Ford's next TV interview, live on NBC, Tom Brokaw hemmed and hawed, stammered and stuttered, but finally came out with it: "I have a question that isn't easy to phrase, so I will just bore straight ahead with it. As you know, I'm certain, because I have been told that you have commented on this before, but it has been speculated on in print not only in Washington but elsewhere and it crops up in conversation from time to time in this town—the question of whether or not you are intellectually up to the job of being president of the United States." Ford, ever earnest, again reiterated his academic record and his knowledge accumulated in a quarter-century of public service.[38]

The effect of these kinds of questions was damaging to Ford, both personally and politically. As Nessen explained, "By asking the president repeatedly to defend his intelligence, reporters in effect forced Ford to declare again and again, 'Your president is no dummy.'"[39] And, of course, the more one has to deny something like being a dummy, the more people are likely to think of that person as a dummy.

Ron Nessen talked about one tactic Ford and his advisors tried to dispel the image of Ford as unintelligent. Nessen said:

> You know, one of the things we dealt with was, "Ford is too dumb to be President." Here's how we dealt with that: the first budget that he proposed, which I would guess would have been in the spring of '76, right? You know, federal budget even in those days was a couple of volumes like that ... and the tradition was you give out the budget, hold for release at noon tomorrow. You know, you've got to give people time to absorb it and figure out what's in it, and then you give them a briefing to answer their questions and explain the more difficult concepts. And traditionally, the head of the council and economic advisors or somebody like that has done this budget briefing, or the head of the budget office, OMB, Office of Management and Budget. Well, Ford did the briefing himself. It was a Saturday morning, and we went to the State Department auditorium and it was packed with reporters, and they asked him the most obscure questions about items in the budget, and he knew it. I mean, he had been on the budget committee, I guess in the House. He understood that stuff.... Ford had been on the budget committee and really did understand these issues and he certainly was beloved by the people of Grand Rapids. Kissinger has a theory that you cannot understand the significance of historic personalities and events except through the perspective of thirty years of subsequence.[40]

Nessen and Kissinger are right—it often takes a long time for people to have perspective about something like the performance of a president, and many views of Ford held by the public are different now than they were in the mid–1970s. However, the act of having Ford deliver the budget statement himself certainly did nothing to diminish the attacks comedians made on him at the time. Even now, in the 21st century, for many Americans the mid–1970s view of Ford is the view they still hold today.

3

Live from New York, It's *Saturday Night!*

During the first episode of *SNL*, which aired on October 11, 1975, "Weekend Update" anchor Chevy Chase told several jokes at Ford's expense, which played on Ford's alleged clumsiness and lack of intelligence, suggesting that the Secret Service needed to protect him from his handkerchief and the doorway of his helicopter. Chase ended this sequence of jokes saying that Ford had a new slogan for his campaign, "If he's so dumb, how come he's president?"

Ford's alleged dimness and clumsiness were frequent, easy themes for jokes, incorporated into "Weekend Update" along with the show's regular sketches.

Much of the political humor on *SNL*—in its first season and in its 40th—is contained in the "Weekend Update" segment. As Dan Aykroyd said of "Update": "*SNL's* political humor has always been well recognized as the best in the entertainment and comedy world. The originators of 'Weekend Update,' writers Herb Sargent and Alan Zweibel, are the inventors of this popular format which we see today in the *Daily Show* and others."[1] In a 1977 *Playboy* interview with the cast and crew of *SNL*, Zweibel talked about "Weekend Update," noting that it originated as Lorne Michaels's concept and that the live format meant that they could incorporate things that happened on Saturday into the show that night. Zweibel explained that the writing of "Weekend Update" continued until the show went on the air, incorporating the very latest developing news. To illustrate his point, he explained a joke written between the dress rehearsal and the live show about a rapidly developing situation during the Patty Hearst kidnapping saga. They were so in tune to late-breaking events, he said, that "Sometimes we even pre-empt the real news that way."[2]

28

The show has waxed and waned in audience and quality over the decades, but it has continuously been a reflection of current events, much as Michaels envisioned it to be. This finger on the pulse of the American zeitgeist has been most frequently demonstrated in "Weekend Update," and making fun of Ford was de rigueur on "Update" from that first episode.

The *SNL* team was also never reluctant to remind voters about Ford's ties to Richard Nixon. On the third episode of the series, broadcast on October 25, Chase told a joke during Weekend Update that Ford was recovering slowly from a bad cold and noting that the last time he had a cold, he "...inadvertently pardoned Richard Nixon."[3]

To the cast and writers of *SNL*, Ford was a legitimate target and a goldmine of humor. In *Playboy*, Chase said, "When I first heard that the ribbing Ford was getting hurt his feelings, it bothered me. On the other hand, he was a man in the public eye, who had to be held accountable for falling on little girls in wheelchairs, just the way Nixon should be held accountable for bombing Cambodia. Thank God, Ford didn't try to bomb Cambodia. God knows who he would have bombed first by mistake."[4] *SNL* writer Rosie Shuster added, "If an individual is being hurt gratuitously, that's where I draw the line. If a person is well enough known to be a target, I think it's all right to attack him, because he's put himself in that role. It comes with the territory. But no one here ever suggested doing Betty Ford mastectomy jokes—it's just too cheap a shot. It's too easy."[5] Ford was a politician who put himself in position to become the butt of jokes and *SNL*'s writers never let concerns about hurting Ford's feelings get in the way of making those jokes.

When *SNL* debuted, it was not the first television show to take shots at prominent people, nor was it the first show to have a political edge to it. By the time it hit the airwaves, two shows that many compare it to, *Laugh-In*, on which *SNL* creator Lorne Michaels served as a writer for one season, and the *Smothers Brothers Comedy Hour*, had come and gone. *SNL* was designed from the beginning to be its own thing, although it is impossible to deny the influence of the Smothers Brothers, Rowan & Martin and others.

SNL was, however, a fresh combination of many influences from TV's earlier days. It was live, and NBC hadn't aired any live programming for a decade; it was the first try at original late-night programming on Saturday night; it appealed to an audience of mostly young people who didn't ordinarily watch television; and it was an almost instant hit. As Timothy White observed in a profile of Michaels for *Rolling Stone*:

As we look back ... it becomes apparent that, like it or not, there has never been another program on television to compare with *Saturday Night Live*. Granted, it owes as great a debt to Ernie Kovacs, Milton Berle, Red Skelton, Steve Allen, Jack Paar, Johnny Carson, *Your Show of Shows* and *That Was the Week That Was* as it does to improvisational comedy. But *Saturday Night Live* is truly greater than the sum of its current parts and historical appendages. It is living comedy, intensely personal, sophisticated, topical with a cutting edge and, while uneven, utterly riveting in its riskiness.[6]

At its inception, *SNL* was designed to be a show written and performed by a young generation *for* a young generation, but it wasn't conceived in a vacuum. As Michaels observed, *SNL* certainly owed something to other shows, especially the Smothers Brothers. Michaels praised the Smothers Brothers, saying, "If Bob Hope was doing a sketch on marijuana on TV at that time, the people acted like they were drunk. I was outraged. The Smothers Brothers broke through, I thought, to some degree. That was a much hipper show than *Laugh-In* was at that time. I was very envious of the people who worked on the Smothers Brothers show because they were people of my generation who were working in television. *Laugh-In* had that appearance because it had performers of my generation, but the writers and the style were very much from another time and another place."[7] From the beginning, Michaels and the group he brought together to produce *SNL* saw themselves as being on a mission to offer the world something that was "not ready for prime time."

If Jimmy Carter was new to most of America in the early stages of the 1976 election cycle, so too was *SNL* and, like Carter, it was an overnight sensation. The show quickly earned a weekly audience of 22 million people and devoted significant energy to the politics of the day, especially by taking jabs at President Ford, for an audience that was particularly receptive to the show's anti-authoritarian message. This exchange among head writer Michael O'Donoghue and cast members of the "Not Ready for Prime-Time Players," from the early days of *SNL* in an interview with *Playboy* magazine, illustrates where the show's creative team was coming from and to whom they believed they were playing. Cast members John Belushi, Chevy Chase, and Dan Aykroyd, all seemed to share the view that television, in general, didn't have a great deal of merit. Chase and Belushi expressed the view that the *SNL* audience was largely comprised of young people who didn't otherwise watch television. Chase said that he felt that doing *SNL* was like performing on the "off Broadway" of television, giving them the opportunity to laugh at the rest of the television world. But Akyroyd made perhaps the most important observation about the nature of *SNL*, responding to a question about why it was important for the show to be live. He said, the reason was, "Feedback from the audience. All the laughs on this show are honest laughs."[8]

In this interview, writer Michael O'Donoghue was absurd in his statements, revealing a sarcastic and cynical attitude toward the world around him, disagreeing with the notion that *SNL* dealt more than other shows with "real life," saying that the drama, *Emergency*, "...says everything that could be said about human life. I look to it for guidance. I pray to it."[9] This attitude pervaded the early generation of writers and performers on *SNL*, who saw themselves as filling a void for a generation looking for something different from their parents. The conversation about what made the show different for that younger generation continued with Michaels, writers Anne Beatts, Rosie Shuster, and Alan Zweibel, and cast member Laraine Newman, responding to a question about whether or not the show contained outrageous and shocking humor. Michaels agreed that the show did a lot of material other shows wouldn't do, but didn't accept the idea that it was just for shock value. He lamented that the state of television was such that *SNL* was the only show that could get away with what it was doing.

They all seemed to argue that pushing the envelope was not the same as shocking for the sake of shocking. Writer Alan Zweibel said, "It's never the intention of the show to shock people. It's just perceived as shocking because this kind of stuff has never been done on television before." Writer Rosie Shuster agreed with this, suggesting that because the show played with societal taboos, but that they did so on the show to make points, not just to shock. Another writer, Anne Beatts suggested that accusing the show of having too much shock value was simply hypocritical, because *everyone* is interested in what they have on the show: "sex, drugs, and rock and roll."[10]

The members of the cast and writing staff saw themselves delivering a new kind of entertainment to a hungry young generation, through a medium none of them—viewers or creators—especially respected.

In designing the show, Michaels worked on his vision with the head of late-night television at NBC, Dick Ebersol, and his proposal was for an intelligent show aimed at young, urban adults.[11] Michaels described his strategy: "I held out for three things with the support of Ebersol. One, no pilot, because if they saw it beforehand they'd say, 'You can't do that on television.' That was solved by the second demand—making it live. Lastly, I wanted a commitment for twenty shows.... I believed the show should look, for the first few times, as if the network had closed down for the night, and these guys snuck into the studio. I wanted the show always to be perceived as an underdog."[12] He further explains, "I respond to whatever is happening at the time to keep the show fresh and topical. I think people look forward to us going after the big story of the week.... I always felt that the show at its best was a record of what had gone on that week in the country, the world, and the lives of the people doing the show."[13] That mission—being a record of what had gone on in the preceding week—is one that *SNL* has fulfilled for forty seasons. Regardless of the show's frequently oscillating quality, it has always served as a mirror, reflecting, if a bit imperfectly, America.

As the television critic from *The Washington Post*, Tom Shales, wrote admiringly of the program at the time of its debut:

> Not behaving is what they do for a living. They have made their show a weekly 90-minute TV revolution that ironically takes the medium back to its origins: live, surprising, spontaneity—albeit with a smidgen of vengeance. Their satire has evolved from the *National Lampoon* and other sources of nihilistic unrest. They bar as few holds as a network TV show can and they would have the NBC brass quivering except that the show is a big hit: commercial time costs $28,000 a minute and sponsors are fighting to get in. This is the television generation discovering, and decimating, television. The film generation is burning out and selling out. The rock generation creates only for its own culture. Michaels and his crew are trailblazers, they are making television respectable by slinging some mud around on Saturday nights. Sometimes they are brilliant—brilliant, I tell you! And sometimes they have the great courage to fall flat on their faces.[14]

In the beginning, the show made a huge splash that was on par with, or exceeded, the attention that cable programs like *The Daily Show* occasionally get today. In fact, for all the attention Jimmy Kimmel and Stephen Colbert receive, they are lauded for drawing an audience of around a million viewers in today's fragmented media marketplace. *SNL* regularly drew 20 times that in its first season. If for no other reason than the fact that the number of media outlets has multiplied exponentially since 1976, *SNL*, at its birth, was uniquely positioned, in terms of content, platform, and audience to have a major impact on both popular and political culture in 1976. The audience it played to was enormous.

In 1976, John Blumenthal and Lindsay Maracotta of *Playboy* assessed the show's impact in this way: "On the second Saturday in October 1975, a live, 90-minute comedy show, titled, appropriately, 'NBC's Saturday Night,' premiered on that network in what used to be the time slot for "Tonight Show" reruns.... News of the show spread rapidly by word of mouth, especially among those 20-to-40-year-olds who rarely, if ever, watch prime time. Advertisers began to take note. So did the press and, though several critics lambasted the show as 'tasteless,' 'sophomoric,' or 'subversive,' most hailed it as a 'breakthrough,' and compared it with enthusiasm to the pioneering days of television, especially to Sid Caesar's *Your Show of Shows*. It soon became necessary for anyone giving a party on Saturday night to have a television set turned to NBC at the crucial hour. In less than a year, the show's estimated viewing audience was twenty-two million and the show went on to win four 1975–1976 Emmy Awards."[15] Similarly, Timothy White observed in *Rolling Stone* that "contrary to popular belief and its underdog image, *Saturday Night Live* has been a resounding success from the start, its ratings steadily climbing."[16] The program quickly became must-watch-television for many American viewers in a way that it is virtually impossible for TV shows to be in today's much more fractured and micro-targeted media environment.

Because of its popularity, the show had the potential to influence—or, at the very least, reinforce—people's views about many things, including politics. If they had wanted to, the writers and cast could have loaded each episode with political satire and parody. Instead, they used politics as source material strategically, and to great effect. The fact that *SNL* was not ninety minutes of political screed, week after week, undoubtedly made the political material they did more impactful. Because politics did not drive the show, when they addressed political topics, what they did was often discussed in the media, such as this observation by Shales on November 8, 1975, after describing some "Weekend Update" political jokes: "Bad taste? Some viewers might think so. But the show's audacity is refreshing in a medium obsessed with the fear of offending anybody."[17] It was also discussed among politicians and almost certainly either influenced or reinforced the views of the young people tuning in to watch.

Doug Hill and Jeff Weingrad, authors of a book about the first decade of *SNL*, observe that while the show's earliest performers and writers were not overtly political, the political bits they aired made an impression. They wrote, "Senator Eugene McCarthy told Lorne at the correspondents' dinner in Washington that the first topic of conversation on the Senate floor every Monday morning was *Saturday Night*—the senators loved to relate to one another the jokes the show had made at their colleagues' expense on 'Weekend Update.' Maverick presidential candidates like Fred Harris and, later, John Anderson directly approached *Saturday Night* hoping for, and getting, some mention on the show."[18] While Harris never appeared on the show, several jokes about him made their way onto "Weekend Update," such as showing a close-up photo while Chevy Chase said, "On the campaign trail today, Senator Fred Harris of Oklahoma denied allegations that he combs his hair with buttered toast."[19] A few weeks later, "Weekend Update" featured a photo of Harris in which he looked remarkably similar to Johnny Cash, accompanied by this joke: "Harris visited a state prison in New Hampshire today. He is shown here singing 'I Walk the Line' as part of his Johnny Cash impression."[20] Two months later, dropping out of the race earned him this joke: "Senator Fred Harris, of Oklahoma, announced at a press conference last Thursday that he is ending his active campaign for the Democratic nomination. Aides complained that Harris had not received the same amount of news coverage as other candidates. Later, he was asked by the press who he was and what he wanted there."[21] The trend of politicians seeking to use *SNL* as a platform to reach audiences that might not pay attention to more traditional media outlets, has accelerated with each election cycle. The fact that *SNL ever* parodied and satirized politics made it relatively unique in American television at the time. With *TW3* a distant memory; and *Laugh-In* and *The Smothers Brothers Comedy Hour* off the air; and Johnny Carson only rarely telling political jokes, there was not much offered on entertainment television that addressed politics in a comic way. As Fotis (2014) asserts, improvisation-based sketch comedy on *SNL* "changed the way people view and make television."[22]

Assassination Humor

Many early *SNL* jokes about Ford played off the fact that he had two near misses with would-be assassins in the fall of 1975. The first took place on the grounds of the California state capitol on September 4, 1975. The woman was disarmed and no shots were fired. Ford's would-be assassin that day was Lynette "Squeaky" Fromme, a follower of Charles Manson. Fromme was convicted, in December, of attempting to murder Ford and was sentenced to life in prison.

At her trial, Fromme's behavior was both bizarre and *SNL*–sketch-inspiring. Fromme appeared in court wearing a red robe and carrying an apple, which she told the federal judge she had brought for him. When the prosecutor made his sentencing recommendation, characterizing Fromme as full of "hate and violence," Fromme threw the apple at him, knocking off his glasses.[23] She shouted, "He's the one to talk about hate," and when her own lawyer tried to interrupt her, telling her that prison would give her a chance to be rehabilitated, she shouted, "I can't be rehabilitated because I haven't done anything wrong. I want Manson out. I want a world at peace. You have only ten years of air and water."[24] This behavior inspired a segment on "Weekend Update," which was illustrated with a series of amateurish courtroom drawings.

Several days after, on September 22, Ford was again in northern California, this time in San Francisco, when a woman named Sara Jane Moore began shooting at him from across the street.[25] Like Fromme, Moore served more than thirty years in jail and was paroled after Ford's death in 2006.

Dick Cheney, Ford's longest-serving chief of staff, commented on the fact that bad things just seemed to keep happening to the President.

> Sometimes we were just plain unlucky. I can remember a trip in which Ford went out to California and spoke to a large group. He was upstairs in the room they had set aside for him after the speech and was getting ready to leave to go to the airport. The Secret Service likes to move the president on the freight elevators because they are more secure and in this instance, it was one of these elevators with doors that open vertically instead of horizontally. Well, he was on that elevator and as the elevator landed on the main floor, the top door went up and the president started to step out. The door went up, caught and then bounced back down and hit him right across the top of the head, knocking him to his knees. We got him back on the elevator and took him back upstairs to the suite. I still have a picture of Dr. Lukash, his personal physician, holding an ice bag on the president's head to stop the bleeding. We took care of that incident, got back on the elevator, went back downstairs to the ground floor, walked outside on the street and Sara Jane Moore took a shot at him. It was all in the same day within about thirty minutes. Now that was just a bum day.[26]

These incidents became fodder for many jokes about Ford's Secret Service protection in sketches and "Weekend Update" segments throughout Ford's presidency.[27] In the second episode of the series, which aired on October 18, 1975, Chase joked during "Weekend Update" about "Ford's regular weekly accident," showing a photo of a damaged presidential limo. Chase said that the car which hit the limo was tackled by Secret Service Agents. Ford, Chase reported, was uninjured in the crash, but poked himself in the eye with his thumb afterward. The thumb, Chase said, was "wrestled to the ground" by Ford's protective detail.[28]

The joke was, once again, inspired by real world events. On October 14, Ford was in Hartford, Connecticut, to speak at a Republican fundraiser. After the event, Ford was on his way to the airport to return to Washington when his limousine was struck at an unguarded intersection by a car full of six teenagers. The photo that *SNL* displayed on the screen while Chase told his joke was of the teens' heavily damaged car.

A few weeks later, on November 15, "Weekend Update" featured another joke about Ford's haplessness. Showing a picture of Ford and a little girl, Chase said, "Our top story tonight: President Ford flew to Paris today for a joint economic summit conference! Overworked and exhausted from his flight, the president mistakenly bumped his head on the face of a little girl who was presenting him with flowers at the airport. Smiling but alert Secret Service agents seized the child and wrestled her to the ground. Commented Ford later: 'It's okay, the kid's too young to vote anyway. Have you seen my flowers?' Ford will visit China in December, making stops in Indonesia and the Philippines. While in China, Mr. Ford plans to fall off the Great Wall by mistake."[29]

There was yet another "Weekend Update" assassination joke the next week, when Chase reported that a Senate investigation revealed there had been many CIA assassination plots against the leaders of other countries. When the President heard this, Chase said, he responded, "Boy, I'm sure glad I'm not foreign." Showing a picture of one hand stabbing another hand with a fork, Chase added that Ford had accidentally stabbed himself with a salad fork. The fork, Chase assured the audience, had been "wrestled to the ground" by the Secret Service.[30]

4

Chase-ing Ford

*There is no single media institution that embodies every element
of the cultural, technological, political and aesthetic evolution embed-
ded in the history of television. However,* SNL *comes as close as any
program does.*—Nick Marx, Matt Sienkiwicz and Ron Becker[1]

In general, the "Weekend Update" jokes about Ford played to stereo-
types about his alleged stupidity and clumsiness. The most impactful part
of the early days of *SNL* for Gerald Ford was Chevy Chase's impersonation
of him in sketches. The physical humor that was created in Chase's characterization of Ford left an everlasting imprint on the U.S. audience's perception of the president. As Jeffrey Jones notes, "With the impersonation
of a sitting president, the sketches became a standout and defining fea-
ture of the new show."[2] Ford's reputation as a clumsy bumbler began with
one actual misstep and grew into a legend of enormous proportions. In
late May and early June of 1975, Ford went on a European trip in which
he addressed a NATO conference and met with Egypt's president, Anwar
Sadat. Two of the most embarrassing real missteps of Ford's presidential
career—one physical and one verbal—came in his dealings with Sadat. It
was from these incidents—as well as press coverage of them and Ford's
subsequent occasional missteps—that Chase's devastating impression of
Ford was born.

Ford's meeting with Sadat was significant because, as Ford noted in
his autobiography, "Only after I'd talked with him would I meet with
Rabin. Always before, American presidents had met with the Israelis first.
The fact that I had said I wanted to establish a personal relationship with
Sadat seemed to worry the Israelis."[3] On June 1, four months before *SNL*
would premiere on NBC, Ford flew to Salzburg, Austria, for the meeting
with Sadat. On the way, something happened that gave birth to the idea
of Ford being a klutz.

Upon arriving in Austria, Ford tripped and fell down several stairs as he was leaving Air Force One. He quickly regained his balance and went on with the arrival ceremony as if nothing had happened. Ford's White House counselor and speechwriter Bob Hartmann described the scene like this:

> It was raining when we landed.... A rickety metal ramp, without rubber treads on the steps, was wheeled out to Air Force One. An aide opened an umbrella for the bare-headed President but Ford took it from him and held it over Betty. He also took the First Lady's arm, instinctively, as together they started down the ramp. A few steps from the bottom, his foot either caught or slipped and he tumbled onto the pavement, landing very agilely on both hands and one knee ... the President bounced quickly to his feet and had a ready quip for his waiting host, Austrian Chancellor Bruno Kreisky, who was more distressed than Ford. "I thought I'd just drop in," he said, grinning. The battery of news and television cameras caught the action but not the joke. Reporters besieged Ron Nessen with questions, and from that day forward they never ceased to be alert for every stumble or halting step, every time the tall President ducked through a helicopter door or took a spill on the ski slopes. The cartoonists and nightclub comics, including some of Ford's own amateur wits, took it from there.[4]

Press Secretary Ron Nessen described the event in his autobiography and noted that its occurrence would forever mark Ford: "Later that day there was another incident [after the slip on the stairs] which furthered the impression among the press that Ford was ungainly. Ford's foot slid twice on a long, rain-slick staircase at the Residenz Palace in Salzburg when he arrived for conferences.... Of course, the president's slips in Salzburg were overplayed, and were exaggerated in some accounts.... The Great Salzburg Stumbling Episode then faded from the news. But the image of Ford as a klutz would never fade away after that."[5] In his memoir, Ford wrote of his reaction to the attention the stumble received. "I jumped to my feet, unhurt, and thought nothing of the fall. So I was quite surprised when Ron Nessen told me later that reporters covering my trip were bombarding him with questions about my missteps.... There was no doubt in my mind that I was the most athletic President to occupy the White House in years. 'I'm an activist,' I said, 'Activists are more prone to stumble than anyone else. If you don't let their questions get under your skin, they'll realize that they're just wasting time, and they'll start to focus on something else.' I was wrong. From that moment on, every time I stumbled or bumped my head or fell in the snow, reporters zeroed in on that to the exclusion of almost everything else."[6] Ford was right—reporters did zero in on his falls and that, at least in part, was due to the fact that when Chevy Chase started falling as Gerald Ford on one of the nation's biggest television hits, people started to see Ford one-dimensionally, as the Stumbler-in-Chief.

For the rest of Ford's presidency, every stumble, trip, and errant golf shot hit by the president became part of the popular image of him as a man who couldn't get out of his own way or one who, as Lyndon Johnson is reputed to have said of Ford before he became president, was "so dumb, he can't walk and chew gum at the same time."[7] Dick Cheney, Ford's chief of staff, said, "The image was a problem, and I must say that Lyndon Johnson had contributed to its being rather negative. That false image was strong enough so that when Ford came on board, it was something we had to deal with on a regular basis. I think it was accentuated by the President's speaking style. On occasion, his remarks may have sounded less than articulate and I think that contributed to his problem."[8]

Another quote attributed to Johnson is that he felt that Ford had played football for too long without a helmet. Bob Orben addressed the jokes Johnson used to tell about Ford as being politically motivated, because of the role Ford played in Congress as the house minority leader for the entirety of Johnson's elected term in office.[9] Orben said, "The reason Lyndon Johnson came up with the two hurtful remarks is that Ford confounded a lot of what Johnson wanted to do and Johnson was furious about it."[10] As for Ford's speaking style, Orben told this story:

> Ford was not a natural joke teller and I have often thought that Ford's monotone and delivery—when I was a kid in the Bronx, they would try kids out for singing and they would point somebody out and say you're a listener, which meant that they didn't know how to carry a tune. I think Ford's natural monotone is the way they speak in Michigan and later on some of the things that he was criticized for, for instance in a speech he said I "gar-en-tee," that's what they say, so it was perfectly natural. Another thing that he used to say is 'judge-a-mint'—if you listen to any of the speeches, judge-a-mint. And I remember asking Bob Hartmann, who was a counselor to the president, "Does he always say 'judge-a-mint?'" And Hartmann smiled and said, "If you want to tell the president of the United States that judgment isn't a three-syllable word, go ahead." And I think I did, I didn't particularly want to be there and I had no fear, but again, Ford just smiled and said, 'That's the way I say it.' He had a tremendous amount of self-confidence, and with good reason.[11]

Ford addressed LBJ's jokes and the frequent comments from critics and the media about his intellect and his athleticism in *Humor and the Presidency*. Ford wrote, "To be sure, the first expression of that kind of remark was certainly disparaging. However, over a period of time, some of my speechwriters and I were able to turn it around and have it become a useful ice-breaker in certain situations."[12]

Although he was gracious in his description of Johnson's statement, it undoubtedly irritated Ford and probably hurt his feelings, not only to have been publicly humiliated by Johnson, but to have the jokes so widely distributed. In writing of the Salzburg incident in *Humor and the Presidency*, with the benefit of more than a decade's worth of hindsight, Ford wrote, "Falling down the stairs from Air Force One while bands are playing and troops are presenting honors is embarrassing. There was no way the press was not going to run that photo. Something like that doesn't help one's stature, but it comes with the turf when you hold public office."[13]

One of the most striking things about Ford's comments regarding his treatment in the press was the constraint he felt about how he could respond to it. Ford wrote, "Some people have suggested that I handled the jokes at my expense very well, and that I thought such things 'came with the turf' of being president. Let me put it this way: I developed a good exterior posture. The truth of the matter is that some of my favorite pipes have teeth marks in their stems that you wouldn't believe. This is a fact. You cannot cry out dramatically about your outrage or your indignity. That, as sure as tomorrow's sunrise, will open a floodgate that you'll never be able to close."[14] It is never easy to be the butt of jokes, even when you hold the most powerful position on Earth. But Ford was exceptionally good at not letting anyone see that they were getting to him.

The November 8 episode was loaded with Ford material that became image-defining for America's thirty-eighth president. After his initial meeting with Sadat in Europe, Ford welcomed the Egyptian president to Washington, D.C., on October 28. In his toast to Sadat, Ford said, "Let me simply conclude ... that it is a pleasure and a privilege for me to offer a toast to you and the people that you represent, the great people of the Government of Israel—Egypt, excuse me."[15] Bob Hartmann commented on this incident in his autobiography, writing, "I approved (and often edited) every word purporting to be Ford's own until the end of his term of office. I could not, of course, do anything about extemporaneous comments for which there was no prepared text—such as in the Ford-Carter debates, his news conference responses or after-dinner toasts. The most memorable of these was his state-dinner toast to Egypt's President Sadat and 'the great people of the government of Israel.' Ford quickly corrected himself. Sadat never blinked, but the guests choked on their chocolate mousse."[16]

The press noted the gaffe. The *New York Times* reported: "President Anwar el-Sadat and President Ford got a laugh out of a slip by Mr. Ford during a dinner toast last night honoring the Egyptian chief of state, Mr. Ford's spokesman said today. Mr. Ford proposed a toast to 'the great people of the Government of Israel.' Recovering quickly, he added: 'Excuse me, of Egypt.' At the time, Mr. Sadat showed no visible reaction to Mr. Ford's mistake. But the White House press secretary, Ron Nessen, said today that the two leaders had 'laughed about it afterward.'"[17] The story itself is not remarkable, but the headline leaves a slightly less than accurate impression: "Ford, in Slip of Tongue, Hails Sadat as Israeli," and it was fodder for Chevy Chase in "Weekend Update" on the November 8 episode, along with several other jokes about Ford and his administration. In the segment, Chase joked that when President Sadat left the United States after a lengthy visit, he gave several gifts to Ford and his family, including knee pads and a helmet for the President. The segment also included jokes about the so-called "Halloween Massacre" at the White House, which involved removing several administration officials. Chase joked that this included Ford asking his son, Jack, to resign as his son. Chase also reported that when Nelson Rockefeller announced that he would not be running with Ford in 1976, he said that Ford was the only leader he knew who could accidentally assassinate himself.[18]

In early November Vice President Rockefeller announced that he would not be Ford's running mate in 1976. Although it was presented publicly as Rockefeller's decision, there is no doubt that Ford asked Rockefeller to step aside in response to the primary challenge from the conservative Ronald Reagan. Rockefeller, a liberal Republican, was never liked by conservative Republicans.[19]

In addition, there was tension between Ford and Rockefeller, a former governor of New York, which stemmed from Ford's refusal to allow the federal government to bail out the financially stricken city of New York and prevent it from defaulting on its many debts. In the fall of 1975, the U.S. economy was in shambles, with both high inflation and high unemployment. Ford adopted an overall economic policy of government fiscal responsibility that was heavily influenced by his tough-minded economic advisors.

Ford gave a speech to the National Press Club on October 29 in which he outlined a very hardline stance against the city of New York.[20] The speech was not well-received in New York, although national polls tended to favor the president's tough stance, which Ford was counting on. In New York, the speech prompted one of the most famous headlines of the 1970s from the *New York Daily News*. On October 30, the *Daily News* led with the headline, "Ford to City: Drop Dead."

The increasingly negative relationship between the White House and New York City was too good for the team at *SNL* to pass up, and in the November 8th episode, which was the first since Ford's speech, "Weekend Update" began with this joke: "The top story tonight: The White House today released another enemies list. It's the New York City telephone directory."[21]

Later, "Congresswoman" Jane Curtin spoke sarcastically in support of Ford's New York policy, saying that even if New York was the "Big Apple," apples all rot eventually and Ford couldn't be expected to stop nature. The money that might be spent in New York, Curtin said, could much better be spent protecting the American people from "an inevitable nuclear attack."[22]

Although at the White House it must have seemed like it would be popular nationally for Ford to oppose a New York bailout, it quickly turned against him. Early on, while the New York City crisis was becoming a serious issue, few Americans knew anything about it. As the crisis evolved, the public became more engaged. In late August, a Roper Poll found that only 19 percent of the public was paying attention to the story.[23] In late September, another Roper poll found that 25 percent of the public was closely following the story.[24] In a subsequent Roper poll taken over a period which included Ford's speech, in late October and early November, the percentage of the public that was closely following the story rose to 45 percent.[25] There was a similar change in public opinion regarding federal aid to New York. Prior to the president's speech, a Gallup Poll found that 47 percent of the public did not think the federal government should provide financial aid to New York, while 43 percent felt it should.[26] In a Roper Poll taken over the period which included Ford's speech, a similar percentage of people, 46 percent, were opposed to federal aid, while 37 percent felt the federal government should help and 9 percent felt both self-help and a bailout were needed.[27] However, in the immediate aftermath of Ford's speech, there was a significant swing in public opinion *in favor* of helping New York. The change noted by Harris Poll data was dramatic, showing support for federal aid to New York by a margin of 69 percent to 18 percent.[28] As Lou Harris, the pollster, said, "The president's attitude of 'New York be damned' has changed the attitude of the American people."[29]

The sudden change in public opinion was certainly noticed by the president, who was by that time actively campaigning for the presidency. By early December, the administration and Congress worked out legislation guaranteeing loans to the city of New York. However, the city, the state, municipal unions, and New York banks were compelled to agree to difficult terms, including steep tax increases, a promise of a balanced state budget, and union and private contributions to the bailout.[30]

So, how did Ford fare electorally in New York after this brouhaha? The Republican primary was an uncontested affair in New York. Neither Ford nor Reagan actively campaigned there because of the state Republican Party's loyalty to Nelson Rockefeller, who many state party leaders hoped might emerge as a candidate for the presidency.[31] In the general election, Carter won the state by nearly five percentage points. This was significantly narrower than some of the margins by which Ford trailed Carter during the campaign in New York in public opinion polls, but 5 percentage points is a significant margin of victory in most American elections. The margin nationwide was just 2 percentage points. It is not difficult to imagine that the continued battering of Ford's image on *SNL* had an impact on the outcome of the election in the city *SNL* called home. To Ron Nessen, the fight with New York was a much bigger factor in the election than anything broadcast on *SNL*, but the two were linked.[32] Ford raised the ire of many New Yorkers, and *SNL* was more than happy to remind them how angry they were.

The announcement by Rockefeller that he would not be Ford's running mate was part of a bigger shake-up in the Ford administration in the fall of 1975, when Ford replaced his secretary of defense and director of the CIA. The shake-up was undertaken largely as an effort to demonstrate that Ford was in charge of his own administration which, up to that point, was questioned by many Americans.

November 8, 1975: Chase Appears as Ford for the First Time

Ford's assertion of power did nothing, however, to slow down *SNL*'s jokes. It also gave *SNL* a new category of jokes to mine for material. On the January 24, 1976, episode, Chase joked about Ford's efforts to pick a new running mate. He listed several possible names and ended with Senator Edward Brooke, an African American Republican Senator from Massachusetts. Chase said that sources at the White House indicated Brook was not going to be picked but was on the list as a "token" of Ford's appreciation for the Senator.[33] In addition to jokes about running mates, Ford's Sadat gaffe, and the fiscal situation in New York City, the November 8 episode began with Chase making his first appearance as a bumbling, stumbling Ford.

In the show's cold open, Chase, as Ford, talked to the nation about the upcoming presidential campaign and the challenge Ford faced from Ronald Reagan. (Although Reagan's formal announcement didn't come for a couple of weeks, he had a national organization and was already campaigning in early primary states.) Lorne Michaels talked about this historic introduction of presidential impersonation to *SNL* in an interview with *Rolling Stone*. He said, "The first time Chevy did Ford, it was because I love cold openings, no predictable introduction, except that we didn't have one and it was Friday night. As usual, we were pacing his office, desperate. Chevy suddenly said, 'Let me do Ford in the opening.'"[34]

This was the first episode of *SNL* to air since Ford's gaffe of introducing Sadat as the leader of Israel, and when Chase-as-Ford gets settled at the podium, he seems to be referencing Ford's difficulty with Egypt and Israel by wrongly referring to Howard Cosell as "Harvey."[35] Chase continued, speaking in the third person and saying he had an announcement to make. The announcement was about someone he knew who was running in several presidential primaries. This mystery man was going to win, Ford predicted, falling behind the podium as he spoke. Picking himself up and switching from third person to first person, he then said that if he didn't win in the primaries, he would continue to compete in them, whether or not there were any to run in. Tripping over some chairs, he then made his second announcement of the evening, the famous "Live, from New York! It's Saturday Night!"[36]

Chase became famous, in part, for his falls and, in part, for his portrayal of Gerald Ford, in which he made no attempt to look or sound like Ford. He took his first tumble in the cold open of the show's second episode on October 18. It was not until the November 8 sketch, at the beginning of episode four, that Chase's falling was married to his impression of Ford.

From that point forward, playing Gerald Ford became Chase's best-known activity on *SNL*. He also continued to tell many jokes about Ford's dim-witted clumsiness on "Weekend Update." In January of 1976, Chase told this joke: "While campaigning for the upcoming primary in New Hampshire, President Ford kissed a snowball and threw a baby."[37]

The Extra Campaign Fun of Ronald Reagan and George Wallace

Ronald Reagan, who first ran for president in 1968, ran a serious, and nearly successful, campaign to take the Republican nomination from Ford in 1976, and his presence in the race offered more material for *SNL*. This was not a positive development for Ford, who was often included in the punch lines of *SNL*'s Reagan jokes. The May 8, 1976, episode of *SNL* opened cold with Chevy Chase as Ronald Reagan but, as was the case with his portrayal of Gerald Ford, with no make-up or attempt to sound like Reagan. He played an organ with the *SNL* band and Garrett Morris standing behind him, holding a saxophone, who Chase-as-Reagan repeatedly called "Boy."

Although Chase only appeared as Reagan once during his time on the show, he told many "Weekend Update" jokes about him. Many managed to contain jokes about Ford as well. A joke from May of 1976 poked fun at both Ford and Reagan, taking aim at their intellects suggesting that doctors had declared both men dead, based on their inability to detect any brain activity.

A word-association sketch served as the cold open for the February 21 episode. In it, "Dr. Speck," played by Dan Aykroyd, becomes increasingly frustrated with his dim-witted patient as he gives words to Ford only to have the President continually repeat the same words. Ford got the hang of it eventually and, at the end of the game, when the doctor said "primary," Ford said, "Lose." The last word from the doctor, right after "primary," was the name of his primary opponent, "Reagan." Ford responded, "Hair dye."

During the same episode, Chase joked in "Weekend Update," that when Ford accused Reagan of being too conservative for the presidency, Reagan responded that Ford twice offered him spots in his cabinet. These positions were, Chase said, "Secretary of Witchcraft" and, joking about Reagan's age, "Director of the Pony Express."[38]

Reagan gave "Weekend Update" a wealth of material on the March 13, 1976, episode, following a gaffe Reagan made during a speech in Aurora, Illinois, in which he said, "Gerald Ford was a communist." Catching himself, Reagan then said, "I mean, Gerald Ford was a Congressman. It must have been a Freudian slip. I will make several criticisms of him tonight, but not in that regard."[39] On *SNL*, Chase joked about the incident, saying that when Reagan apologized for his slip he said he'd done so because he had communists on his mind. When he was asked for comment about Reagan's remark, Ford called him a "fatuous ass." Ford then apologized for his own Freudian slip, saying that he meant to call Reagan a mediocre actor, but he'd had "fatuous asses" on his mind.

As the primary campaign remained tight, *SNL* continued to comment on the battle between Ford and Reagan. Chase made a series of jokes about Ford's faltering campaign and continued to remind the audience of the *SNL* take on Ford as a stumbling, bumbling fool. He mentioned Ford's determination to not only win the primary election in New Hampshire, but the "secondary" election as well. He joked that the Ford campaign staff was trimming expenses by firing a number of aides whose job it was to coach Ford's walking and speaking. Finally, he reported that Ford was now promising to stop campaigning to lose and start campaigning to win.

In addition to jokes about Ford and Reagan, the crew at *SNL* also took notice of the fact that George Wallace was making his third run for the presidency, after nearly being assassinated during his 1972 campaign, leaving him paralyzed and confined to a wheelchair. "Weekend Update" was peppered with jokes in which Wallace was a frequent subject. Jokes about Wallace mostly centered on the wheelchair. In October, 1975, for instance, Chase said that when Wallace was denied an audience with the Pope, a spokesman said that the Pope was always being asked for audiences by the disabled and he had recognized Wallace. Chase added that Ronald Reagan decided to campaign from a wheelchair to make things more fair for Wallace.[40]

The wheelchair jokes continued with regularity. A month later, in November 1975, Chase joked that Wallace would "roll" to the Democratic nomination and quoted Wallace as saying that he would never let his handicap get in the way of the extremist and racist policies he supported.[41]

The next week, Chase joked that the FCC had ruled that the equal time rule required the showing of clips from Reagan movies every time a Ford campaign ad aired. He added that Wallace responded to this ruling by demanding equal time in the form of one-minute clips of the show *Ironsides* be aired.[42] (The television show *Ironsides* starred Raymond Burr as a wheelchair-bound, mystery-solving former police chief of detectives in San Francisco.) Much later in the campaign, in April 1976, Chase again joked about Wallace's physical condition, noting that to prove he was not weakened too much for the presidency by his injury, Wallace had promised to demonstrate his strength by using his bare hands to crush a child.

Wallace's dim views on racial equality came out a couple of weeks later in this joke on "Weekend Update," when Chase said that Wallace denied being a racist and that he judged people not by skin color but by how well he could see them in the dark when they smiled. A week later, Chase revisited this joke, reporting a "correction" from Wallace who, Chase said, denied making such a statement but, rather, said that he judged people by how well they can "fast-dance." *SNL* returned to the air in July, after Carter wrapped up the Democratic nomination, and on "Weekend Update," Chase told one final Wallace joke, sarcastically reporting that he had endorsed Carter by saying it was time for the Democrats to have a candidate without an accent.

After a hiatus of several weeks, in which the show was off the air for the month of June, the July episodes allowed *SNL* to make plenty of jokes about the two parties' national conventions. The Republican nomination was in doubt all the way up to its convention in Kansas City in mid–August and on July 31, *SNL* aired a sketch about the extreme closeness of the race, entitled "Ford Delegate."

In the sketch, Chase's clueless Ford tries to convince an uncommitted delegate from Mississippi, played by Kris Kristofferson, to support him over Reagan. Ford is saved by Betty Ford (as played by Jane Curtin), who was often portrayed as the brains of the operation in *SNL's* treatment of the Ford White House. The "negotiation" with Kristofferson's delegate is finally brokered by the first lady in this exchange. It was Betty who easily understood the favors the Mississippi delegate was requesting in return for support at the convention and she sealed the deal with Kristofferson, promising him that the President will make some calls to free up the money for the water treatment project he wants. Happy to hear this, he tells Betty that he can't see any reason for his delegates not to support Ford now.[43]

In the end, Ford ended up winning the Republican nomination by a little over 100 delegates in Kansas City, and the full attention of the nation, and *Saturday Night*, turned to the competition between Ford and Carter.

5

Ron Nessen
Discovers *SNL*

After Salzburg, the press seemed to keep a special watch to catch and transmit every presidential stumble, real and imagined, physical and verbal. Any incident that supported the image was reported and filmed: Ford wrapped in the leashes of his frisky dogs; Ford bumping his head on the door of a helicopter; Ford locked out of his own news conference by a broken door handle; Ford falling down on skis. They were the kind of everyday minor mishaps that befall everyone, but when they happened to Ford, cameras were always trained on him.—
Ron Nessen[1]

While *SNL* joked about many candidates, with those such as George Wallace and Ronald Reagan making the attractive occasional target, most of the focus remained on Ford and Carter. For instance, the February 14, 1976, "Weekend Update" segment included a series of jokes first about Ford's clumsiness and stupidity. It was Valentine's Day and Ford was reported to have searched for eggs under the Christmas tree to celebrate the holiday. After watching Dorothy Hamill skate at the Olympics, performing a series of complicated jumps and spins, Chase reported that Ford said he couldn't see what the big deal was, since he did those things just getting out of the car. Finally, Chase turned back to Ford's incompetence for the Presidency, alluding to a statement Ford made after a visit to China, in which he said he wasn't sure if he had met the country's new leader. Chase said that the leader, Hua Guofeng, responded to Ford's comments by saying that he wasn't sure if he'd met Ford either, since "All those presidents look alike to me." To show there were no hard feelings between the two countries, Chase said, Ford formally forgave the Chinese for the attack on Pearl Harbor that started World War II.[2]

These kinds of jokes were bad enough, but it is important to remember that it wasn't just *SNL* that was making fun of Ford. As 1975 turned into the bicentennial year of 1976, it seemed that everyone was telling jokes about the president. In a December 1975 column, Ford's former press secretary, Jerry terHorst, observed, "The cartoons are brutal. The jokes are savage. And the derision is everywhere present, even among Republicans. We are witnessing—and participating in—a trendy political game the object of which seems to be to jeer President Ford out of office." He noted that even the highly cautious Johnny Carson, who was slow to tell political jokes for fear of offending half his audience, no matter which politician the jokes were about, was telling Ford jokes: "One of the most telling aspects of the trend is its acceptance on network television, even on Johnny Carson's *Tonight Show*. Nothing happens by accident on that one; it's taped for later broadcast. After years of experience, Carson and the NBC brass know how far they can go in pushing the outer limits of good taste. Treating President Ford with ridicule, therefore, has been judged by the networks to be inoffensive to national audiences."[3] Political columnists Lou Cannon and David Broder further observed in January, "In the last few weeks, President Ford has become the butt of a hundred jokes and cartoons, all embellishing on the theme that he is what *Newsweek* called 'an amiable bumbler.'"[4]

While Ford may have felt it was impossible to become visibly angry with the press for the way he was covered, his press secretary felt obliged to publicly defend his boss. Ron Nessen was troubled by what he, and most of Ford's loyal supporters in the administration, felt was an unfair characterization of the president in the news media.

In his autobiography, Nessen described an incident that had an impact on people's perception of his performance as press secretary. Nessen described complaining to the traveling press corps about their treatment of the president in Vail during the Ford family's holiday vacation in December 1975 on a day in which the nation's newspapers were full of pictures of Ford falling down on the ski slope. His complaint came after he consulted with Dick Cheney, then Ford's chief of staff, about how to respond to the press's incessant focus on Ford as a bumbler. Nessen wrote,

> Cheney replied that in private meetings and interviews with reporters he let them know he was angry about the inaccurate image of the president being portrayed in the press. He suggested that I also express anger in background sessions with newsmen. The next morning, I wandered into the press room and found half a dozen reporters sipping coffee and reading the Sunday newspapers ... naturally the conversation turned to Ford's supposed clumsiness. Thinking I was chatting informally.... I decided to try Cheney's suggestion. I told reporters that stories portraying Ford as a bumbler were "the most unconscionable misrepresentation of the president"...

> It was a Sunday, there was no other news for the White House press corps, and thus my little informal complaint became a lead story."[5]

Nessen was quoted in stories saying, "This president is healthy, he is graceful, and he is by far the most athletic president within memory."[6]

Nessen's affection for his boss—as well as his outrage at the treatment of Ford—was genuine, built in covering Ford as vice president while he crisscrossed the nation campaigning for Republicans in the 1974 midterm election season. Nessen said this of the experience and the connection it allowed him to build with Ford:

> When Ford was Vice President, the Nixon people gave him this old two-engine conveyer to fly in, and this was coming up on the congressional election of '74. Well, Nixon was already a prisoner in the White House from Watergate, so Ford had to do all the campaigning, and of course he loved it. He would do it every day of his life if he could. They gave him this old conveyer to fly in, and there were five of us reporters who traveled everywhere with him. I'm going through some of my own notes, he has this full schedule at the White House, then he goes to New York to make an evening speech, then he flies to California all on the same day. We traveled I think two-hundred-and-some thousand miles on the campaign. But anyhow, he had a close relationship with these five or six reporters, and I was one of them. I think the people who spent a lot of time with Ford like that really did appreciate the depth of his character and experience and so forth.[7]

It was this affectionate feeling for Ford that sparked Nessen's anger. That anger on Ford's behalf did not play well in the press. For example, a story in *Newsweek*, entitled "Nessen's Report Card," took the press secretary to task for what was portrayed as an angry tirade against the press for its coverage of Ford's fall on the ski slopes in Vail. "But if Ford's performance on the slippery slopes was pardonable, Nessen's seemed less so. 'To sensible people,' editorialized the *Wall Street Journal*, 'the whole idea of a Presidential press secretary bragging about his boss's gracefulness makes the whole team look comic.' It was not the first time Nessen had managed to seem maladroit in his boss's behalf.... Last week, a six-man committee of the National Press Club handed Nessen an embarrassing report card, based on an eight-month study of White House press relations."[8] In hindsight, it is hard to blame Nessen. Faced with the many public relations troubles of the Ford administration, not the least of which being what he felt were unfair characterizations of his boss's intelligence and physical aptitude, Nessen was frequently frustrated as press secretary, thanks to the way the reporters—some of whom had been his colleagues in the not-too-distant past—portrayed Gerald Ford.

During the January 24, 1976, "Weekend Update" segment, Chase began with an "apology" for treating Ford unfairly and ended with a joke inspired by Ford's fall on the ski slopes. Chase apologized that "Weekend Update" had treated Ford unfairly with stories that could be, "interpreted as accusing the President of stupidity and clumsiness." He promised that going forward they would treat the presidency with respect and cut unfair references to Ford. Having made this promise, he then reported a story about "an unidentified man" who was seen falling out a window, tripping on his way to board Marine One, hitting his head on a helicopter blade, and departing the White House for Vail, Colorado.[9]

Given his anger with the news media, Nessen's reaction to *SNL* was surprising.

As Nessen told the story in his autobiography, one Saturday night, January 17, 1976, unable to sleep, he happened upon *SNL* for the first time and watched in fascination as Chevy Chase portrayed Ford, and Buck Henry took on the role of Ron Nessen, preparing Ford for a press conference, in a sketch entitled "Operation Stumblebum." Unlike the news reports which angered him, the sketch made him laugh and, ultimately, led him to the decision to appear on the show as its guest host a few months later. The sketch included an exchange about Nessen's job security in which Ford asked Nessen if he knew anything about the rumors that he, Ford, was planning to fire Nessen. When Nessen tells Ford that decision is up to him, Ford responds, "Well, I guess we'll find out sooner or later then, won't we?"

The sketch also addressed an imagined White House strategy to deal with the "stumblebum" problem. The solution, Nessen told Ford, was called "Operation Stumblebum," in which everyone at the White House would make an effort to make Ford's malapropisms and clumsy moments appear perfectly normal. Every time Ford did something that could be interpreted as a gaffe, those around him would do whatever he had done, thereby making it look perfectly normal. As he speaks to Ford, the President attempts to light the bottom of his pipe. Nessen does the same thing, telling him this is a perfect example of his plan.

It could not have been a less flattering picture of the president. As Nessen related, it didn't take long for it to occur to him that, maybe, in this new television program, there was a way for Ford to improve his reputation with the American people by joining in and playing along with the jokes being made about him. Journalists Doug Hill and Jeff Weingrad asserted in their book that Nessen became an instant fan of the program, obsessed with its portrayal of the president. They wrote,

> Nessen was amused in spite of himself. The sketch had accurately reflected the fact that Nessen, among others in the White House, considered the media's portrayal

of Ford as a bumbler one of the most serious public relations liabilities of his administration. Nessen had spent a significant amount of time and energy trying to overcome that image. Yet here was Chevy Chase taking Ford's buffoonery almost as far as it could go in the opposite direction. Nessen asked an aide to get a cassette of the show, and he watched *Saturday Night* religiously from then on.[10]

This story was confirmed by Lorne Michaels in a story by Tom Shales, the television critic for the *Washington Post*. Shales wrote, "Lorne Michaels, young producer of 'Saturday Night,' said yesterday Nessen requested videotape of the sketch and Michaels had one sent to the White House, where Nessen watched it again. The President did not see it, however."[11] Nessen was quoted by Shales as saying, "When I'm home on Saturday nights, I almost always watch it."[12] That was certainly untrue, since in his own autobiography, Nessen reported it was the first time he had seen the show, but he undoubtedly wanted to look hip enough to be watching it and it also sent a signal that must have made the folks at *SNL* feel important—the White House was watching them.

Shales observed, "Nessen considers the show 'very pointed satirical humor' and that he has 'never seen anything that's gone over the line,'" and further noted that "Nessen seemed less tolerant of jokes about presidential clumsiness late last December when, at Vail, Colo., with the first family, he lashed out at what he called the 'most unconscionable representation' in history and described the President as 'healthy' and 'graceful.'"[13]

Shales was pointing out an inconsistency—if Nessen was so angry about the reporting, why wasn't he angry about Chase and *SNL*? However, this inconsistency is really an issue of timing. This observation was made by Shales in February. While Nessen may well have come to feel that *Saturday Night* was being unfair to Ford *after* he hosted the show in April, in February Nessen was vexed by the news media's coverage of Ford and still saw *Saturday Night*, an entertainment program, as a possible solution to his boss's public relations problem.

As Nessen tells the story, he finally resolved to go on the show after Ford's own performance at the Radio & Television Correspondents' Association dinner in March 1976, which was hosted by Chase. After Chase, impersonating Ford, made some jokes and took some predictable falls, Ford took to the podium, but not before *accidentally* coming close to pulling the tablecloth off his table. He upset some place settings, knocked his script to the ground, and said, "Mr. Chevy Chase, you are a very, very funny suburb." Ford speechwriter Bob Orben described how the president's routine came about:

About a month or two before that event, I got a call at 6:00, 6:30 in the morning—the President wants to see you right away. And so I go right in and I figure, oh my god, there's something wrong with the speech, or there's a problem, and he said, "Have you done anything for the radio and TV correspondents' dinner," and I said no, I really haven't, except for an opening. I said the opening, if you're game, is really right out of the Red Skelton playbook, and that's your responding to all the Chevy Chase craziness of being clumsy. So at the point where you're introduced, you're sitting at the head table. Obviously, that will have all manner of clutter, dishes and serving bowls and that sort of thing in front of you, and when you're introduced, you grab hold of the bottom part of the tablecloth and stand up and, holding onto that with your left hand, start to walk to the lectern, dragging all of this off the table, dragging all of this clutter onto the floor, and you're totally unaware of this. And as you get to the lectern you put your speech, which is a phony speech which is about 400 pages, on the very lip of the lectern so that it cascades off into the audience, and this is as far as I got, and that's the way he started.[14]

The dinner led to what seemed like a friendly relationship between the *SNL* star, Lorne Michaels, Ron Nessen, and the president, who was suddenly getting national attention for being funny while making fun of himself. It was this success at the correspondents' dinner that led Nessen to believe the solution to Ford's public relations problems could be found on *SNL*, the show that had been making such terrible fun of him.

Shales reported, "During their visit to Washington, the gang met with Nessen, toured the White House, and on a rare free day for them, ran around the town acting silly."[15] Following the correspondents' dinner and the time spent hanging out with Chase, Nessen made the fateful decision to do the show. He wrote, "Encouraged by Ford's enthusiastic spoofing of his klutz image, I resolved my lingering doubts and confirmed that I would appear as guest host on 'Saturday Night.'"[16] Nessen elaborated on these events in an interview on the same day, March 19, 2009, that Barack Obama was to become the first sitting U.S. president to appear on *The Tonight Show*. Nessen said:

Now you see, the president is gonna go on with Leno.... You know, I understand a couple of things. One, he has a huge audience and can reach a lot of people. You also say something about yourself. "Hey, I'm not pompous. I can go out there and mix it up with them." There was some of that behind some of the Ford stuff. I mean, I think it was a little bit different. I think one of the reasons for it was to show that Ford was a regular guy and he could make fun of himself. The way this all started, Chevy Chase was doing his routine on *Saturday Night Live*. We have a big annual banquet here in Washington for the Radio and Television Correspondents Association and Chevy Chase was the entertainment in the spring of '76. He comes in the far door and he's stumbling and bumping into tables and tripping over things and gets up on the stage and does the whole routine. Now Ford was sitting right there. Well, Ford had a guy on his speechwriting staff who was a former Hollywood humor writer. This guy had worked with Ford and prepared him, and they introduce Ford. He gets up and pretends to pull the placemat off with him. Then he puts his speech on the podium and knocks it over. Well, in Washington the only type of humor that goes over is self-deprecating humor. You cannot make fun of somebody else.

Nessen explains that this culture of humor has remained throughout the following decades. He continues:

Now, two years ago they had a comedian [Stephen Colbert] at the White House Correspondents' dinner. You probably read about it … and it was a disaster because he didn't understand that and he really went after Bush…. Self-deprecating humor is the only kind that goes over in Washington and that was part of the *Saturday Night Live* thing, which is if Ford can come on the show himself and make fun of himself, it really diffuses the situation. Chevy Chase comes from a wealthy family. He liked to play tennis and of course Ford liked to play tennis. So Ford invited him to come to the White House the next day and play tennis on the White House court, and they did.[17]

With this confluence of events—sleepless night that led him to run across *SNL*; the appearance of America's newest comedy sensation at the Radio and Television Correspondents' dinner; a visit by Chevy Chase to the White House to play tennis with the President; and an added element, a chance meeting with *SNL* writer Al Franken in New Hampshire—Ron Nessen was ready to do what politicians always do: try to turn a disadvantage into an advantage. In both his interview for this book and in his autobiography, it is clear that what Nessen hoped to do was to humanize Ford and to make him part of the jokes, rather than the butt of them. Nessen wrote of Chevy Chase and the program, "I worried that the act could further damage Ford's public image, but stirring in the back of my mind was the notion that perhaps the popularity of 'Saturday Night' might make it the vehicle to counteract the bumbler image."[18]

The problem, however, was that Nessen—and Ford—didn't understand something Bob Orben, a show business veteran, understood very well. It was one thing for Ford to use a little slapstick at a Washington banquet. It was entirely different to try and take control of the comic narrative on the home turf of the comedians. Having spent one career writing for performers like Red Skelton, Jack Paar, and Dick Gregory and then a second career writing jokes and speeches for politicians such as Barry Goldwater and Gerald Ford, Orben is in a unique position to understand why jokes that work in entertainment might not work for politicians. In 1964, Orben was writing material for both comedians and politicians. In 1964, Orben was writing a great deal of material for both comedians and politicians. As Orben said:

I was writing, sending a page of material a day to Dick Gregory. I was sending a page of material a day to Barry Goldwater, who was running for president. I've often been asked, "Are jokes interchangeable?" Obviously not. You can't do Gregory material for Goldwater. I was also a writer on the Red Skelton TV show in California, and I was doing my own humor service called Orben's Current Comedy, which was published twice a month.... Orben's Current Comedy started essentially as a show business [venture], but politicians and speakers and ministers and God knows who else quickly learned about it and so—once in a while I'd look at the subscribers list and a good part of Washington was subscribing to it.... The Goldwater people got in touch with me and said they expected to get the nomination and they'd want special material. So that was the first major politician that I recall [contacting me]. Goldwater had a good reputation for humor and so it didn't surprise me when he got in touch with me and he wanted humor for the campaign. Goldwater had a good natural sense of humor and he used a lot of the material during the campaign.[19]

But Goldwater used it on *his* turf—the hustings—where he got to rely on his own sense of humor and to tell jokes that were crafted for him, not on a show like *SNL*, where all of the writing was done by people with unknown motives. In February 1964, Goldwater appeared on *The Jack Paar Show*. Jack Gould reviewed his appearance with favor, writing, "His major guest last night was Senator Goldwater, whose quick sense of humor was more of a revelation than his political pronouncements. The Senator held his own nicely in exchanging cracks with the humorist."[20] In that environment, Goldwater was both capable of holding his own and was given the chance to do so.

On a scripted show like *SNL*, and being people who had, perhaps, less natural comedic ability than Barry Goldwater, Ron Nessen and Gerald Ford had much less chance to hold their own. In writing for Goldwater and Ford, Orben was able to tailor material to the situation and each man's strength. Orben said, "I have through the years counseled people if you don't want to get up in front of an audience and do a 'Pat and Mike' joke, you want to do something that is relevant to that audience. I had a demonstration of that that was done at the University of Notre Dame that Ford got 28 seconds of roaring reaction. Now, 28 seconds doesn't sound like much but the average big laugh in show business is about five seconds, so this just electrified the place and why? Because it had a special relevance to the audience."[21]

The joke at Notre Dame came in his opening lines and went like this: "As your next-door neighbor from Michigan, I have always been impressed by the outstanding record of the students of the University of Notre Dame. They have always been leaders in academic achievement and social concern and sports prowess. And now once again you are blazing new paths in the development of new concepts in mass transportation. Some communities have the monorail. Some have the subway. Notre Dame has the Quickie."[22] The "Quickie" was a bus that students had purchased, after Indiana raised its drinking age to twenty-one, to take trips to Michigan, where the drinking age was eighteen. Orben wrote:

> It isn't that the audience automatically bought everything the President had to say after that, but you can bet they were an attentive and friendly group—because the President had taken the trouble to find out about them. Now employing humor involves taking a risk. It requires a lot of guts to lay yourself out before thousands of people and the national press with a long, yawn-producing set-up that leads eventually to an unmistakable punch line. If the joke had not worked, it would have been very embarrassing. The alternative would have been to play it safe. You can always get an acceptable reaction from a college audience by joking about the mystery meat in the cafeteria or praising the football team. But that sort of thing won't get the audience out of their seats. President Ford went for the touchdown.[23]

How the President's Press Secretary Came to Host SNL

In three accounts of how Nessen's guest-hosting gig on *SNL* came about, including Nessen's autobiography, the story is basically the same: Nessen was in New Hampshire on a campaign trip with Ford when he ran into a writer from *SNL*, Al Franken (who is now a U.S. senator from Minnesota). In early 1976, Franken was on hiatus from the show, traveling the campaign trail with his brother Owen, a press photographer. Tom Davis, Franken's *SNL* writing partner, said that Owen "befriended Jimmy and Rosalynn Carter and Al went with him."[24] According to Hill and Weingrad's account, "Thinking he might get some material he could use for the show, Franken spent a day or two riding on the press bus, following the candidates as they stumped the state…. At a campaign stop on the same trip, Franken met Ford's press secretary." According to this account Nessen "told Franken how much he liked the show. Franken, thinking how perfect it would be to have the real press secretary play opposite Chevy Chase's Gerald Ford, broached the idea of Nessen appearing on the show. To Franken's surprise, Nessen said, 'Oh, I'd love to be on it.' Franken said he'd talk to Lorne. After a few phone conversations with Lorne, Nessen agreed to host the show on April 17."[25]

In Tom Shales and James Miller's book of interviews about *SNL*, Franken confirmed the story. He said, "I went up to New Hampshire with my brother, who is a press photographer, to follow the campaign in '76. And I ran into Ron Nessen, who was the White House press secretary. And I was surprised that he had seen it—and that he liked it. I said, 'Well, you should be on the show,' and I went back to the office a few days later and I told Lorne. He kind of had to remind me that he was the producer of the show, and that I had only been in show business for about ten minutes. I was a writer. But anyway, Nessen ended up coming on."[26]

Nessen told another version of the story of how—and why—he came to be a *SNL* guest host. "Ford had three teenaged kids in the White House, so he was familiar with the show. He didn't want to do it but he told me I should do it. So, they asked me and I did it. I had been with NBC for twelve years so when I got there to do the show I knew everybody in the studio crew and everybody in the control crew because I worked with them when I was at NBC ... I think it probably had the desired effect of diffusing it and showing he could make fun of himself."[27] As a longtime television reporter before becoming the presidential press secretary, Nessen was comfortable on camera.

Nessen's opinion of whether or not it "had the desired effect," was not universally shared and, in fact, Nessen's opinion is rather variable. In 1978, when he wrote his autobiography, Nessen was quite sure that it did not help. For his part, Ford also believed in the power of self-deprecating humor. Ford wrote, in his book about humor and the presidency, "Self-deprecating humor is probably the most effective kind of humor for a president. But not everyone knows how to use it."[28] One might conclude from this sentence, though he didn't add it, that Ford felt like appearing on *SNL* turned out to be the wrong way to use it.

Ford and Humor

Bob Orben started helping to guide Ford's use of humor in the late 1960s when Ford was the house minority leader. Orben first wrote jokes for Ford to use in a speech at the Gridiron Club. Orben said this of the beginning of his relationship with Ford:

> Ford gave maybe two hundred speeches a year but humor wasn't a big part of it so they figured maybe they needed professional help. A good part of what Ford did at the Gridiron Dinner that year I provided. And everybody had assumed that Hubert Humphrey would be the star of the evening. The surprise star of the evening was Ford. He closed with something that was amazingly prophetic. Johnson was out of the race at that point—so Hubert Humphrey was the obvious Democratic nominee, and Ford said as he looked around, "I have no designs on the White House, unlike

some in the audience. But I have to admit as I'm tired and I'm hungry leaving Congress, as I drive past 1600 Pennsylvania Avenue I do seem to hear a little voice within me saying 'If you lived here you'd be home now.'" That was a big hit.

Orben continued, noting that Ford was very aware of the power of humor. Orben asserts:

Ford realized that humor, topical humor, was an important communication device and so we kept in touch and I did occasional material for him. In 1973 when he became Vice President, the Ford people were in touch with me and I became a consultant to Ford and started to write on a regular basis and then when he became President I got a call from Bob Hartmann: "The president wants you down here," and I said, "When?" And he said, "Now!" That's how it all started.[29]

Journalist Richard Reeves noted, rather derisively, of the need Ford, and nearly every other politician, had for a joke writer, although Ford still couldn't be guaranteed to get the jokes right which was, according to Reeves, a problem common to politicians. He wrote: "Orben writes jokes for Gerald R. Ford.... Ford tells the jokes very badly, which is the way most politicians tell jokes.... Orben, for instance, wrote the joke that Ford classically botched a couple of months ago in Indianapolis. A routine political self-deprecator, it had the president being stopped by a lady in the hall who said, 'You look familiar' and Ford was supposed to answer, 'Jerry Ford?' Then she comes back, 'No, no, but you're close.' The way Ford actually told it, the lines were, 'I am Jerry Ford,' and 'No, but you're close.'"[30]

When Ford became president, his use of humor was well received by the country, playing into the high popularity Ford experienced in the month before he pardoned Richard Nixon. As Orben said:

There was a huge amount of positive publicity about Ford and his sense of humor and use of humor. That perked up a lot of ears in Washington. In fact it was in editorials saying "it's good to have laughter in the White House again." ... I do think Ford, particularly in that first month before the Nixon pardon, was getting a huge amount of publicity all over the place on the Ford humor; and this was a big factor. The very second speech he ever made as President was at Ohio State University. Fifteen thousand in the field house and this was just two weeks after he became president. He started off by saying, "So much has happened since I accepted this invitation to be here. I was then America's first instant Vice President and today I find myself to be America's first instant President. The U.S. Marine Corps band was so confused they didn't know whether to play 'Hail to the Chief' or 'You've Come a Long Way, Baby.'" My heart was in my mouth because there was a split second of silence where people were thinking, "Did he really say that?" And then it was tremendous and it was essentially saying that he realizes that he is an accidental president but that he has full confidence in his ability to do the job.[31]

Ford, from Orben's perspective, first made himself known to a national audience with his humor, even though he was a politician, not a stand-up comedian. As Orben said, "Well, there was always a certain amount of coaching, but Ford—my whole point in dealing with anybody is if the material is right and you have the courage to get the words out, that's all that's required."[32]

To Richard Reeves, Ford received the benefit of the doubt from reporters when he told jokes. Reeves wrote, "There is the Yogi Berra phenomenon—Berra doesn't really have much of a sense of humor, but baseball writers work with the essentially dumb things he says to give him the aura of a peasant philosopher.... President Ford, for instance, is getting some benefit of the Yogi Berra phenomenon. In profile after profile, he is reported to have said, 'I don't think Ronald Reagan dyes his hair, it's just prematurely orange.' I may be wrong, but I don't believe Ford is physically capable of cracking a line like that. What probably happened is that he said something like, 'Reagan's hair sure is a funny color,' and aides or reporters took care of the rest."[33] To Ford's credit, Reeves further notes that he believes the same is true for most other politicians, such as Henry Kissinger or Barry Goldwater.

Even after Ford's popularity took a hit for pardoning Nixon, Orben and the president understood that humor was an important way to try and relate to the American people, particularly on the always-growing perception that Ford was clumsy and dumb. Orben spoke of the administration's concern about Ford's image problem:

> Well, we were all aware of it—you couldn't not be aware of it. I had a continual debate with others and I think the President sided with me in feeling—the question is should we respond to this? My feeling was always that you had to respond to it because the nation was talking about it and if you don't respond to it, you just look foolish. In fact, one time he went up to the Yale law school for the sesquicentennial celebration. He started off his remarks by saying, "It is a great honor to be here at the Yale Law School Sesquicentennial Celebration, and I defy anyone to say that and chew gum at the same time." And it started off all three networks in their coverage.

Orben continued to explain that Ford's response was spot-on because he was aware of the clumsiness critique, but it was a false accusation. Orben added:

> Now that was just right in the sense that it indicated that, yes, he was aware of the criticism, but he could just shrug it off because it wasn't true. I've always wanted to point-blank ask him, although I know what his answer would have been about the criticism. Here's a guy—he was captain of the Michigan football team, he was offered two pro football spots on graduation, he was an athlete. You know, he could pin anyone that was criticizing him down to the mat, and yet he suffered all this. Klutz he wasn't, it was rather known at the time that women liked to dance with him because he was very light on his feet.[34]

The Yale speech was delivered on April 25, 1975, before *SNL* went on the air and started poking regular fun at him, but after many in the press had been openly questioning his intelligence. In addition to the gum-chewing joke, Ford joked about his perceived lack of intellect, saying, "At that time, one of the entrance requirements to the Yale Law School was a personal interview with three distinguished members of the faculty. In my case, one of them was Professor Myres McDougal, whom I'm delighted to see is with us tonight.... You might be interested to know that Professor McDougal ... mentioned the fact that he still had his notes from that interview. He said that under the appropriate headings there were entries like the following: good looking, well dressed, plenty of poise, personality—excellent. Then, under another heading: informational background—not too good.... I won't go into any more details about that interview. Suffice it to say that Professor McDougal was extraordinarily impressed with my capabilities and so caught up with my capabilities and my vision of my potentialities that in a whirlwind of enthusiasm, he wrote, 'I see no reason why we should not take him.'"[35] Ford's jokes were well-received and it gave Ford and aides like Orben the idea that humor was a key to political success.

But despite the gains Ford made through the use of humor, Orben was very wary about having anything to do with *SNL*. Orben worried because, unlike having Chevy Chase host an event in Washington, D.C., where Chase was playing on the president's home field, this time the opposite would be true—Nessen and Ford would be in *SNL*'s arena and at their mercy. To Orben, the trouble with appearing on *SNL* was that Nessen and Ford would be giving up too much control and taking *too much* of a risk. He summed up the difference, saying of the Washington correspondents' dinner, "Chevy Chase now was in our ballpark, mainly Washington with journalists and, as you know, most of the professional performers do not do well at the White House correspondents' dinner or the radio–TV dinner because they don't know the ballpark.... I never realized until I came to Washington how much of an advantage that whoever was doing the material in Washington had over the California writers or anybody else, because we knew the territory, we knew where the bodies were buried, and we knew what would turn on an audience."[36] When he got to New York to host *SNL*, Nessen no longer knew where the bodies were buried. He was at the mercy of *SNL*'s writers and performers.

When he heard about the possibility of a *SNL* appearance, Orben tried to talk Nessen out of it. He said, "When Ron first said he was gonna do *Saturday Night Live*, I said, 'Don't do it, Ron,' and he said 'I have script control,' and all that. I said 'You have nothing. This is your ballpark and this is their ballpark and it's not good.'"[37] For Orben, having control over the jokes was the key to successful use of humor. The Radio and TV dinner worked well because he and the president were able to orchestrate the jokes. At *SNL*, the former television writer Orben knew, things would be very different.

SNL really wanted Ford to host, not Nessen. Tom Shales wrote, "Later, Michaels approached Nessen about appearing on the show, after a bid to get the President himself failed."[38] One question is how much discussion there was between Nessen and Ford before Nessen agreed to do the show. When Nessen's forthcoming appearance was announced, Shales reported that Nessen made the decision on his own, writing, "Nessen said he did not check with the President before agreeing to host the show, but did confer with legal counsel Philip W. Buchen about accepting payment. Nessen said he will either waive the payment or donate it to charity. NBC—where Nessen worked as a reporter from 1962 to 1974—will pay only his expenses, Nessen said."[39]

However, Nessen remembered the decision differently, asserting that appearing on the program was Ford's idea, largely at his children's urging. This version of the story doesn't appear anywhere else. Ford himself didn't write about the show, either in his autobiography or his book on humor and the presidency, so it is impossible to confirm. However, it seems implausible that such a decision—unlike anything any representative of a presidential administration had done before—would be made *without* the president's approval, especially since the president himself agreed to do three taped cameos for the episode.

Regardless of advice to the contrary from Orben, Nessen guest-hosted *SNL* and made history when he did so, taking many people—even those at *SNL*—by surprise. As veteran *SNL* writer Tom Davis said three decades later, "We were amazed that with Chevy's handle on Ford that Nessen would agree to appear."[40] The surprise stemmed from the fact that Chase's portrayal of Ford was plenty damaging to the president all on its own, without the many other things reported about Ford's physical and mental capacities in the news media. Orben credits (or blames) Chase with being the single greatest cause of damage to Ford's reputation, saying, "Of course. How can anyone deny that?"[41] Expanding on this, Orben said, "The problem with humor is if you gave me enough money, a few million dollars and pinpointed any politician or public figure of any sort and gave me the time to write jokes on a particular point—he's a drunk, he's a chaser—whatever you come up with as the subject, very quickly the public will believe that he *is* a drunk or a chaser or whatever, and that was the problem that we had. That the media picked up from Chevy Chase—and others, but mostly Chevy Chase—and that became the reality."[42] That reality was something Nessen—and Ford—thought he could modify by interfacing directly with Ford's most popular tormenters, and which Orben feared Nessen would make worse by appearing on the show.

6

The Episode

It didn't do us any good.—Bob Orben[1]

Well, I think if the goal was to show that Ford had a good sense of humor, I guess you could say that it didn't work out. Again, like I said, Ford had a good sense of humor. He could make fun of himself and he was comfortable with it. That's all I could really say.—Ron Nessen[2]

Ron Nessen hosted *SNL* on April 17, 1976, before "a studio audience of 300 persons, including such celebrities as actresses Candice Bergen and Louise Lasser, cartoonist Garry Trudeau, and pop star Paul Simon, and such NBC honchos as Julian Goodman, chairman of the board, and Herbert Schlosser, network president."[3] This was ten days before the start of a string of Republican primaries, starting with Pennsylvania on April 27 and ending in Ohio, New Jersey, and California on June 8. Nessen's description of the appearance is confined to roughly two and a half pages in his book, with an additional page about the reaction to his appearance from Ford, Ford's family, and the news media. Nessen's description of the event reflects conflicted feelings. While he writes of his regret for doing it and the negative impact it had, he also remembers much of the experience fondly, reflecting positively on his experience in New York during the week before the show. He wrote,

When I arrived at the NBC studios in Rockefeller Plaza in New York City three days before the program to begin rehearsals, there was a wariness on both sides. In person, the mostly young cast and production team turned out to be even more eccentric in their language, dress, and conduct than I had expected. As a spokesman for a Republican president, dressed in a suit and tie, I must have appeared to them to be a direct descendant of Herbert Hoover. After going through a few scenes in practice, however, I realized that the people I was working with were extremely talented and professional. And they realized that I was willing and competent to take part in the fun, having appeared on live TV probably more than they had during twelve years as an NBC news correspondent.[4]

The cold open duties on Nessen's episode were handled by Gerald Ford, who was taped in the White House uttering three phrases, including the famous opening line. They were: "Live from New York, it's Saturday Night"; "Ladies and gentlemen, the press secretary to the President of the United States," which played after the credits and immediately before Nessen took the stage; and "Good evening. I'm Gerald Ford and you're not," which played at the beginning of "Weekend Update" and was a spoof on Chevy Chase's signature Update line, "I'm Chevy Chase and you're not." It was longer than Nixon's two seconds of airtime on *Laugh-In* in 1968, but not by much. As *SNL* producer Dick Ebersol put it, "We are prepared to give equal time to Ronald Reagan, who obviously qualifies. That equal time would equal approximately 13 to 15 seconds."[5] In his autobiography, Nessen's version of the taping of Ford's lines is short and positive. He wrote, "A few days before the show, I asked Ford to film three short lines to be inserted in the program. He agreed. Standing in the Cabinet Room, looking into a camera, Ford intoned, 'Live from New York, it's *Saturday Night*,' 'Ladies and gentlemen, the press secretary to the president of the United States,' and 'I'm Gerald Ford and you're not.'"[6] In Hill's and Weingrad's account, however, getting Ford to say those lines was not nearly as smooth or matter of fact as Nessen's brief account suggests. According to the two writers, the taping session took place in the presence of Lorne Michaels, *SNL*'s then-resident filmmaker Gary Weis, and a couple of NBC officials, including Dick Ebersol. Hill and Weingrad assert that the session was filled with the kinds of gaffes that haunted Ford throughout his presidency. As they chronicle, with Nessen signed up to host, Lorne Michaels asked Ford to appear in a few videotaped segments during the show. Ford agreed to this and a few days before the show was broadcast, Michaels traveled to Washington with a small group that included Dick Ebersol and Gary Weis. As they write,

> The film crew, provided by the NBC News bureau in Washington, set up their equipment and waited. At 3:30 on the dot Ford marched into the room. It was clear to Lorne and Weis that this was but another stop in a blur of engagements the President walked through every day. With a glimmer of recognition in his eyes, Ford shook Lorne's hand and said, "Chevy, how are you?" As Weis attached a microphone to Ford's lapel, Lorne tried to put the President at ease. "Mr. President," he said, "if this works out, who knows where it could lead."[7]

According to Hill and Weingrad, Ford smiled, appearing a little confused and it took several takes for Ford to get his three short lines recorded. They conclude,

> When they were through, Ford got up to leave for the next event on his schedule. He forgot, however, to remove the microphone from his lapel. The NBC News crew

had used a relatively old-fashioned microphone, one that was attached by a wire directly to the camera. When the President reached the full length of the cord, he was jerked backward, faltering a step while the camera swayed and almost tipped over. Ford regained his footing, removed the microphone, and left. Nessen implored Lorne, Weis, and Ebersol never to mention the incident to anyone.[8]

Clearly, the request was not honored by someone at the taping, since the story appeared in the Hill and Weingrad account.

Weis recalls:

I wasn't allowed to bring my own camera or cinematographer. I had to use an NBC news man to do that piece of business. It was off the Rose Garden area because afterwards he was going to make a speech. And three minutes 'til two, the doors open and the Secret Service walks in and line up. Exactly bang on the dot 2:00, he walks in the door. We meet him. I put a lavalier lapel microphone on him. We do a couple of takes. I am obviously not going to ask him to do it with a little more emotion. But I think we did a couple of takes. One of the interesting things was that he did walk away with the lavalier mic still on, which was one of those things that he would do, or was the rumor back then, anyway. But he walked away with it on, it didn't pull him back comically, but it did stick. So, they said, "Hold on, Mr. President." I did have some stills printed up of that.[9]

Nessen forcefully denies that Ford had any moments of clumsiness in the taping of his lines. When asked about the incident, Nessen replied, "If I were you, I'd be very suspicious of all the 'Jerry Ford was clumsy and stupid' stories. My experience is that these second-hand third-hand-fourth-hand-fifth-hand stories grow more ridiculous with each retelling. Unless you're looking for the most ridiculous 'Jerry Ford was clumsy and stupid' stories, in which case there are lots of folks out there who will provide you with lots of examples, mostly imagined and/or widely exaggerated."[10]

In Tom Shales and James Miller's oral history of *SNL*, Michaels recalled the visit to the White House. Michaels said: "I had to shoot Ford saying 'Live from New York' and 'I'm Gerald Ford and you're not' for the show. And I suddenly find myself in the Oval Office, and it's just me, the President, and this little crew. There's security too, I'm sure. And Ford does it, but the line reading is wrong, and I realized that it's just the same as working with anybody else and getting them to relax and do the line properly to the camera. We'd done two or three takes, and to relax him, I said to him—my sense of humor at the time—'Mr. President, if this works out, who knows where it will lead?' Which was completely lost on him."[11] In another interview, Michaels remembered the president fondly, saying, "In the Oval Office he couldn't have been more gracious or kind when we were doing it."[12] Regardless of the stories, some of which are undoubtedly made less reliable with the passage of many years, it is certainly true that, on screen, Ford appears somewhat uncomfortable when he delivers his lines.

Nessen's opening monologue was filled with jokes which played directly on the President's alleged flaws. He described his job duties, saying that his job was to interpret the complicated doings at the White House for the public. In the course of doing this job for the Ford administration, he said, he had learned several useful phrases, such as, "What the president really said was," and "What the president really bumped into was."[13]

In retrospect, it is easy to see the opening monologue as the first dark clouds on the horizon before a storm strikes. When considering Nessen's monologue, as well as other controversial material in the episode, it is puzzling that Nessen didn't fight against any of it or let the president know what was coming. Apparently, however, Nessen did neither. In his autobiography, Nessen wrote about the press reaction to the show, but not whether he had any discussions with the president prior to broadcast about the tone of the show's material, in light of the fact that both he, as a high profile representative of the administration, and the president himself, would be appearing on it. In an interview, Nessen explained, "I did not discuss the content of the *Saturday Night Live* show with Ford in advance because I really didn't know the content until I went to New York City and started the rehearsals."[14] If he really did participate in writing some of the sketches, as Nessen also said, then ignorance of the content doesn't stand up as an explanation. What seems more plausible is that Nessen thought that the whole point was to show the president could take the jokes and, if Nessen complained about them, his complaints would get out and defeat the whole purpose for being there.

As for the sketches he was in, Nessen appeared to have done little editing or attempting to restrain the writers' satiric impulses. Given how many jokes Nessen made at the boss's expense, it is hard to imagine, if he did edit some, how rough they might have been. A *Chicago Tribune* reporter, Johanna Steinmetz, who was on the *SNL* set during rehearsals for Nessen's appearance, wrote, "Nessen vetoed none of his material on the show and appeared to enjoy other sketches in which he did not participate.... The most controversial sketch in which Nessen appeared was one in which he played himself to Chase's hilarious rendering of an uncoordinated, obtuse President Ford.... During the dress rehearsal of that sketch, an Emmy Award winning writer on the show's staff was heard to remark to a colleague: 'What we are watching may be the most amazing piece of TV ever done.' Replied the second writer: 'It's almost like heresy on Nessen's part, isn't it?'"[15]

After the show aired, critics repeatedly questioned why Nessen didn't do something to moderate the show or, perhaps, simply refuse to do it when he saw what was coming. Hill and Weigand assert that Nessen was unable to do anything because he didn't show up to begin rehearsals until the show had largely taken shape and that there was little he could have done to influence the episode's tone. They also contend that Nessen was largely hands-off in the writing of the show, which allowed the writers to get away with comedy murder. Hill and Weigand report that Nessen accepted this reality, writing that Nessen said, "'What could I do? Walk off in a huff on Thursday, two days before the show?' So Nessen didn't object to a comma of what had been written."[16] When asked how much Nessen was involved in the writing, Tom Davis concurred with Johanna Steinmetz's report, remembering Nessen positively, but also suggesting that Nessen was not very involved in the writing. As Davis recalled, Nessen did not interact much with anyone but Lorne Michaels prior to the broadcast, saying, "Al and I were not included in the meetings in Lorne's office at that time. During blocking and read-through he seemed like a really smart, nice guy."[17]

Nessen's own recollection of the writing of the show and his involvement is occasionally different from the version presented by Hill and Weigand. In an interview, Nessen confirmed that he did not voice any objections to the writing. He said, "I don't think they would have ever agreed to it and I certainly don't recall it ever coming up."[18] Shales quoted Nessen as saying, "When we first talked about this, I told them, I can't do anything truly embarrassing or in bad taste to the White House ... and they agreed there would be nothing like that on the show."[19] Shales reported, "Michaels was asked if the show would ease up on its satire during Nessen's visit. 'Absolutely not,' he said, 'We do our show regardless.'"[20]

Nessen didn't portray himself to Shales as being as hands-off in the writing process, nor does he remember not showing up in New York until Thursday. Nessen said, "They asked me to come up on Monday before the show to take part in the writing. The way it used to work then, they used to sit around this big table in a conference room all week and threw lines at each other. This was a group exercise in writing the show and they wanted me to take part in writing the show. I couldn't get there on Monday but I got there on Tuesday. So Tuesday, Wednesday, Thursday, Friday, and Saturday morning I took part in the writing. So I had some impact on the writing. I looked at it and read the script for a long time and I had stuff that I wrote that was used on the show," and said that one of the sketches, a bit about press secretaries throughout history which recurred several times during the episode, was his idea.[21] A story about Michaels and *SNL* that was written during the week Nessen hosted is more in line with the Hill and Weigand timeline of Nessen's arrival. The reporter, Tom Burke, writes, "Though *Saturday Night* doggedly makes sport of the president, Ron Nessen wants very much to be guest host this week. But it *is* Wednesday and he's still unsure whether the president can spare him. Lorne's demeanor toward Nessen exactly matches his demeanor toward everyone, as though he has determined that, because of his position, his pleasantness will *not* be graded according to anyone's status. 'Nice guy, Nessen,' he offers. This is read, as is so much around *SN*, inscrutably. 'Hmmm? No, I'm not panicked whether he'll come or not. I mean, I am. The show's written around him. This time of the week, we're *always* in a state of controlled panic. He'll come.' In that, there's a sense of willed results which is startling."[22]

One X-factor in Nessen's appearance on *SNL* is that it came in the midst of a strike at NBC. The strike involved the National Association of Broadcast Employees and Technicians, which was the union that represented NBC's technical workers—including camera operators, sound technicians, and lighting technicians. The nationwide strike began on March 31, 1976, following several weeks of contract negotiations, and lasted until the employees returned to work on May 24, 1976. Because Ford had been taped to appear on *SNL*, Steinmetz reported, "NBC, fearing the striking NABET workers would storm the White House with protests, kept the surprise inserts secret until the show went live."[23] Prior to his appearance as host, Nessen received a telegram from NABET, requesting that he not appear on the program during the strike.

In the telegram, Arthur Kent, the president of Local 11 of NABET, wrote,

> It has come to our attention that you are to appear on "NBC's Saturday Night" on Saturday, April 17. To do so would mean crossing NABET'S picket line and, thus, we would appreciate your postponing this appearance. The 1750 members of NABET, primarily technicians and newswriters, have been locked out of their jobs by NBC since April 7, and we believe NBC is trying to break the union. At issue in our contract dispute are seniority, pensions, medical benefits, and the maintenance of decent working conditions. As a former member of the working press, we believe you will appreciate our insistence on maintaining fair and decent conditions for our members and will refuse to cross our picket line.[24]

Nessen responded to Kent, but not until after his appearance on the show. On April 19, two days after his hosting appearance, he wrote to Kent,

> Your telegram requesting that I not cross the NABET picket line at NBC just reached my desk this afternoon, following my return from New York. Obviously, it arrived

too late for me to consider the issues you list before my appearance on "NBC's Saturday Night." I am not informed on the issues of this strike; I am a member of AFTRA, whose members are not honoring the picket line; and I feel it would have been irresponsible of me not to keep my commitment to the producers of "Saturday Night."[25]

Fortunately for the administration, the fact that Nessen crossed a union's picket line to host *SNL* did not create any kind of media stir, although Nessen was clearly edgy about it when he showed up at NBC studios in New York. "Nessen arrived in New York last Thursday to begin rehearsal.... The former NBC newsman appeared somber at first, having crossed picket lines to make his comedic debut...'John Chancellor and Barbara Walters cross the picket lines every day, you crossed them, Hubert Humphrey crossed them,' he complained. 'Why all this attention on me?'"[26]

In his autobiography, Nessen made no mention of the strike, but he wrote of his ease working with the *Saturday Night* staff: "In fact, I discovered that I had worked on news broadcasts over the years with several members of the technical crew."[27] The reason Nessen knew the people working the technical side of the show was because they were veteran managers and supervisors, called into service because of the strike. As Hill and Weingrad wrote:

Nessen happened to host the show while NBC was in the midst of a strike by its technical union. Much of the studio equipment that week was manned by management personnel, so that the complexity the show might ordinarily have had was reduced. All week long Lorne was telling the writers to "simplify, simplify," and by Saturday he was forced to use sketches that called for as little camera movement as possible. That ruled out, Lorne says, a lot of the more subtle political material that had been written for the show.[28]

In an interview, Michaels said, "As for that specific program, one of the problems we had to solve *that* week was dealing with a technicians' strike at NBC. We had to come up with sketches that were stand-up presentations—such as ad parodies—because the cameras couldn't move. That's why we had sketches like the 'Flucker's' and 'Autumn Fizz' commercials—not because we stacked them for that particular show."[29]

Whether or not the strike had an influence on the available material, why didn't Nessen try harder to moderate what was going to be broadcast on his episode, regardless of when he arrived in New York? It wasn't just sketches that were critical of Ford that brought Nessen criticism after the fact, but also the sketches that filled the rest of the show, such as the "Flucker's" sketch mentioned by Lorne Michaels, which were quite crude. In Nessen's defense, his ultimate goal was to take ownership of Ford's image problem by playing along with the jokes. It was his calculation that the public would give Ford credit for having a sense of humor. But perhaps not for being un-presidential.

It is easy to believe that, in his mind, fighting with the writers or leaving were not really options for Nessen. If he had "walked off in a huff" as Hill and Weigand assert he should have done, several things, all negative from Nessen's perspective, could have happened, although it is hard to imagine that the show could have turned even more negatively against the president. If Nessen left, he would have lost the opportunity to put his theory to the test—that showing the president to be in on the joke before a huge national audience would help the administration take control of Ford's image. Many in the press ripped him for allowing such a negative and crude episode to be broadcast with the president so intimately involved, but if Nessen had stormed off, no doubt the reporting would have focused on administration tantrums and attempts to control the media, just as the news media critiqued Nessen for his behavior in Vail.

Hill and Weingrad contend that the NBC censors decided that Nessen "knew what he was doing and that he could take care of himself."[30] It is important to consider the NBC censors. The Smothers Brothers were driven off (or they drove themselves off) the air after fighting a quixotic battle with the CBS censors and management.[31] The relationship between the crew at *SNL* and the censors appears to have been much calmer (at least during that first season while the campaign was going on) than the one the Smothers Brothers had at CBS. When, for instance, two famously blue comedians, Richard Pryor and George Carlin, hosted the show in the first season, the show was put on a five-second delay, but the censors cut only two words from Pryor's monologues. Nothing else, including the word "Nigger," was cut from Pryor's episode. As Lorne Michaels said, "Ultimately, they came around on everything."[32] At *SNL*, the censors were for the most part tolerated as a "necessary evil,"[33] and the truth is that the cuts imposed by NBC censors were relatively rare. The censor assigned to the show the first season was a man named James Otley. According to one account, most of the staff at *SNL* considered him to be a "reasonable man," so reasonable, in fact, that, according to writer Tom Schiller, he didn't like working on Saturday nights."[34] Otley left after the first season and the censoring seems to have stepped up, angering writers such as Michael O'Donoghue, who said the new censor, Jane Crawley, was "ruining the show," and vowed "to sell all cut jokes to *Hustler* magazine to embarrass NBC."[35] Regardless of feelings about the new censor in season two, during the first season, the show was given a relative free hand.[36]

Washington Post television critic Tom Shales described the show's relationship with NBC censors like this: "Michaels says 'Saturday Night' keeps the resident NBC censors 'on the edge of their seats' and some battles have been lost—a planned adult version of 'Sesame Street' teaching sex education was nixed and words like 'schmuck' get the blue pencil. But Michaels says he isn't playing 'games' with the censors or trying to sneak naughty words onto the air. 'We really censor ourselves,' says Jane Curtin, another resident player. 'We're a television generation; we know what can be done and what can't."[37]

The executive in charge of standards and practices—censorship—for the network was Herminio Traviesas and, according to *SNL* executive producer Dick Ebersol, "We have a great working relationship with Travie.... There are some no-no's, such as language and sexuality—you don't hear four-letter words on the show. But there's never been any problem about political freedom."[38]

Regardless of how much control he tried to assert over the content of sketches, what Nessen really wanted to take control of was Ford's image. Hill and Weingrad wrote, "Lorne understood Nessen's motivation, and it caused him some reservations about having Nessen on the show. Lorne had never liked the way Bob Hope would make jokes about the President one day and play golf with him the next. It led, he was sure, to pulling punches. He wouldn't have it that way with Nessen. When he talked to Nessen on the phone, he told him that the show wouldn't change the way it did things in deference to Nessen's position.... Already the lines were drawn."[39]

At the same time Michaels protested that Ford's people weren't going to be able to use his show for political appearances, he also appeared to enjoy the attention he and the show received because of their connection with the Ford White House and the benefit it had for the show's bottom line. In a different interview, Shales asked Michaels if he was worried he and the show were being co-opted by the president. Shales wrote, "Michaels was a staff writer for 'Laugh In!' the day Nixon dropped by to tape 'Sock it to me,' part of a campaign to humanize him. But Michaels says he is not worried that the court jesters will lose their integrity. 'What's the danger—we go into the White House and come out as David Eisenhower? We just want to be ourselves—and make a fortune.'"[40] This sentiment suggests there was more than just political animosity against Ford at play. Chase reflected a similar attitude, telling Shales, "'It's a once-in-a-lifetime thing.... We've been on the periphery of show business and politics all our lives, and this is a chance to see the inside.'"[41]

Orben was a contemporary of, though not acquainted with, one of *SNL's* writers, Herb Sargent, a fellow television veteran. When he was asked if he considered reaching out to Sargent or anyone at *SNL* to express displeasure with the jokes the show frequently made about Ford, Orben said, "No, it's not good form to complain," and went on to talk about the only comedian he ever collaborated with when he worked in the White House— Bob Hope.

> I would call Hope's head writer and I would say, "Look, we're gonna do jokes about this, that, and the other thing, so don't do any jokes about this, that, and the other thing. You tell me what you're working on and I will stay away from that." So, it was an area of cooperation that worked out very well, and if I had a good joke that fit into them, I would give it to them, and vice versa.[42]

Hope worked in familiar territory and he was the kind of entertainer with whom Orben knew how to deal. The group at *SNL* was very different and it was why Orben feared having Ford and Nessen engage with them.

Following Nessen's opening monologue came a fake advertisement that featured Dan Aykroyd as a manic TV pitchman selling a product he called the Bass-o-matic. The high point of the skit comes when Aykroyd drops a bass in the Bass-o-matic, which is nothing but a standard blender, grinds the fish to liquid, and pours it into a glass. The scene cuts to Laraine Newman, holding a glass of pink liquid. She takes a sip and exclaims, "Wow, that's terrific bass!"[43] This sketch, which would no doubt raise the ire of animal rights groups were it to air today, was, by far, the least offensive part of the episode, which featured a number of sketches that pushed the limits of good taste, using the standards even of today.

Following the Bass-o-matic skit was what Nessen described in his autobiography as his "major contribution to the program," in which he played himself to Chase's Gerald Ford. In the sketch, playing off of every Ford stereotype, Nessen and the faux Ford went over the president's schedule and referred directly to Nessen's stated reason for doing the show— to improve Ford's image. He meets with Ford in the Oval Office and tells him that he needs his permission to host *SNL*, explaining that he thinks it is a good idea to show the country that Ford is in on all the jokes *SNL* has been making about him. He points out to Ford that this worked out well for Richard Nixon, who appeared on the show *Laugh-In* during the 1968 presidential campaign. Ford nods and comments about how funny Nixon is, spurring a large laugh from the audience. When Ford tells Nessen he may do the show, Nessen tells him he thinks it would be a good idea for Ford to appear on the show too. Ford protests, telling Nessen, as he stumbles around the office, tripping over everything in sight, that he won't have the presidency demeaned by going on *SNL* and falling all over the place.

The sketch leaned heavily on the audience's comedic perceptions of Ford, from his clumsiness and dim wit to the pardon of Nixon. Its tone was certainly what everyone at the White House had come to expect from comedians. The difference this time was that one of Ford's intimates, Nessen, was part of the joke-making that was mostly at Ford's expense. One (partial) exception was a joke told by Nessen. Ford told Nessen that he wanted to know how his dog, Liberty, had gotten pregnant. He said he might launch an investigation, maybe even call CBS reporter Daniel Schorr to look into it. He then asks Nessen what they should tell the press about Liberty's embarrassing pregnancy. Nessen responds that they should simply call the puppies, "our ethnic treasures."

This was a reference to Jimmy Carter for a campaign gaffe in which he told a reporter that he saw nothing wrong with maintaining "ethnic purity" in neighborhoods, and at Ford for his attempt to capitalize on Carter's remark. CBS reporter Daniel Schorr had recently been at the forefront of reporting misdeeds by the CIA.

This was the last Ford-related sketch in Nessen's episode. As Davis explained, "After Chevy's piece we were loath to do anything more sharply critical or political, except for Update jokes."[44] That does not mean that the rest of the show was a gentle romp, or that it was not political. Instead of taking direct shots at Ford, what followed the Oval Office sketch was a line-up of edgy skits that were described afterward by many critics as raunchy, outrageous, and disrespectful of the fact that the president and his press secretary were so involved with the episode. Immediately following Nessen's big skit was a fake advertisement for "Flucker's Jam," a takeoff on the Smucker's jam slogan "with a name like Smucker's, it has to be good" which hawked a series of jams, each one more outrageous than the last, such as "Nose Hair" jam, "Painful Rectal Itch" jam, and "Mangled Baby Ducks" jam.

Tom Davis reflected on the appropriateness of the "Flucker's Jam" sketch being in Nessen's episode, saying, "That was Michael O'Donoghue who wrote that. He took weeks to write things; so, I think that it was more of a decision on Lorne's part to put it in the show. Asked if Michaels deliberately loaded the show with raunchy material, Davis said, "I think he didn't want every piece to be political.... I don't think he was looking for raunchiness, but I'm sure he got it that week. It's more of a coincidence, I think.... There's usually a raunchy sketch or two every week. Now, if there were two or three in the show, it might have been loaded up, but I doubt that it was a deliberate thing by Lorne. It might have just been a flowering of raunchy pieces on a week where Lorne was looking for things that were not political. But, it's possible that we have Ron Nessen on, no one's watching, let's give 'em some raunch. I guess it's possible, but I don't think a lot of time was spent thinking that way, certainly not by me."[45] Tom Davis might not have felt that the show was deliberately raunchy, but many people certainly did.

The Flucker's sketch got a special level of attention from the network's head censor, Herminio Traviesas. In an account of Nessen's episode, reporter Johanna Steinmetz wrote, "Word spreads that…. NBC's Department of Standards and Practices has reservations about Flucker's." Noting that the *SNL* staff "thus far has won more latitude than any show in the history of TV," Steinmetz quoted Lorne Michaels: "'I'm not going to defend it on the grounds of taste…. All those words are already on the air in some form or another, and the reason this gets a laugh is that people are just releasing the irritations they already feel about it.'"[46] After a day of no action on the sketch, Traviesas took over the job of *SNL* from Jay Otley: "In the studio the skit is performed for the cameras. In the control room, sitting before the monitors, Traviesas gives it the go-ahead. Later he says: 'I'm not too keen about some of the words, but the young kids will probably think that's very funny—in that context.'"[47]

The "Flucker's Jam" sketch was followed by the first of several vignettes in which Nessen played the part of press secretaries through history. In the first one, he appeared in late 18th century costume as the press secretary to Catherine the Great, "Leonid Pushnev," and made an announcement that played on an enduring, but false, version of how Catherine died (during sexual intercourse with a horse). Standing behind a podium, Pushnev reported Catherine's tragic death as a riding accident. She died, he said, "in the saddle," and would henceforth be known as "Catherine the Mashed."[48] Catherine in fact, is believed to have died of a stroke, but the sexual innuendo in this sketch contributed to the overall tone of the show.

Next was a sketch that featured Julie Nixon Eisenhower and David Eisenhower, portrayed by Gilda Radner and Dan Aykroyd, hooked up to a lie detector giving untruthful responses to questions about Richard Nixon's sanity and the state of their marriage. Nixon and his family were frequently fodder for *SNL* during the early years of the show and, while Ford was president, the references certainly helped to remind people of Ford's connection to Nixon.

The David and Julie sketch was followed by John Belushi playing a pot smoking Army lieutenant colonel in a recruiting commercial, referring to the "new" Army as "a joint venture that works," and uttering lines such as, "You have your own life to lead, you have stuff to do. But so do *we*. The *best* stuff an Army helicopter can carry in from all over the world!"[49] Pot humor was another frequently occurring theme on *SNL* in the early days.

SNL aired several sketches that tied marijuana to the Ford family. These were inspired by a series of events in the second half of 1975, including a remarkably frank interview that Betty Ford did for *60 Minutes*, which aired on August 10, 1975. Ford said of her children, "I'm sure they've all probably tried marijuana," and added she might have tried it when she was young if it was something that other young people were trying at the time and she compared such experimentation with having "your first beer or your first cigarette."[50]

In October of 1975, one of the Ford children, Jack, made national news when he admitted that he had, in fact, tried marijuana, saying, "I've smoked marijuana before and I don't think that's so exceptional for people growing up in the nineteen sixties.... The important thing to me is that I do have friends who use drugs, and I don't think that will exclude them as my friends."[51] This admission prompted statements from President Ford, who refused to publicly criticize his son. Ford said that he did not "approve of young people using marijuana," but said it was "a very honorable thing" for Jack to acknowledge using it, adding, "I believe the preponderance of the evidence so far is that it's not a healthy thing to have," but that his children had "been brought up to be honest with their parents and honest otherwise."[52]

And Now for the News, "Weekend Update" Style— More of Nessen's Episode

Belushi's marijuana skit was followed by the "Weekend Update" segment, which was especially heavy with jokes at Ford's expense. The segment began with Chase's signature line, "Good evening. I'm Chevy Chase and you're not." The scene then shifted to Ford saying, "Good evening. I'm Gerald Ford and you're not." Chase responded to this with a shake of his head and said that the President's doctor was in therapy for his "identity crisis." He continued, noting that Ford gave an interview to "Underachiever's Weekly," in which he told the reporter that the middle initial, R, was in his name to separate Gerald from Ford. Describing Richard

Nixon's work on his forthcoming autobiography, Chase showed a picture of Nixon with his dog, named "Tricky." Ford, Chase said, had announced he planned to pardon the dog.[53]

The pardon joke—Ford's pardon of Nixon was a frequently occurring subject for jokes on the show—was followed by an interview, "Live from Madrid," in which Laraine Newman asked questions of the press secretary for the late Francisco Franco, played by Nessen. The bit was both a continuation of the series of "Press Secretaries throughout History" and of a long-running "Weekend Update" gag about the death of Spanish dictator Franco. Playing "Mr. Boyardee," Nessen gave a statement about Franco's condition, refusing to acknowledge that Franco was dead. Instead, he repeated that Franco was "stable."[54]

The newscast ended with Gilda Radner appearing as her recurring character, Emily Litella, to give an "Editorial Reply" in which she complained about presidential politics. The Emily Litella editorials were always based on Emily's misunderstanding of a word or concept, such as complaining about "busting schoolchildren," instead of "bussing." In this case, Litella was upset about all the news coverage of "presidential erections." The audience laughs, thinking of sex, but she launches into a discussion of monuments built to honor former presidents such as Washington and Lincoln. After going on at great length about these presidential erections and how money should be spent on elections and not erections, Chevy Chase stops her and tells her the news coverage is about the presidential election. She responds, "Oh, that's very different. Never mind."

Radner and writer Alan Zweibel discussed the editorial in *Playboy* with surprise and humor about the sketch and its ability to be aired on live television. Radner speculated that while the joke obviously had a sexual connotation, the censor let them get away with it because in her monologue, she kept referring to buildings that had been erected to honor presidents. She and writer Alan Zweibel agreed that if the jokes had been about presidents and sex, the censor would have cut the commentary.[55]

Following "Weekend Update," Nessen introduced a film by Gary Weis about New York City garbage collectors. This was followed by Radner and Chase in a faux commercial for a carbonated douche called "Autumn Fizz." Radner and Zweibel also commented on this sketch to *Playboy* discussing a line that was left out of the sketch. Radner said that they originally had her say, "Don't leave him holding the bag." It was cut not because of a censor but because, Zweibel explained, it was too easy of a joke, based on people being shocked about, "a reference to a douche bag on television."

Here, Radner added how proud she was of the episode, because they hadn't held back on the tone of the humor just because the presidential press secretary was hosting the show.[56]

Next was a spoof of Tom Snyder's "Tomorrow Show," with Dan Aykroyd playing Snyder and interviewing Ron Nessen, as himself. Snyder proceeded to question Nessen about all kinds of potentially uncomfortable topics such as sexual misbehavior by politicians, including presidents, in Washington. Nessen denied there was any truth to such stories and said that in the Ford White House, each night the President had milk and cookies with everyone who worked there and then tucked them into bed and read them a story at 9 p.m.[57]

After the politically charged *Tomorrow* sketch, the next segment was the weekly home movie, which was a regular segment in the early days of the show. The home movie during Nessen's week was as crass as anything else that appeared in the episode. It featured a man walking into a bathroom, stepping up to a urinal, and beginning to sing. Two urinals down, another man begins to sing with him, in harmony. A third man walks up to the urinals and also begins to sing. The skit goes on for approximately another minute as a fourth man walks up. The four men flush and turn around simultaneously, zipping their zippers.

The home movie was followed by another "Press Secretaries throughout History" segment, with Nessen as "Julius Marcellus," the press secretary to Oedipus, the king of the Greek city state, Thebe. "Marcellus" announces a name change for the King's mother, playing on Greek myth that Oedipus killed his father so he could marry his mother. Marcellus says, that from now on the mother of Oedipus will be known as the "Queen Wife," instead of "Queen Mother." He then asks revolutionaries to adjust their graffiti to reflect her new name.[58] The next sketch took on a different branch of the federal government, the judiciary. While it is raunchy and suggestive, like nearly everything else in the episode, it was also right on the cutting edge of current events, in the greatest tradition of *SNL*.

The sketch, "Supreme Court Spot Check," features Chevy Chase and Jane Curtin as Dwayne and Rhonda, a couple in bed having sex. The door bursts open and the nine members of the Supreme Court file in. "Justice Belushi," and "Justice Aykroyd" inform the couple that they are there because of a recent ruling by the court about the criminal nature of certain sexual acts, even when they are engaged in by consenting adults. They tell the couple to continue with what they were doing so the Court can decide if they are breaking any laws. When they tell the couple what they are doing is okay, Rhonda stops them and asks them why there are no women on the Supreme Court. They stumble awkwardly trying to answer this question and file out of the room.[59]

Like much of *SNL*'s content, this skit was both potentially offensive and very topical. On the potentially offensive question, Herminio Traviesas personally reviewed this sketch, as he did with the Flucker's sketch. As Steinmetz reported, "Specific references to Chief Justice Warren Burger and a few words such as 'tongue' are changed at the outset. Otherwise, Traviesas is enjoying it hugely. 'Best thing in the show,' he chuckles. He checks with Jane to be sure she is planning to wear something on top. She says she will wear a tube. Reassured, he exits smiling."[60]

On the question of being topical, around the time of this program's airing, two high-profile cases involving sodomy laws were working their way through the courts that apparently caught the attention of the *SNL* writers. One was *State of Iowa v. Roger Eugene Pilcher*, which involved a state sodomy law that outlawed several sexual practices, including consensual heterosexual sodomy, which was the issue in this case. In May of 1976, the Iowa Supreme Court found this law to be unconstitutional and the state legislature subsequently repealed the law, joining several other states that had done the same.

A much higher profile decision on sodomy was made by the U.S. Supreme Court on March 30, 1976, just two weeks before the Nessen episode aired, and it garnered national attention, thanks to the fact that it dealt not only with the hot-button issue of homosexual conduct, but also with the issue of privacy. Since the mid–1960s, the Supreme Court had made a series of decisions, such as *Griswold v. Connecticut* (1965), *Stanley v. Georgia* (1969), and *Roe v. Wade* (1973) that found there was a privacy right where sexually related matters were concerned, such as the use of birth control, the possession of pornography, and the right to have an abortion. In such cases, the Supreme Court consistently found that consenting adults had a right to privacy and freedom from government interference. In the case *Doe v. Commonwealth's Attorney for the City of Richmond* (1976), however, two gay men—"consenting adults"—filed suit seeking to have Virginia's sodomy law overturned, particularly where it applied to homosexual conduct. In a clear deviation from its recent decisions, the Supreme Court summarily concurred with a lower federal court's decision that found that the law's ban on sodomy and oral sex was constitutional and did not violate the right to privacy found in other recent cases. "Justice Aykroyd's" comment that it didn't matter if Dwayne and Rhonda were consenting adults was directly related to the Court's decision and the Nessen episode was the first chance the show had to comment on the decision.

"Rhonda's" question about the lack of women on the Supreme Court was also very timely. Ongoing debate about women's rights and what impact the Equal Rights Amendment might have coincided with the recent appointment of John Paul Stevens to the Supreme Court on December 19, 1975. Stevens was asked about the E.R.A. during his confirmation hearings. In having Jane Curtin's character ask about the lack of women on the Court, the sketch reminded viewers of the politics of the day. It was a sketch that was criticized, like so many of the other sketches that comprised Nessen's episode, for the sheer gall of having a sketch with two people having sex in "the Ford/Nessen episode," but it was also a sketch chock full of socio-political commentary.

Following the "Supreme Court Spot Check," Nessen appeared in another "Press Secretaries throughout History" sketch, this time as Thomas Jefferson's press secretary, "John Quincy Ross." It was an amusing, but also very pointed, critique of the third president, in the year of the bicentennial, when Jefferson was being widely lauded, along with the rest of the Founding Fathers, as a great visionary. Ross announced that there were no slaves on Jefferson's plantation. Rather, the black people working there are close relatives of Jefferson who enjoy hard labor. He added that Jefferson wants reporters to know that the Louisiana Purchase was a good idea. It will double the size of the country and, he says, will give the nation the future home for the Dinah Shore Women's Golf Classic.[61]

Given the now widely shared consensus that Jefferson fathered several children with slave Sally Hemings, Nessen's joke is even more pointed.

The remaining minutes of the show were filled with a stand-up routine by Billy Crystal, a fake ad for a pacemaker battery, and a very brief sketch, introduced by Nessen, called "Misconception," for a show whose mission was to disprove clichés. In this case, the cliché was "too many cooks spoil the broth," and it involved a large group of chefs standing around a pot, arguing about the broth. The maître d', John Belushi, steps in, tastes the broth, and pronounces it the best broth he's ever tasted. Next week, Nessen announces at the end, the show will try to prove that a cat really only has one life. Patti Smith performed a second song, a cover of The Who's "My Generation." Her first song was a cover of Them's "Gloria." When Smith was finished, it was time for the farewells.

As the host and cast gathered onstage for the traditional farewell, Nessen said that there had been some moments when he wasn't sure if he'd be able to "get through" the show but now that it was over, he was happy he'd done it and was sad that the experience was over. He'd had fun, he said, and enjoyed working with the team that put on the show.

With that, the first appearance of major political figures on *SNL* came to an end and it could hardly have been described as a rousing success by anyone in the Ford Administration.

Judgment Time

The tone of the sketches that filled Nessen's episode was roundly questioned in the press and there was a good deal of criticism of Nessen's judgment, both from members of Ford's administration and by critics in the media. A *Newsweek* article, published three weeks after Nessen's appearance, contained the following observation:

> When Nessen flubbed a line, Chase quickly ad-libbed, "Oh, that's all right, Ron, you're pardoned." Not all of the President's men were left laughing. "It was the kind of stuff you'd expect to see between two strippers," groaned one.... Another aide worried that while Nessen's performance would hardly cause the President to lose this weekend's Texas primary, as Ford was a serious underdog anyway, it wouldn't particularly help him in a string of upcoming primaries.[62]

While it will remain forever unknown what impact, if any, Ford's association with *SNL* had on the primary campaign, the reality is that while Ford resoundingly won the Pennsylvania primary on April 27, he was soundly beaten in Texas, on May 1, Georgia, and Nebraska on May 11. He also lost a closer contest in Indiana on May 4.

First reports portrayed the president as being as upset as his aides, but Ford himself announced otherwise: "You have to expect some sharp barbs in a political campaign."[63] This was a vintage Ford response to the jokes about him. He never let people know if they hurt his feelings. The *Washington Post*'s television critic, Tom Shales, who was an early fan of the program, reviewed the show in comparison with Nixon's appearance on *Laugh-In* and observed, "There were many jokes about Mr. Ford's predecessor, Richard M. Nixon.... Mr. Ford's participation in—and apparent sanction of—the 'Saturday Night' satire has been compared to Nixon's 'Laugh-in' appearance, but in fact the 'Saturday Night' sketches and gags about sex, marijuana and politics are far more explicit and outrageous than the 'Laugh-In' material ever was."[64] Shales's clear implication is that *Laugh-In* may have helped Nixon, but *SNL* did nothing for Ford.

An editorial in the *Chicago Tribune*, published several days after Nessen's episode, was blunt in its assessment of the press secretary's appearance on the show. With the headline, "It wasn't funny, Mr. Nessen," the editorial pulled no punches. "It's been nearly a week since White House press secretary Ron Nessen disgraced himself by appearing—along with a good deal of obscene humor—on NBC's 'Saturday Night' program. And we've yet to see even an effort to excuse it.... This simply can't be brushed off as the kind of humor that must be expected. The President and Mrs. Ford have tried to conceal any embarrassment, partly no doubt because Mr. Ford himself contributed to the program.... Mr. Ford should have been more careful and Mr. Nessen has done his boss a great disservice. If he wants to resume his career on television, he had better give up his job at the White House."[65]

The editorial also referred to an earlier column by Jerald terHorst, Ford's former press secretary, who was blistering in his criticism of NBC for broadcasting the program, of Nessen's performance, and of Ford's decision to let him do it:

> Acting on the belief that presidential sanction makes everything all right, NBC held a privy party last Saturday night. The fact that President Ford and White House press secretary Ron Nessen participated in the network's travesty on good taste tells us more about them than we should like to know.... But that doesn't excuse the network of NBC executives for inflicting trash on the rest of the nation, even if the excuse is that the show is aimed at the sophisticated disco set and not at Middle America or young children...

After this, terHorst poses the question of what was the motivation for the president to let Nessen appear on *SNL*. He wrote:

> What motivated Ford to give Nessen permission to participate in this show? It was the idea that if you can't lick 'em, join 'em. So the same press secretary who berated reporters and photographers for calling attention to Ford's clumsier moments went on NBC to joke about it. And the President, good sport that he is, went along with it. And NBC, apparently assuming that Ford's permissiveness meant more than it did, used the occasion to air distasteful material ... surely there must still be some staffing mechanism within the White House that can prevent such gross errors in judgment from being committed by a press secretary and compounded by a President. And it should have started with the question: "Why?" What good, for the government, for Ford, for the country, would be served by Nessen's participating in such a show? Apparently that question wasn't asked, or it certainly would have had to be answered in the negative.[66]

Jerald terHorst's harsh indictment even included the suggestion, which was also voiced by the *New York Times'* television critic John O'Connor, that Nessen did damage to U.S.–Spanish relations by portraying Francisco Franco's press secretary and participating in *SNL*'s long-running joke about Franco's death (with Chevy Chase finding many different ways to say, "Francisco Franco is still dead."). O'Connor wrote, "Suddenly, however, the satire took on questionable undertones with the participation of the Presidential press secretary. A skit about the death of Spain's late Generalissimo Francisco Franco became undiplomatic, to say the least."[67] The criticism from terHorst was harsher. He wrote, "During his daily briefings at the White House, Nessen would never think of spoofing about the death of Spain's Generalissimo Franco. The late dictator is no American hero, to be sure, but good relations with Spain and Franco's hand-picked successor, Juan Carlos, remain high on the U.S. agenda. So why is it all right for a high government official, the spokesman for the President of the U.S., to poke fun at a dead Franco on a TV comedy show? The fact is, it's not all right. It bespeaks a callous insensitivity to foreign affairs that is perturbing to all who wonder if the Ford staff is up to the job."[68]

In an article published in the *Chicago Tribune* by reporter Johanna Steinmetz, who was in the studio during the week of Nessen's episode, it was reported that there was dissension in the White House over Nessen's appearance. Steinmetz wrote:

> Some, including longtime Nessen critics, were whispering in the corridors that the press secretary's appearance accompanied by a film clip of Ford introducing the show had not helped the administration's image. One aide described his reaction to the Nessen performance as "unmitigated horror." Another said, "I haven't heard anyone say they thought it was a good idea."

Steinmetz wrote that most of the aids reported that Ford didn't display any reaction:

> Most said the President did not react at all. Nessen reportedly opened the Monday staff meeting by saying, "I guess you'll want to kid me about the 'Saturday Night' show." The President responded by saying it kept him up later than usual. Nessen attempted to follow up the commentary by saying, "And it wasn't worth it?" But others present said the President ignored the questions and shifted the discussion to other topics. One friend of Nessen's said the President suggested to the press secretary later that the television performance "may have opened up a whole new constituency." Nessen said the President was kidding.[69]

Regardless of what the president may or may not have said about Nessen's appearance, most of the post-show coverage in the press was negative and suggested Nessen had made a major misstep. Some also suggested that, perhaps, Nessen was motivated by self-interest. Steinmetz wrote, "Nessen, who prides himself on his one-liners, once confided to a friend that a post–White House career as a television personality or even a standup comedian was not unappealing to him," and she quoted Nessen talking about why he agreed to host the show, saying, "'I had watched the show. This is sort of my Walter Mitty period.'"[70]

Nessen was, according to many of the reports, prickly over criticism of his appearance and asserted that the president was not unhappy with him. One story in the *Chicago Tribune* chronicled Nessen's reaction in this way: "While his act as press secretary never has won rave reviews, his one-night stint as a White House Don Rickles and straight man for comic Chevy Chase has dismayed some White House colleagues and evoked 'stony silence' from the big critic in the Oval Office. It's the Oval Office reaction, or lack of it, that has Nessen a little testy. 'That's bull——, [sic]' he snapped, when asked about reports that President Ford was 'not pleased' with his performance... 'The President was not irritated. He found parts of it amusing, very imaginative.' Nessen said the President kidded him twice, 'for a total of about 10 seconds.' When asked what Ford kidded him about, the press secretary was hardly a Bob Hope. 'This is too silly to talk about,' he said. 'I'm too busy.... There's a lot of serious business going on here today. I don't have time to talk about this any longer. I have about 50 calls to answer and a lot of people waiting for me.'"[71]

In an interview, Gary Weis, the filmmaker who shot Ford's segments for the program, said that Nessen was initially quite angry at the post-show party, but then took a very different tone in letters he sent to the folks at *SNL*. Weis said, "I remember after the show—you know there was a party and after the party there was an after party. This was very late. Nessen flipped out in Lorne's apartment. He went nutso. 'You all think that you all have got this on us, well, fuck you!' He just snapped. He snapped. He got up and left. He thought we were trying to make fun of everything and that we outsmarted you. Then he wrote a letter it was on White House stationery to everyone."[72] In a letter to Weis and others at *SNL*, Nessen wrote, "Thank you for your thoughtfulness in sending me the blowups of your film frames taken here at the White House. The pictures will be a prized memory of a very enjoyable interlude in my life. Don't believe the stories suggesting that the White House disapproved of my appearance on 'Saturday Night.' That is not true, and in fact, the reaction has been quite good."[73] In an interview, Nessen said he did not remember losing his temper at the party.[74] In Nessen's recollection of the post-show party the most outstanding thing about it was the drug use that was taking place. Nessen said, "Well, there's always a party after *Saturday Night Live* and I assume there still is, down in Rockefeller Center. So the show was over and there was a party there. They invite all the advertisers to come meet the crew and staff. Well, then everyone adjourns to the party after the party, at Paul Simon's apartment. Paul Simon is, I guess, a good friend of Lorne. This is up on Central Park West in one of those wonderful apartment buildings. So we went up to the house and there was lot of marijuana smoking going on. And I stayed a while and it must've been late. They put the guests up at the Essex House, which is on Central Park South. I walked back from Paul Simon's apartment to the Essex House and the sky was getting light. I saw all this marijuana being smoked and if you read the books you know there was a hell of a lot of cocaine being sniffed too. I never saw any of that at the party."[75]

It is hard to know exactly what Gerald Ford's reaction was, because he never made any public comment. There was the quote attributed to him in *Newsweek*, and reports out of the White House were mixed. As one Associated Press report put it, "Earlier in the week, some White House aides had said the President was displeased with the show, but other aides denied that Ford was upset."[76] Nessen said enigmatically to reporters at a press briefing that the president had "basically no reaction" to the show.[77] In his autobiography, Nessen wrote, "When I returned to the White House on Monday morning after the program, Ford told me he had watched at Camp David, laughed at some parts of it, didn't like others and couldn't understand why some subjects were topics of humor (presumably a mock commercial for a carbonated vaginal douche and a sketch about the Supreme Court inspecting a couple's bedroom habits)."[78]

While it is true that the president, himself, made very little public comment about Nessen's and his appearance on *SNL*, Betty Ford did make some comments at a press conference in Corpus Christi, while campaigning for her husband. What she said fits with the Associated Press assessment—some of the show irritated the Fords and some of it made them laugh. In her statements, Betty Ford was not overwhelmingly critical, but she was clearly in damage control mode, responding to the criticism Ford was receiving from people like terHorst for being involved with what so many saw as a crass program. Betty Ford said, "I must say I was a little disappointed in some of the skits. I thought they were a little distasteful and so did the President. It was something we would not have had a part in. Although he was not involved in it, it looked like he was endorsing the 'Saturday Night' show. But when he did it, he didn't know what was going to take place," and complained specifically about the "Supreme Court Spot Check" sketch, referring to it as the skit which "took place in sort of intimate quarters."[79] However, when she was asked if she and the president felt that Nessen's parts in the show had been inappropriate, including the Oval Office sketch, Betty Ford said "No," and added "I thought the White House material was very funny and so did the President. We both laughed at it and had a good time."[80]

In his autobiography, Nessen tells the story of one member of the

Ford family who was quite unhappy with his appearance on *SNL*. He writes:

> Jack Ford, the president's twenty-five-year-old son, who often complained about the quality and loyalty of the White House staff, was deeply displeased by my appearance on "Saturday Night." He was traveling through the country, campaigning for the president, and grew angry when he started receiving more questions about the show than about Ford's policies.

Nessen explains:

> He dashed off an angry note in red ink on White House stationery and had it hand-delivered to me in Austin, Texas, where I was appearing at a seminar at the University of Texas. "I thought as Press Sec. you're supposed to make professional decisions that get the Pres. good press!" Jack steamed. "If you get a min. I'd be happy to explain to you that your job is to further the Pres. interests, not yours or your family's!" Jack's private plane happened to touch down that afternoon at Austin to refuel and I went out to the airport to try to mollify him. I explained that I had no intention of advancing my own interests at his father's expense, that I went on "Saturday Night" primarily to demonstrate that the Ford White House could laugh at itself and, thereby, defuse jokes about the president's clumsiness. Jack did not seem convinced.[81]

Thirty-five years later, Nessen continued to deny that the president was unhappy with his appearance on the program, though he did acknowledge that there were some in the White House who questioned his judgment for doing the show. No doubt, Nessen could find comfort in words that Ford wrote nearly a decade later in his book on humor and the presidency that seems as though they were written specifically with Nessen in mind.

> The willingness to take a chance with humor is not a frivolous characteristic of an administration. The fact is, a staff member who does not fear reprisal and is not generally intimidated is going to come up with a lot more ideas and be much more creative in his or her thinking. It's bad enough to be without lighthearted moments, but it's even worse to have silence when you need a good analysis, proposal, or speech. It wouldn't surprise me if there was a measurable correlation between humor in an administration and the popularity of that administration's policies. If a president starts to put restraints on humor, the isolation and insulation to which I referred earlier will soon follow. Avoiding that state of affairs will keep a lot of people on your side during tough times.[82]

Although he doesn't make specific reference to the April 17, 1976, episode of *SNL* in this passage, it seems clear that this was exactly the kind of creative thinking he was looking for in his advisors. It may not have worked out as he hoped, but Ford appears not to have carried a grudge about the misfire.

Nessen did not specify which staffers were so negative and neither did press reports at the time. One White House insider whose opinion about the Nessen *SNL* experience is clear is speechwriter Bob Orben. No doubt, Nessen and Ford agreed beforehand that there was value in having the administration interact with the show as a way of showing that Ford "got it" and could be part of the joke. Orben did not agree, and he was particularly troubled by Ford's cameo appearances on the show. Orben said that he was unaware of what other Ford staffers said after the episode aired, but he speculated that no one, especially Ford, could have been very happy with it. He said, "I'm sure that there was discussion. I would have loved to have known if President Ford had ever seen the show before. It was a particularly raunchy show, and knowing President Ford, I have the feeling that he wasn't thrilled with the show. I don't know that, I never discussed it afterwards ... if he had known I don't think we would have gone near it."[83] As for Ford's own appearance on the show, Orben said, "I didn't know that Ron had asked the President to do a cameo there. If I had known that, I would have gone in to the President and argued 'don't do it!'"[84] With regard to Nessen's decision to push ahead, despite his advice against it, Orben said, "All his motivation was admirable," but he knew that show was not going to do what Nessen wanted it to do for Ford's image, "Because it, if you look at the totality of the show, it wasn't going to do Ford any good," and, he concluded, "I was right."[85]

Although the majority of press commentary about the Nessen *SNL* episode ran along the "what were they thinking in the White House?" line of thought, a few reporters were more charitable. One of the most positive reviews of the episode came from Jay Sharbutt, the Associated Press's television critic. He wrote, "Last Saturday's show was good, bizarre fun and showed the man in the White House might be a good deal hipper than anyone ever suspected. And any controversy it caused probably will be overshadowed when an even more prominent White House figure hosts next week's show—the late Millard Fillmore."[86]

In his memoir, Nessen was not quite as confrontational and defensive as the *Chicago Tribune* reported, but he was still clearly annoyed by the reactions of most reporters. Nessen wrote, "Some press reaction to my appearance was downright silly. At my first press briefing following the program, Sarah McClendon demanded: 'Is this the type of thing that the president believes that the Federal Communications Commission should allow general audiences in the United States to see? Does he approve of the Federal Communications Commission permitting mixed audiences to see this?'"[87] This exchange came in the midst of a lengthy interrogation

Nessen received during his daily press briefing on the Monday after he hosted the show which touched on many topics—did the President know about the script ahead of time, how did the President react, how did the public react, was it appropriate to be involved with such a show? Much of the interchange between Nessen, McClendon, and the other reporters was good-natured, but the reporters also continued to press Nessen, prompting him to sound both puzzled and annoyed with the reaction to his hosting of the show.

When Nessen was asked if Ford knew about the content of the show in advance, he said Ford did not know. A reporter pressed, "Didn't you think it was your duty to tell him?" Nessen replied, "I did not," which prompted another reporter to ask, "Ron, did you think any part of that show was tasteless, that you should not really lend your name to that kind of an enterprise?" Nessen responded, "Well, I will let you make that judgment."

Reporters also wanted to know Ford's reaction. After telling them he thought Ford had watched "most" of the episode, he was asked, "Ron, about the question I proposed, what was the President's reaction to the *Saturday Night* show?" Nessen replied, "I didn't really talk to him that much about it, Les." The reporter responded, "He just had no reaction at all, is that it?" Nessen said, "Basically no reaction." When asked what the public response was, Nessen said, "I have no idea." A reporter followed up, "You don't know whether he got phone calls or anything? Did he say anything to you?" Nessen responded, jokingly, "My mother called." The campaign came up when Sarah McClendon asked, "Did the President's advisors say anything about whether they thought this would affect his campaign?" Nessen, clearly not telling the truth if Bob Orben's story of cautioning him is true, replied, "No, they have not. I don't even know. I don't know that they are thinking in those terms, Sarah."

Nessen was asked, "Before we leave the *SNL* show, since the President didn't know what the script was, he apparently didn't give much thought to any connection between his own tape-recorded appearances and the content of the show, is that right?" Nessen professed not to understand the question and a follow-up was asked: "Some of the material in the show is certainly controversial and the President's appearance in a tape-recorded way identifies him, in some people's minds, with the questionable content. Since the President did not have a script, does he now have any reservations about his appearance?" Nessen replied, "As I say, we just didn't talk about it."

Another question clearly reflected a sense of disbelief about Nessen's responses. "Ron, as the President's advisor on public relations, press and so forth, is it your feeling that this was any more appropriate for you and him to participate in than, say, Congressman Mills to be on stage with a close friend of his?" The question invoked the Wilbur Mills—Fanne Foxe scandal. When the laughter in the briefing room subsided, Nessen responded, "I never actually thought of that, Les." The reporter followed up, "Now that I have stimulated your thinking, do you think you could think fast on this one and tell me where you think this is more appropriate? I mean, you know, hemorrhoid jam and carbonated douches and that sort of thing? Ron, I just wondered, do you think this identifies with most of the American people, or what?" Nessen responded, "I am no TV critic, Les, so I would leave that." The conversation continued with this exchange with Sarah McClendon: "Did the President see all of the show, Ron?" Nessen answered, "I think he saw most of it, Sarah." Nessen was then asked, "Was he seeing it with Mrs. Ford or anybody?" Nessen replied, "They were up at Camp David. I don't know who..." and was interrupted with two follow-up questions, "Do you think they saw it all?" and "In mixed company?"

McClendon continued to press, asking Nessen, "I am serious. Was there anything you thought should not go on the air?" Nessen replied, "Obviously, the things I did were things that I felt comfortable doing." This brought a natural follow up, which was to ask Nessen if there was *anything* he rejected. Nessen replied, with apparent frustration, "Oh, Sarah, look, the thing was Saturday night and this is Monday morning and it strikes me that there must be more important things in the world than my appearance on *Saturday Night*." McClendon pressed ahead, saying, "I am serious about this, Ron. This has to do with you and the President, but mainly the President, being in a show like this. Is this the type of thing that the President believes that the Federal Communications Commission should allow general audiences in the United States to see.... I think this is the type of thing that the American people should know." Nessen responded, "I just didn't frankly talk to him about this. I didn't anticipate that there would be this vast amount of interest." McClendon responded, "There is some real sensitivity about this," and another reporter asked, "Did the President chide you about it?" "He did not," Nessen responded, and the press conference shifted away from *SNL*.[88]

The press conference itself influenced some press coverage of Nessen's hosting of *SNL*. For instance, this small item appeared in the *Washington Post* the day after Nessen's press conference: "Is Gerald Ford unhappy about a comedy show that starred laugh-a-minute Ron Nessen? Some

White House aides say yes, and some say no, and Nessen told reporters that there was 'basically no reaction.'" After a brief description of the episode, reporter Judy Bachrach wrote, "A top-level Ford assistant said, 'The whole thing was childish and ill-advised, not the type of thing the President should have been connected with.' Nessen said, 'There must be more serious issues in the world than my appearance on *Saturday Night*.'"[89]

In the episode following Nessen's and Ford's appearances on the show, Chevy Chase told this joke: "Our top story tonight, President Ford has been criticized all week by conservative supporters for his appearance on and endorsement of a late-night comedy TV show, which specializes in bad taste, cheap-shot humor, and filthy language wherever possible. Replying to allegations that the program made the President look stupid, Mr. Ford reportedly said, quote, 'Nonsense, pass the soup on to my face please.' He is seen here, reading the statement from a blank piece of paper."[90]

The tone of the sketches, from the carbonated douche and jam commercials, to the minstrels at the urinals and the justices of the Supreme Court watching a couple have sex, was bawdy, even by the more relaxed standards of today. According to Hill and Weingrad, "Lorne will forever maintain that *Saturday Night* did not intentionally, as he put it, 'take the President and shove his press secretary up his ass.' But many of the show's writers say there was more to it than that. They say, without equivocation, that *Saturday Night* was out to get Nessen.... The writers knew that Nessen would be on guard for material that was politically dangerous. Thus, they went in a different direction—'feinted left and went right,' as one put it—by writing instead some of the raunchiest material ever presented on *Saturday Night*."[91] In the *Playboy* interview, writer Michael O'Donoghue saw the Nessen episode as a symbiotic experience, saying, "Nessen did it to co-opt us and we did it to co-opt him, so that was a trade-off."[92] Writer Rosie Shuster said that the attitude of the writers was, "The President's watching. Let's make him cringe and squirm."[93]

Despite the fact that Chevy Chase later came to feel fondly toward Ford, in 1975 and 1976 Chase was very public with his negative feelings about Ford, both in interviews and in the way he portrayed him on *SNL*. As his biographer, Rena Fruchter, observes, "Chevy was always a political liberal, and although he knew and liked Gerald Ford, the president became an endless target of Chevy's physical humor. Some of Chevy's all-time favorite sketches were mercilessly at his expense."[94] Chase seems to have had real animosity for Ford when he was an *SNL* cast member, although he professed even then to like him personally. In interviews in the mid–1970s, Chase made his feelings about Ford, whom he met at the television correspondents' dinner and at the White House for tennis, clear before the episode aired, saying to Tom Shales, "'He's never supported any legislation to help people in his life.... He is a totally compassionless man. But a nice guy."[95]

The lengthy interview many of the writers and cast members gave to *Playboy* in 1977 included the following exchange with Chase about his feelings about Ford and his portrayal of the president. Chase stated that he thought Ford was a bad guy who didn't care about the people of the country. Asked why Ford made such a good subject for parody, Chase responded that it was inherently funny to make fun of a guy who felt so guilty about being the President that he kept trying to kill himself by falling all the time.

Commenting about the time he hosted the Radio and Television Correspondents' Banquet in Washington, with Ford in the audience, Chase said that all he did was his "terrible impression of Ford." He told the reporter that he didn't have a plan beyond stumbling and crashing into the podium, with Aykroyd and Belushi accompanying him as Secret Service agents.

Playboy then asked if Ford thought it was funny and Chase said he laughed and didn't appear offended. The next question was simply about what the two of them discussed when they met. Chase was dismissive of Ford. He said they made small talk and that while they spoke, he came to a realization about the president. Ford was, he said, not a bad guy like Nixon. He wasn't strong enough to be bad like Nixon. What he realized about Ford, Chase said, was that speaking to him was, "like looking into the eyes of 50 milligrams of Valium."[96]

Following his appearance on *SNL*, in a letter to Lorne Michaels dated April 20, 1976, Nessen wrote, "The President has asked me to notify you that if you continue to make fun of him on television, he will be forced to destroy your studio with tactical nuclear weapons. There will be no pardon this time, Michaels! But seriously, I had fun, as must have been obvious. You and the others on the show are talented and nice to be around. Don't let it all become chic."[97] Despite the positive tenor of this note, however, Nessen was less than thrilled with the outcome of his appearance on the show. Hill and Weingrad assert that what *SNL* did to Nessen was "fake the pants off the press secretary of the President of the United States."[98] In both his autobiography and an interview, Nessen acknowledged that, with hindsight, he came to believe that it was the goal of many at *SNL* to embarrass Ford, although Lorne Michaels strongly denied it. In the *Playboy* interview, Michaels was asked if there had been a plan to shock Ford with all of the blue material on the episode. Michaels denied this in a roundabout way, saying that they didn't write the show trying to shock the president because the pace of *SNL* didn't allow for such specificity.[99]

It is hard to imagine the members of the press reacting more negatively to Nessen's guest hosting gig than they did, but if the show had been more political and less raunchy, it could have been far worse for Nessen and President Ford than it was. For Bob Orben, it was bad enough. He said, "I don't think the whole episode did us any good. In a way it was validating it was drawing even more attention to the situation and not in a positive way."[100]

Nessen reviewed comments made by O'Donoghue and Chase, and acknowledged that it seemed like the show's team had been out to get him and Ford, but he denied that he or Ford had been fooled. Nessen said, "Well, I think the goal of the staff people, as revealed in their books afterward, was to really tear down Ford. But again, Ford had a good sense of humor, he had kids in the White House. You know, he understood that. I didn't get that impression. I really didn't."[101] Nessen also concluded that their appearances did not accomplish what he hoped they would. He wrote, "Looking back, it's obvious that my attempt to smother the ridicule of Ford by joining the laughter on 'Saturday Night' was a failure. Ford's reputation as a bumbler persisted and was a factor in the election outcome, as Chevy Chase claimed."[102] This was a reference to a comment Chase made in the *Playboy* interview. Chase pointed out that the election had been very close and that Ford had lost New York. If Ford had won in New York and everything else remained the same, Ford would have ended up with the same number of Electoral votes as Carter. He went on, "It's the most heinously egotistical thing to say I had anything to do with it, but I think I must have had some influence. I was clearly not a Ford man; I was, in fact, a Udall man," and after Carter sealed up the nomination, Chase said, "I supported Carter. Carter's a better man."[103]

While most of the criticism in the press and the White House was aimed at Nessen and Ford, some negative commentary was also aimed at *SNL*. Following the broadcast, John J. O'Connor, the television critic for the *New York Times*, wrote a review of the show that has criticism for Nessen and the president, the news media, and *SNL* in equal doses. He wrote, "Chevy Chase ... happens to be especially successful with his interpretations of an incredibly clumsy and dense Gerald Ford. Obviously, the Ford people would be anxious to lick this image-making threat. So, in a familiar but still treacherous ploy, they decided to join their taunters.... Suddenly, however, the satire took on questionable undertones with the participation of the Presidential press secretary. A skit about the death of Spain's late Generalissimo Francisco Franco became undiplomatic, to say the least. Jokes about Richard M. Nixon and a clever routine casting doubt on the various capacities of David Eisenhower turned curiously squeamish. So too, the show's standard parcel of sex jokes—some hilarious, some dreadful—did not mix easily with White House representation."[104]

O'Connor continued with a fascinating suggestion that much of the news media's reaction to the show was negative because of the president who was involved. It might have been much different, he argued, if a different president had been on the show: "Still, if the young John F. Kennedy had taken a similar gamble with his critics, he probably would have been praised for his refreshing charm and media sophistication."[105] This is an interesting point. It is not difficult to imagine that if it had been Kennedy saying, "I'm JFK and you're not," the press might have reacted differently because many people saw Kennedy as a handsome, witty, charming, media genius. On the other hand, many were primed to see Ford as dim, bumbling, clownish, and quite possibly corrupt—because of his pardon of Nixon. It was through that lens that his appearance on *SNL* was reviewed by the press and public. Nessen's appearance appeared to the public through the prism of news media that were jaded by Vietnam and Watergate, and cynical about anything the president who pardoned Nixon tried to do. To many in the media, Nessen's visit to *SNL* would never be seen as anything other than an attempt—in bad taste—to baldly try to control them.

Lastly, in his review, O'Connor wondered if Ford might have helped himself while the program's staff damaged themselves—the cooptation that Lorne Michaels denied being worried about. O'Connor wrote, "Perhaps President Ford has defused the 'clumsiness issue' by good-naturedly joining his detractors. But, also perhaps, the 'Saturday Night' series itself may have lost something crucial in the process. The general effectiveness of the show's political satire is directly related to its ability to be outrageous or simply naughty. But with the President's press secretary amiably participating, the same material is reduced to a symbiotic routine between the Establishment and its court jesters. Far from being outrageous, it is reassuring. Far from being naughty, it is a resounding endorsement."[106] The question that arises is whether sketch comedy's role is to resolve strife or provoke thought. Some might argue that having Ford be a dimwit is a cautionary tale to *SNL*'s audience not to be comfortable after the country's anxiety over Nixon, then often characterized as an evil genius.

Ron Nessen, thirty-five years after the fact, addressed the question of whether Ford's (and his own) appearance on *SNL* degraded the presidency as an institution, as many commentators claimed. He said things reminiscent of O'Connor's closing words in his 1976 review. Nessen talked about Ford's appearance changing—in a positive way—how presidents relate to the public. He said:

> Is President Obama going on the Leno show degrading the Presidency? Look, I think you can make the exact opposite argument. Here's a Republican President, Ford. Most people think Republicans are stuffy and look down their noses at popular entertainment and so forth. Here's a guy willing to get involved in a show that makes fun of him. It seems to me that you diffuse and you make friends. You don't lose friends by going on the show. I think that might be some over-analysis. Look, the way people get their news, information and make up their mind on political issues, is changing.

Nessen noted a trend that has become even more pronounced in the age of social media, saying that polls show that young people are finding their news in different ways, looking at sources other than the traditional media for news. He suggested there is an ever-increasing blurring of the lines between shows people watch for entertainment and the news. This, he argued, was a positive development, at least for presidents. He said:

> That has changed people's opinion of the Presidency. If anything I think it's changed their opinion for the better. As you know, you have these dinners in Washington, the Gridiron dinner, the Correspondents Association dinner. If the President comes … they always make a speech that's supposed to be a humorous speech and if they're smart, it is a self-deprecating speech. I just don't see how engaging in something that has a wide audience and lot of people watching, especially if you're a Republican that has a reputation for being stuffy and kind of out of touch with the popular culture, seems to me that it would help you, not hurt.[107]

Comments about Nessen's appearance on *SNL*, made more than thirty-five years after the fact by Lorne Michaels, lend credence to the notion, suggested by O'Connor, that the show was actually endorsing Ford, at least insofar that *SNL* saw him as a breath of fresh air after Nixon. Michaels said, when asked if the show's writers and cast had been out to "get" Nessen and Ford, "Oh no, I don't think so at all. I think it was very warm towards him. I think everyone was very excited he was doing it, we were doing it. I think it was much more playful than that. I don't think there was any attempt to spring anything on him or whatever. I think he saw and approved everything that we were doing as we were doing it. And I think the fact that the Ford White House was as open as it was and allowed this kind of thing showed the end of that kind of paranoid period and enemies list and all of that. As I said, I thought, you know, sunlight is the best disinfectant and we were part of that—the country going back towards some sort of normalcy."[108]

In a visit to the *SNL* studios during the week Ron Nessen guest-hosted, *Rolling Stone* reporter Tom Burke also argued, as O'Connor suggested, that the Nessen/Ford episode was pro–Ford. Burke wrote: "'We're *not* endorsing *any* candidate,' Lorne's stated, but the Nessen week, though funny enough, appears to be either *SN*'s blatant Washington ass-kiss, reciprocation for everyone being asked there for dinner the week before, or a thorough duping by the White House of *SN*, which produces on Saturday a long slow-motion replay of Nixon's Sock-It-to-Me. Ford himself has lots of spots (taped) on the show; never has a president so benevolently blessed, in front of millions, those who make sport of him. It's disquieting to watch, and you expect the next week, starring Raquel Welch, a funny, camp, professional performer, to be an oasis."[109]

Reminding writer Tom Davis of reviews like that suggested *SNL* was being co-opted by the politicians, prompted him to comment, "Like most reviewers, he is full of shit," but the questions raised by O'Connor, Burke and others, are worth considering.[110] Questions such as who co-opted whom and what impact *SNL* had on politics, both in the short term of the 1976 election and over the longer term of 1975 to the present, are ones that are difficult to answer with certainty, but are worth asking. Chevy Chase's impersonation of Gerald Ford had an impact on viewers and left them with an indelible impression. Supporters of Ford, of course, take issue with that impression, and in this book, it has been argued that Ford was not the bumbler *SNL* and others made him out to be. The impression, however, was powerful.

7

"Hello! My Name Is Jimmy Carter, and I'm Running for President"[1]

After winning this week's primaries, Jimmy Carter has amassed a total of 624 delegates. He now has five more delegates than he has teeth. —"Weekend Update"[2]

By April, Jimmy Carter was the clear frontrunner of the Democratic field. For their part, members of Carter's team insist that they paid little attention to Nessen and Ford's appearances on the show. Carter media advisor Jerry Rafshoon said, "I don't remember.... I remember when Ford was on there, Ford and Nessen, but it seems to me it was before the general election. April of '76, you know, we were so tensely involved in the primary campaign trying to put that away. And we were winning early, we were seriously contested by everybody at the party, we had the 'anybody but Carter' movement and we really didn't have that much time for television."[3] Rafshoon said there was no particular reaction in the Carter campaign to Nessen and Ford's appearances on the show. He said, "I've got to admit I don't remember anything like that. I mean, the '76 campaign was so intense and we were living in Atlanta and running around the country, and I'm not sure that that was really on our radar screen."[4]

Pat Caddell, Carter's pollster, said that the Carter campaign did not interact with *SNL* and he also spoke negatively of the Ford campaign's interaction with *SNL* and dismissed the show's influence during the campaign, saying, "No, I don't think I had met anybody from *Saturday Night Live* until well after the campaign.... So no, there was none [contact] whatsoever. The difference is that we would have never thought of having one. That's a difference of politics at that time and now. It never occurred to someone that you should call them up and curry favor with them, it just wasn't done. I got to know Lorne Michaels much later and a lot of people in the cast and so forth, you know, later, but that was more social than anything else."[5]

Jimmy Carter's treatment by the folks at *SNL* was not always pleasant, but during the campaign there was a significant and important difference between how the show treated Carter and how it treated Ford. Ford was portrayed endlessly, unmercifully, as a buffoon, and a corrupt buffoon at that. No matter how nice he might have been, *SNL* did a lot to reinforce the image of Ford as someone who was just not smart enough to be president and who had only been chosen for the post through political dirty dealing. The image of Ford perpetuated on the small screen by the "Not Ready for Prime-Time Players" not only influenced the audience who watched the show, but contributed greatly to a more general public discussion about Ford's fitness for office. As media researchers Lichter, et al., conclude, "But it wasn't TV news that cemented Ford's reputation as a stumblebum. It was late-night TV comedy.... Ironically, the real Ford was anything but clumsy.... But the real-life All-Star athlete couldn't compete with the bumbling comic creation of *Saturday Night's* weekly skits."[6]

Jimmy Carter's pollster, Pat Caddell, commented on *SNL*'s impact on people's impressions of Ford in 1975 and 1976. On one hand, Caddell was dismissive, saying it was "a very minor factor, it was an interesting cultural phenomenon." However, he also suggested that it had a very real impact on Ford's reputation, saying, "I think that to an extent it created, you know it added to, the image that he was a stumblebum...[it] just adds to the image held of the sense of not being in charge, not being that competent, which is ironic because he was probably the most athletic president we ever had.... The problem was, or were, the pictures, and of course, Chevy Chase was having a ball with that. So to that extent it contributed to the cultural sense of Ford."[7] Carter did not have the same problems from *SNL* during the campaign. This is not to say that the show left Carter alone— the general impression of Carter during the campaign on *SNL* was of a man who was supremely confident to the point of arrogance, and a man who was somewhat disingenuous, but he was most definitely not portrayed as incompetent. And although arrogance is not generally admired by the American public any more than incompetence, Carter was offering uncorrupt arrogance, whereas Ford's alleged incompetence suggested that if he was not part of the corruption problem of Nixon's administration, he certainly wasn't the solution to it.

In 1975, Carter wrote a campaign autobiography entitled *Why Not the Best?* The title, which might sound arrogant out of context, originated, as Carter explains in the book, from his days as a graduate of the Naval Academy, when he was applying for the Navy's nuclear submarine program. Carter was interviewed by the legendary Admiral Hyman Rickover. The admiral concluded the interview, according to Carter, with this line of questioning: "How did you stand in your class at the Naval Academy?" Carter answered, "Sir, I stood fifty-ninth in a class of 820!" Rickover responded, "Did you do your best?" Carter writes, "I started to say, 'Yes, sir,' but I remembered who this was, and recalled several of the many times at the Academy when I could have learned more about our allies, our enemies, weapons, strategy, and so forth. I was just human. I finally gulped and said, 'No, sir, I didn't always do my best.'" To which, Carter reports, Rickover said, "'Why not?' I sat there for a while, shaken, and then slowly left the room."[8]

Despite the seeming self-deprecation in the way he tells the story there is obvious ego behind the title and Carter's smiling face on the cover, which suggests, "I *am* the best. Why would you vote for anyone else?" It is obvious in the book that Carter felt very highly about himself. Throughout the book, there are passages describing his various vocations, the time he dedicates to his work, the knowledge he has accumulated, and the plans he has for the country. Carter was a man supremely confident in his abilities when he took office and, in the decades since, he has frequently spoken up to defend his record, with the seeming attitude of a man who can't quite believe that the rest of the country doesn't see him as a great president.

Carter and Ford, Aykroyd and Chase

One thing that is obvious in watching the work of Chevy Chase as Ford and Dan Aykroyd as Carter is how different were the two actors' approaches. Chase focused exclusively on physical comedy, with no attempt, or a purposeful avoidance, of looking or sounding like Ford. Aykroyd went about his impersonation of Carter with much more direct focus on his character. In describing his take on Carter, Aykroyd said, "It wasn't that I said oh, 'I want to do Jimmy Carter.' It was an assignment from Lorne Michaels as the producer of the show telling me that this gentleman was a candidate for president and had a good shot and he was in consideration and needed to be parodied so I took a look at Carter, the cardigan sweater, the smile, the eye contact, the sandy hair, and in the

Peter Sellers mode of mode of impersonations and impressions took all of those physical attributes and put them all together, watched hours of video tape and performed the impression based upon basically that premise. Of an assignment and then having to take on the physical attributes and come forth with an impression, so it was really just a function of me being one of the hired actors on the show. I enjoyed doing the impression. It's nice to have a good voice and a good accent to work with, and a good physical look."[9]

At the time he was portraying Carter on *SNL*, Aykroyd was both modest and apprehensive about his Carter impression. He told the *Washington Post*'s Tom Shales, "I'm afraid of that Carter thing a lot. I don't want to be just 'the guy who did Carter' when I go looking for another job. I remember what happened to Vaughn Meader when Kennedy died. Besides, I was in Atlanta on Election Day and that town is filled with people who can do Carter."[10]

Modest or not, the fact that Aykroyd carefully studied Carter was obvious. In this regard, the contrast between Chase and Aykroyd couldn't be starker. Aykroyd worked hard on Carter's voice and facial expressions which were, at times, characterized as off-putting by his critics. *SNL* writer Tom Davis commented on the differences between Aykroyd's Carter and Chase's Ford. "Chevy thought it was funny that no attempt was made to look like Ford.... Well, Chevy was great at playing himself. And then if he played someone else, he was Chevy playing someone else. And that's different from Dan Aykroyd who, when he sets out to do Tom Snyder, or do Jimmy Carter, you get a really good impression of that character, that is studied and perfected; whereas Chevy is always Chevy. Now, it's a little like Cary Grant. Cary Grant was Cary Grant in every part he played. And he became an enormous star, and Chevy Chase is like that, he is always Chevy Chase no matter what he does."[11] This fact was played for laughs in a sketch aired on April 24, 1976, as Chase approached the end of his one and only season as a member of the cast. Set at the Academy Awards, Chase is about to present an award. When he takes the envelope, he reads it and reacts with anger when he sees it is a request for him to "Get to the fall, Chevy." He rants that he's more than the guy who falls. He says, for instance, "I'm a writer. I'm not just the guy who falls and does this newscaster, and, frankly, I'm hurt, and I don't think it's funny. And, um.... I mean, I'm a political satirist, not some guy who just falls for you guys around here, producer Lorne Michaels." He is handed another card and it once again tells him to get to the fall. He storms off stage, yelling, "That is it! I, I'm, I'm out of this, I'm walking." He starts to leave, approaches some folding chairs, and turns back. He says, "I'll tell you something.... I'll tell you something! I am not just a physical comedian—television comedy—I ... I'm walking ... thank you, I've loved doing the show, you're great people, thanks a great deal!" At this point, of course, he stumbles over the chairs, crashes to the ground, and leaps up to shout, "Live, from New York, it's *Saturday Night!*"[12]

While Aykroyd made a much more careful impersonation of Carter, a mustache that Aykroyd wore in his portrayal of Carter stands out, because Carter did not have a mustache. Aykroyd did start to dye it gray in deference to Carter's hair color, but it still stood out. Aykroyd denied keeping the mustache on for comedic effect, stating that he simply had a mustache and didn't want to shave it: "My mustache was worn through all my work until 1977."[13] While the mustache might not have been kept for comedic effect, it was funny nevertheless, and it is in stark contrast with the rest of Aykroyd's detailed impression of Carter.

Davis commented, "Yep, it was a real mustache. Lorne wanted him to shave the mustache but he didn't want to shave the mustache. Maybe he thought it was funny, because he doesn't look like Jimmy Carter, but they did do stuff with makeup to make him look like Jimmy Carter, despite the mustache. So, it wasn't like Chevy just completely ignoring what he looked like. Which was a bold thing though; I'd never seen that done before."[14] Dan Aykroyd said, "One of Chevy's strengths is hazardous physical comedy. Mine was impressionism. We each used our respective talents to elicit laughs, however we could. Chevy's depiction of Ford is induplicable."[15]

Davis said, "Dan Aykroyd is more like, let's compare him to Laurence Olivier, and that he would be startlingly different from one part to another because of the pursuit of his craft."[16] In the first season of *SNL*, Aykroyd also portrayed Nixon with frequency and, if anything, he gave an even more detailed portrayal of the disgraced president than he did of Carter.

Aykroyd's characterization of Carter evolved over time. In his first such appearance, in an episode broadcast on July 24, 1976, Aykroyd adopted a southern accent, but did not dye his hair gray, as he did in subsequent appearances. However, in that first appearance, Aykroyd satirized Carter's style, picking up on the phoniness that some perceived in Carter. Although it seems to many observers that the cast and writers of *SNL*, especially Chevy Chase, preferred Carter to Ford in 1976, Aykroyd denies this, saying, "*SNL* never had a political bias when I was there and to the best of my knowledge it does not now."[17]

Chevy Chase, however, was always clear about his preference for Carter over Ford. When Nessen hosted *SNL*, he spoke openly of what he—and others—saw as the show's favoritism of Carter. One reporter noted of Chase, "The fellow who's become the new idol of the stay-up-late, Saturday night masses verbalizes what has already been apparent on air, that, 'None of us on the show is really a Ford fan. We've shown we are not aligned with White House politics by our satirizations which always have liberal leanings.'"[18]

Even if *SNL* could be argued to have favored Carter over Ford, however, it does not mean that Aykroyd and the writers failed to pick up on the vagueness of Carter's positions or that they favored Carter in the field of Democratic candidates. On February 21, 1976, just after the New Hampshire primary, Chase told this joke about Carter: "After his plurality victory in former Georgia, Governor Jimmy Carter was asked when he would start getting more specific on the issues. Carter said, 'Perhaps sometime in the near future.'"[19] Even Johnny Carson, who was careful to be almost entirely non-political on his show,[20] made jokes about Carter's lack of firm political positions.[21]

In his autobiography, Arizona Congressman Mo Udall reflected on his and Carter's different campaign styles in 1976: "Carter was escaping virtually untouched on the issues. Perhaps blinded by his smile, the reporters traveling with him wrote mostly positive stories about his do-good, feel-good quest for a renewal of trust, goodness, and godliness in Washington.... This strategy, conceived by Jody Powell, Hamilton Jordan, and Pat Caddell, was brilliant—and brilliantly executed. By the time my campaign got tough on Carter, he was so far ahead that my accusations that he was waffling on the issues only served to make me look shrill."[22]

A sketch, "Carter's Campaign," which was broadcast on July 24, 1976, just after Carter secured the nomination, was quite negative, playing on Carter's obviously large ego and the perception of some, such as Udall, that Carter was too slick. One aspect of Aykroyd's performance that really stands out is his big, often inappropriate smile, and obvious attempts to make eye contact which he mentions specifically in the sketch. The sketch is a direct commentary on Carter's campaign style. Aykroyd's Carter talks about the speeches he's planning to make around the country and how, while giving those speeches, making eye contact with members of the audience is critically important. As he outlines this strategy, which he will follow no matter how big or small the audience, he is demonstrating the technique, promising he's going to do it, "just like this."[23]

Bob Dylan, Ted Kennedy, Hubert Humphrey and More to Laugh About on SNL

In addition to jokes about Carter's apparent lack of sincerity, another recurring theme in *SNL*'s treatment of the candidate was his self-professed appreciation of the music of Bob Dylan. Carter frequently invoked Dylan's name in *Why Not the Best?* and in his campaign speeches. He said, "I started to listen to Bob Dylan's music primarily because of my sons, but I got to like it and I used to spend three or four hours a day listening to Paul Simon, Bob Dylan and the Allman Brothers. At home I'd study government reorganization or budgeting techniques while I listened to rock."[24]

Before he had officially declared his candidacy, when he was still governor of Georgia, Carter spoke at the University of Georgia Law School's "Law Day" event. He said, "[One] source of my understanding about what's right and wrong in this society is from a personal, very close friend of mine, a great poet named Bob Dylan. After listening to his records about "The Ballad of Hattie Carrol," [sic] and 'Like a Rolling Stone' and 'The Times, They Are a-Changing,' I've learned to appreciate the dynamism of change in a modern society. I grew up as a landowner's son. But I don't think I ever realized the proper interrelationship between the landowner and those who worked on a farm until I heard Dylan's record, 'I Ain't Gonna Work on Maggie's Farm No More.'"[25]

Carter invoked Dylan's name with frequency, no doubt believing that it lent his campaign credibility with America's youth. In his autobiography, Carter wrote, "I am a Southerner and an American. I am a farmer, an engineer, a father and husband, a Christian, a politician and former governor, a planner, a businessman, a nuclear physicist, a naval officer, a canoeist, and among other things, a lover of Bob Dylan's songs and Dylan Thomas's poetry."[26]

Carter quoted a Dylan line in his speech accepting the Democratic nomination for president, saying, "I have never had more faith in America than I do today. We have an America that, in Bob Dylan's phrase, is busy being born, not busy dying."[27] This turned out to be a bit of an error on Carter's part. The way the lyrics actually read in the song, "It's Alright, Ma (I'm Only Bleeding)," is "That he not busy being born is busy dying."[28] Carter quoted Dylan so frequently, it was easy picking for the parody of *SNL*. For instance, in the peanut warehouse sketch, Aykroyd's Carter said, "You know, I like to quote Bob Dylan. And he said something I think means a lot to Americans and that is, 'You should not feel so all alone, everybody must get stoned.'"[29]

It is Carter's apparent political motivation in quoting Bob Dylan that Aykroyd played with in his portrayal of Carter and, as a result, the treatment of Jimmy Carter on the show was far from unabashedly positive. As Aykroyd said, the writers and he went for the comedy where they saw it and that did not always reflect positively on Carter. However, despite their possibly negative aspects, the Carter sketches did something that the Chase treatment of Ford did not—they treated Carter as intelligent and competent, and that is something that Carter apparently enjoyed. When asked in a written interview, Carter indicated that he had never paid any attention to *SNL* until Tina Fey's famous turn as Sarah Palin in 2008, writing, "I've never watched *SNL* nor had any serious discussions about any episodes (except Sarah Palin)."[30] However, Carter's White House communications director, Gerald Rafshoon, remembered things differently in an interview for this book, saying, "He loved it, he loved it…. Yeah, he did."[31]

Carter and Civil Rights

In an interview with reporter Sam Roberts of the *New York Daily News*, published on April 4, Carter made the biggest gaffe of his campaign when he was asked about "low-income scatter-site housing in the suburbs."[32] He said, "I see nothing wrong with ethnic purity being maintained. I would not force a racial integration of a neighborhood by government action. But I would not permit discrimination against a family moving into the neighborhood."[33] Instead of realizing the danger of a southern candidate for president using such a politically and emotionally charged phrase, Carter reiterated his remarks several times over the next couple of days. For instance, in response to a CBS correspondent, Carter said, "I have nothing against a community that's made up of people who are Polish, Czechoslovakians, French-Canadians, or blacks who are trying to maintain the ethnic purity of their neighborhood."[34] At an event in South Bend, Indiana, Carter said, "I'm not going to use the federal government's authority deliberately to circumvent the natural inclination of people to live in ethnically homogeneous neighborhoods."[35]

However, as the remark continued to draw press attention, Carter finally relented and, six days after it was first published, he issued an apology—though a somewhat defiant one. In Philadelphia, just before the Pennsylvania primary, he said that he apologized for "an unfortunate choice of words.... I don't think there are ethnically pure neighborhoods in this country," and added that the phrase ethnic purity "bothers me too." He concluded, "If the phrase had racial connotations, I've apologized, I hope, to the public, and I've already talked to my supporters."[36]

Unsurprisingly, Carter's opponents tried to take advantage of his comments. Udall said, "It is disturbing, very disturbing language to hear from a presidential candidate, whatever he ends up saying he meant to say."[37] Gerald Ford objected to the use of the phrase "ethnic purity," but did try to take advantage of both sides by saying that "ethnic heritage is a great treasure of this country and I don't think that federal action should be used to destroy that ethnic treasure."[38] Hence the "ethnic treasures" joke in the Ford and Nessen Oval Office sketch.

On Nessen's April 17 episode, two weeks after Carter first made the ethnic purity comment and a week after he apologized for it, Chevy Chase made a joke about the remark during the "Weekend Update" segment, saying that Carter denied that when he referred to "ethnic purity," he was speaking only about white neighborhoods. Carter, Chase reported, was going to get rid of his speechwriter, "Bernie Goebbels."[39]

The joke was biting, and it was one of only a couple of jokes on the show that referred to the incident. In the cold open to an episode broadcast on April 24, Chevy Chase appeared as a presenter on the Oscars and he was there to present an award for the best performance in a political campaign. Carter was nominated for his "ethnic purity" comments, along with several other nominees, including Gerald Ford for, "shortening the nation's attention span," and George Wallace for his support of civil rights.[40] Carter's remark was a major gaffe, but the use of the phrase, along with his stubborn refusal to back away from it for several days, never became an issue of any significance for *SNL* during the campaign—just two short jokes. There is some evidence, in fact, that the *SNL* team made a conscious effort not to play Carter's comments for laughs or politics.

On Nessen's episode, one of the running "Press Secretaries through Time" sketches was supposed to include Hitler's press secretary. *Chicago Tribune* reporter Johanna Steinmetz reported that writer Alan Zweibel told Nessen that Hitler's press secretary would "perhaps make some sense out of an alleged remark his boss made about ethnic purity." But, Steinmetz continued, while Nessen responded enthusiastically, Zweibel added, "But we can't make the joke on Carter. We have to make it on Hitler."[41] Not only did they not make the joke on Carter, there was never a Hitler press secretary sketch in the show. Unlike the ceaseless portrayals of Ford as a bumbling fool, this arguably much more serious gaffe by a candidate who claimed to be a pioneering politician on the issue of civil rights could arguably have been given more attention by both the news media and entertainers like those at *SNL*.

The African American leader Julian Bond, at the time a state senator in Georgia, was not a supporter of Carter and had, in fact, campaigned for Morris Udall during the primary season of 1976. Toward the end of the campaign he worked for Carter's election over Gerald Ford. In 1977, shortly after Carter took office as president, Bond guest-hosted *SNL*.

Bond said there was a real difference in how the show treated the two candidates, giving Carter the benefit of the doubt where they gave Ford none. In response to a question about the difference between how the show dealt with Ford's gaffe on Eastern Europe, which is examined in the next chapter, and Carter's "ethnic purity" remark, Bond said, "I think Ford's error was simply verbal confusion—surely he knew better. Carter's statement seemed to me a deliberate ploy for Northern, urban white ethnic votes—he said them in upstate New York, as I recall. Maybe the lack of *SNL* references reflected the writers themselves—white youngsters with little racial consciousness."[42]

8

Jimmy and Jerry Debate
While Dan and Chevy
Do the Same

There is solid evidence that many funny stories become staples of collective memory. When they are repeated over and over again, memories are refreshed and the humorous story lingers. A good example is the publicity generated about former President Ford when he died in 2006. Old clips from Saturday Night Live *mocking him for clumsiness saturated the airwaves. Were the effects of these clips the same in 2006 as they had been thirty years earlier during the 1976 presidential campaign? We do not know.*—Doris Graber[1]

In 1976, *SNL* began a tradition that endures four decades later—the faux debate. *SNL* actually aired a debate sketch prior to the first "real" debate between Ford and Carter. We are now accustomed to *SNL's* faux debates parodying the actual debates, playing on memorable moments such as Gore's references to the "lock box," or Obama's seemingly sleepy performance in his first debate with Mitt Romney. But the premiere of this now well-known comedy sketch genre came in September of 1976. To contextualize, the political scene had been transformed by television broadcasts of presidential debates in 1960.

Many scholarly, as well as more casual, observers argue that the point in American politics when image came to be more important than substance was the first televised debate between John Kennedy and Richard Nixon. It was the first televised presidential debate in history and those who watched it on television tended to express the opinion that Kennedy won the debate, while those who listened to it on the radio felt as though Nixon's performance was better.[2] So convinced were presidential candidates such as Lyndon Johnson and Richard Nixon that the 1960 debates had a profound impact on the outcome of the election, there were no televised presidential debates from 1960 to 1976. The politicians explained this lack of debating by blaming the FCC's equal time rule, but that was just a convenient excuse which made it possible to say that they would love to debate, but the FCC's rules wouldn't let them to do it unless there were twenty candidates on the stage.

There was no incentive for the candidates—certainly not the frontrunners—to debate in 1964, 1968, or 1972. There was no reason for Johnson, who had every advantage in 1964, not the least of which being the memory of a martyred president to lean on, to engage in a televised debate with Barry Goldwater. Nixon, who learned important lessons from the 1960 debates (chief among these was: don't participate), had no interest in participating in debates in 1968 or 1972. All that Nixon could have accomplished by debating was to endanger comfortable leads in the polls over Hubert Humphrey and George McGovern. In 1976, however, both candidates understood there was potentially much to be gained from debates—they both felt they would win by, among other things, demonstrating to Americans how likable they were.

However, the equal-time rule was still a serious concern. There were close to a dozen third-party candidates running, from former Georgia governor Lester Maddox, who was the American Independent Party candidate, to Socialist Workers candidate Peter Camejo, and the perennial candidate, Lyndon LaRouche. Neither Carter nor Ford had a desire to share the stage with fringe players. The need to do so was negated by an FCC decision in 1975.

In late September of 1975, the FCC ruled, by a five-to-two vote, that the equal-time rule would no longer apply to candidate press conferences or candidate debates (providing the debates were not held in network studios and were sponsored by independent organizations, such as the League of Women Voters). The commission's reasoning was that "the undue stifling of broadcast coverage of news events involving candidates for public office has been unfortunate and we believe that this remedy will go a long way toward ameliorating the paucity of coverage according these events during the past 15 years."[3]

Ford needed to close the gap in the polls and to prove his presidential bearing, knowledge, ability—i.e., intelligence—to be president, and to draw attention to what the Ford campaign believed was a major Carter flaw—his lack of specificity on the issues. As an internal Ford campaign memo from August argued, "Carter's success is largely attributable to three factors: 1. A thematic campaign of national renewal avoiding issues. 2. Relative to other candidates, he's terrific and is perceived as a winner. 3.

He is a superb politician and highly intelligent."[4] By engaging in debates, the Ford campaign hoped to pin Carter down on issue positions and then attack those positions, to make Carter look like less of a winner, and to demonstrate that Ford was also intelligent and a superb politician. Carter, on the other hand, wanted to prove he was presidential material, not just an appealing character from the country that *seemed* like a breath of fresh air after the trauma of Vietnam and LBJ and Watergate and Nixon, but didn't have any real substance.

According to journalist Martin Schram, "Style, both camps had come to believe, was probably more important than substance. In fact, in the debate, style perhaps *was* substance."[5] Style certainly had much to do with the negotiations that preceded the debates. Issues such as how Ford and Carter would be addressed (the Carter side didn't want Ford to be referred to as "President" while Carter was called "Governor"); the positioning of the podiums (the Carter team didn't want Ford and Carter standing side by side, thereby emphasizing Ford's significant height advantage); and the subjects of the debates (Carter, for example, wanted the first debate to be about domestic policy—it was—because he viewed it as a strength for him during a time of economic downturn).[6] The two sides agreed to three debates, the first devoted to domestic policy, the second to foreign policy, and the third was open to any topic. There was also a vice presidential debate between Bob Dole and Walter Mondale.

The strategies for each side were different, but the ultimate goal was the same—to make voters see the positive differences between each man and his opponent. According to Schram, Ford's debate objectives were similar to his reasons for allowing Ron Nessen to appear on *SNL*. Schram wrote, "The President's advisors saw the debates as a chance for the President to dispel the notions that he was not intelligent and not capable of running the government and leading the country."[7] Of Carter's objectives, Schram wrote, "For Carter, the debates were a chance to show, most of all, that this still relatively unknown man from Georgia could be presidential. The debates were a chance for him to demonstrate that he was not fuzzy on the issues. They were a chance for him to show that he had done more in 1976 than just grinning and winning; he could show that he was well acquainted with the issues facing the country."[8]

The first debate took place in Philadelphia on September 23rd in the Walnut Street Theater. It was generally regarded as a victory for Ford, if only because he didn't do nearly as badly as many expected him to do. From a purely aesthetic standpoint Ford was a clear winner. The candidates were positioned so their height difference was obvious and, throughout the debate, Carter was referred to as "Governor," while Ford was referred to as "President." Carter's aide, Greg Schneiders, left the hall where the debate was held to watch it in a bar so he could gauge public reaction. When he returned to the hall after the debate, "Carter aides were slapping their candidate on the back and shaking his hand and telling him he had been great. Schneiders knew better. No, he told one of the other advisors, Carter had not won. Maybe it was even. At best."[9] In addition, the Republican pollster Robert Teeter conducted an ongoing poll throughout the debate in which he measured viewers' reactions with a device equipped with a rheostat knob that they could turn up or down depending on what each candidate said. He found that "the debate ... went clearly to Ford. Various subsequent, independent surveys gave an edge to the President as well."[10] After the first debate, Ford's team felt he had looked and sounded good, and confidently awaited the second debate. And *SNL* created their first in a lengthy run of faux debates.

The First-Ever SNL *Debate*

In its first faux debate, which aired on September 18, 1976, *SNL* predicted many of the events of the first real debate featuring Gerald Ford and Jimmy Carter, but, by going first, they were also unable to take full advantage of some comic gold. Live performance events happened in the real first Ford-Carter debate that seemed ready-made for the *SNL* parody treatment. For instance, toward its end, the debate was interrupted by a strange occurrence that is every bit as memorable as anything the two candidates said, when the networks' audio feed from the theater was lost. Jimmy Carter was in the middle of a response to Ford's answer to a question from panelist Elizabeth Drew about control of the federal government's intelligence agencies. Carter spoke for about half a minute after the audio was lost before he was told what happened. When Carter was informed that the audio feed had been lost he stopped speaking and the candidates stood at their podiums, not speaking and looking uncomfortable, for twenty-seven minutes, until the sound was restored and they finished the debate. Ford speechwriter Bob Orben remembers thinking that Ford would have wanted to handle the uncomfortable wait differently. Orben said, "Remember in the first debate something went wrong with the sound system and for some incredible reason they had both Carter and Ford standing up in front of the lecterns and it was characterized at the time as two guys who had [gone] into a tailor shop and were waiting for their pants to come back. Unfortunately, that's the case. Ford's natural bent, I think, would have been to come up and sit on the lip of the stage and make small talk because he was that sort of person, but at that point there were too many *experts* involved."[11]

When the audio problem was finally resolved, Carter picked up with no reference to the lengthy delay, saying, "There has been too much government secrecy and not, not enough respect for the personal privacy of American citizens."[12] Carter and Ford then gave their closing statements and the debate was over.

During the outage, with what sounded like some tongue-in-cheek commentary, network broadcasters reassured viewers that the CIA had not pulled the plug on debate *about* the CIA. On the CBS broadcast of the debate, anchor Harry Reasoner broke into the broadcast after about thirty seconds of silence and said, "The pool broadcasters in Philadelphia have temporarily lost the audio. It is not a conspiracy against Governor Carter or President Ford and they will fix it as soon as possible."[13] During the outage, NBC anchor David Brinkley also seemed to be addressing potential audience concerns about some kind of a conspiracy when he said, "Again, the pool audio from the Walnut Street Theater in Philadelphia has been lost, we hope, for the moment. We are, needless to say, trying to restore it. Do not know what has happened to it. Both candidates have lost a more or less equal number of, of their words."[14] One thing is certainly true: the loss of audio, emphasized especially by the subject matter of the debate when it was lost—secretive government agencies like the FBI and CIA— should have been ready-made material for parody on a show like *SNL*, if only the debate sketch aired *after* the actual first debate.

The strange audio problem became fodder for a joke, delivered by Jane Curtin, on "Weekend Update." While Ford won the first third of the debate and Carter won the second third, it was the American people, Curtin said, who won the final, largely silent, third of the debate.[15] When interviewed, Tom Davis, who wrote the sketch with Al Franken, Chevy Chase, and Dan Aykroyd, didn't specifically recall the audio gap in the actual debate, or the specific timing of which debate occurred first, but he suggested that it simply wouldn't have fit with the comic flow of the rest of the sketch to include it, saying, "Our plate was full anyway."[16] To Davis, having to worry about the actual occurrence of the audio outage might have interfered with the more substantive material they wrote for the sketch. This attitude is certainly reflected in the fact that they did not revisit the audio loss in their subsequent two 1976 debate sketches.

Regardless of the writing choices that went into preparing the sketches, there is one undeniable fact: this is the only time the parody debate has aired before a real debate on the show. Even if Davis felt like the audio gap wouldn't have contributed much, it seems as though at least someone, perhaps Lorne Michaels, may have looked at the audio gap as a comedic opportunity lost. Debate sketches are now a staple of *SNL* and they always make reference to what has happened in actual debates. We now expect *SNL* sketches to comment on things that have happened. In that first debate sketch, the writers were predicting what they thought would happen. In large measure, they were right on target, which is testament to what keen observers of the campaign Davis and his colleagues were. A twenty-seven-minute loss of audio, of course, would have been impossible to predict, but it would have been interesting to see what *SNL* could have performed.

In that sketch, the themes that the *SNL* writers played on were the same themes which the candidates' teams hoped to turn from weaknesses to strengths with the debate: Ford's alleged dull-witted clumsiness and Carter's slipperiness on the issues. The sketch was hosted by Lily Tomlin, who appeared as Ruth Clusen, the president of the League of Women Voters, the organization which sponsored the debates in 1976. The real Clusen later went on to serve in the Carter administration as an assistant secretary in the Department of Energy. The fictional debate began with a coin toss, as in the beginning of a football game, which was a satiric shot at the president, a former University of Michigan football star. The referee who conducted the coin toss was veteran NFL referee Tommy Bell, as portrayed by Tom Davis. The panel of reporters included Jane Curtin as Liz Montgomery, Garrett Morris as Earl Roland, and John Belushi as Tom Burke. The first question, asked by Jane Curtin, went to Ford about whether he was avoiding the public by staying in the White House. Ford, stumbling on pronouncing her name, said that he wasn't hiding, rather he was lost.

Next was a question from John Belushi for Carter about marijuana, which turned to a discussion of pardons. Belushi asked him where he stood on the question of the legalization of marijuana, since his own son, Chip, said that he smoked marijuana. Carter said he would pardon Chip for smoking marijuana, but only after the legal process had run its course. Jane Curtin then interrupted and pointed out that it seemed like Carter had used the opportunity to raise the issue of pardons, since Ford had pardoned Nixon. Was he, Curtin asked, hoping to gain some advantage by brining up Watergate? Carter denied that this was the case but continued speaking after the buzzer, taking time to spell out the word Watergate while continuing to deny that he was trying to use it for political advantage.

Asked for his rebuttal, Ford stumbled through an answer saying that he agreed, Watergate had no business being discussed in the debate.

Jane Curtin tells Carter that it is obvious he changed the marijuana question to a discussion of pardons and asks if he's hoping to make political "gains" by bringing up Watergate. One of the single-most important issues in the 1976 campaign was the legacy of Richard Nixon's presidency and Ford's decision to pardon him. It is not surprising that, when writing the first debate sketch, the writers also viewed the pardon as excellent material—for comedy.

When pressed on the issue of abortion, on which both candidates were difficult to pin down in the real world, Chase as Ford said that he supported the idea of letting states decide their own policies on abortion, so women who wanted an abortion could just move to a different state. In his rebuttal to Ford, Akroyd as Carter said unequivocally that he saw no need to clarify a "perfectly ambiguous" position on abortion.

During the campaign, Carter's sincerity was questioned frequently, by Carter's opponents and some members of the press. As one *Wall Street Journal* report characterized the primary campaign, "On the Democratic side, most intra-party sniping thus far has been aimed at former Gov. Jimmy Carter of Georgia, a sure sign his fellow candidates are beginning to take him seriously. The central complaint seems to be that he's a rather slippery customer—either deliberately telling different things to different audiences, depending on what each wants to hear, or at least quite content to let different audiences draw different conclusions from deliberately vague statements."[17] On this question about Carter, the "Not Ready for Prime-Time Players" were more than willing to join in.

Ford's proposal on abortion in the campaign was exactly what Chevy Chase voiced as Ford in the faux debate: a constitutional amendment to allow each state to determine its own position on abortion. It was a clever idea on Ford's part, for such an amendment would have forever eliminated the need for federal politicians to get involved in abortion politics and would have, instead, always made abortion a state issue. Belushi and Aykroyd had an exchange about whether or not Carter flip-flopped on the issues. Carter denied ever flip-flopping on the issues. Belushi pointed out several instances of apparent flip-flopping, getting Carter to admit each one. At the end, Carter engaged in a tortured bit of flip-flopping on the subject of flip-flopping, apologizing for it to save himself from, "the embarrassment that normally accompanies flip-flopping.[18]

While this particular line of fake debate touched on questions about Carter, there was far more about Ford's flaws in the sketch. Among other issues addressed in the faux debate was the economy, and an exchange on that topic ended with one of *SNL*'s most famous jokes—at Ford's expense. Jane Curtin began with a question about a complicated piece of economic legislation, the Humphrey-Hawkins bill. As she introduced one economic figure after another, the camera shows Ford looking ever more confused. When she finally finishes the long question, he looks at the camera, face covered in sweat, and says, "It was my understanding that there would be no math during the debates." He then invited Curtin to ask him any other question about domestic policy that she wanted, such as his relationship with Betty Ford.

The Humphrey-Hawkins bill, which was eventually signed into law by Jimmy Carter in 1978, was a sweeping piece of legislation dealing with employment and other aspects of economic policy. Lorne Michaels remembered the line fondly, saying, "My favorite moment on it, I think, is probably the Ford-Carter debate where Chevy's answer is, "Um I was told there would be no math."[19] Writer Tom Davis also cited this line as his favorite moment from *SNL*'s treatment of the 1976 campaign, giving Al Franken credit for writing it.[20] Poking fun at Ford for being ignorant on issues of the federal budget was an especially unfair thing to do because Ford took particular pride in his mastery of everything to do with the budget.

The sketch ended with a bit of physical comedy—a botched attempt by Ford to pour some water and a spectacular crash over the podium which, during rehearsal, injured Chase severely enough that, after the show, he had to be hospitalized.

Chase missed the next couple of weeks' worth of shows. When he was asked about the incident by *Playboy*, he said that he had broken his "podium." The injury occurred during the rehearsal and it was only after the show that he realized the severity of the injury.[21]

Writer Tom Davis described Chase's accident and its aftermath in rather colorful language, saying, "Yeah, he fell over on—there was a metal lectern and he fell off the stage and smashed his balls. And he got up and did the show while he was in tremendous pain. He got up, and he was in great pain during that show, and you'll never notice, he's totally professional. But he banged his balls up bad enough that he had to go to the hospital. Yeah, he was out for a while, yeah."[22]

Never ones to let a potential comic moment go, the *SNL* writers made Chase's injury opening fodder while he was recuperating. The next week's episode began with a cold open featuring Gilda Radner, who reported to the audience that Chase injured himself during the debate sketch and wouldn't be able to do that week's cold open. Since the show must go on, she said that she would go ahead and start the show without him, doing the sketch that she and Chase rehearsed.[23]

The Second Debate(s): Eastern Europe and Playboy—Material from the Real World for the Second SNL Fake Debate

The second debate between Carter and Ford was held on October 6 in San Francisco. Moderated by Pauline Frederick of National Public Radio, the debate quickly became legendary for one of the greatest gaffes ever made by a presidential candidate. The fear of making such gaffes was, of course, one of the prime reasons that front-running candidates avoided televised debates in 1964, 1968, and 1972. The gaffe was made by Ford and his problems began with a question from *New York Times* reporter Max Frankel about the United States' relationship with the Soviet Union and about the Helsinki Accords, signed in 1975 which, Frankel argued, was essentially an agreement from the United States "that the Russians have dominance in Eastern Europe." Ford responded, in part:

> I believe that we have uh—negotiated with the Soviet Union since I've been president from a position of strength.... In the case of Helsinki, thirty-five nations signed an agreement, including the secretary of state for the Vatican—I can't under any circumstances believe that the—His Holiness, the Pope, would agree by signing that agreement that the thirty-five nations have turned over to the Warsaw Pact nations the domination of, uh—Eastern Europe. It just isn't true. And if Mr. Carter alleges that His Holiness by signing that has done it, he is totally inaccurate. Now, what has been accomplished by the Helsinki agreement? Number one, we have an agreement where they notify us and we notify them of any, uh—military maneuvers that are to be undertaken. They have done it. In both cases where they've done so, there is no Soviet domination of Eastern Europe and there never will be under a Ford administration.

As the moderator tried to ask Carter for his response, Frankel interrupted and said:

> I'm sorry. I—could I just follow—did I understand you to say, sir, that the Russians are not ... using Eastern Europe as their own sphere of influence in occupying mo—most of the countries there and in—and making sure with their troops that it's a—that it's a Communist zone, whereas on our side of the line the Italians and the French are still flirting with the possibility of ... Communism?

It is difficult to understand how Ford could have said such a thing and, given a chance to reconsider his words, refuse to retract it. Journalist Martin Schram argues that Ford's misstep was the result of over-preparation:

He had gone into the debate primed to counter a question that was never asked. Ford and his advisors had expected that he would be asked about a position that had been expressed privately by a State Department official, but which had been leaked to the press and had become a political embarrassment to the President. The State Department official, counselor Helmut Sonnenfeldt, had taken the position that the United States should, in its planning, concede the obvious military reality that Eastern Europe is under the military domination of the Soviet Union.... The leaking of Sonnenfeldt's view of the military reality brought Ford political problems from his party's right wing. He had gone into the debate rehearsed to try to ease this political pressure by emphasizing that he did not intend to concede Eastern Europe to the Soviet Union. But once on camera, Ford went too far.[24]

Schram's explanation has merit—it is impossible that Ford really believed there was no Soviet domination of Eastern Europe—but regardless of what prompted Ford to say what he did, the comment—and his refusal to retract it—had tremendous consequences. In the aftermath of the debate, there was hell to pay. Ford was widely scorned as people analyzed his remarks and speculated about what they could mean. Each scenario was more negative than the last. Either Ford was crazy, stupid, or a combination of the two. Many in the media, and in the viewing audience, wondered how there was any way Ford could say that the Soviet satellite states of Central and Eastern Europe were not under Soviet domination.

SNL's *Second Debate*

SNL's second faux debate was billed on the show as the third debate, but it was closely based on the actual second debate. Unlike the first such debate, which was broadcast before the actual first debate, this sketch did not air until October 16, a week after the second debate, and Ford's Poland comments were the basis for many of the sketch's jokes. However, the second *SNL* debate did not stick solely to foreign policy the way the real second debate did and while no one at the San Francisco debate asked Carter about his *Playboy* interview, it was ready-made for *SNL*.

In the sketch, panelists were played by Garrett Morris, Jane Curtin, and John Belushi. Aykroyd was Carter, and Chase was back from medical leave as Ford. *SNL* is not often subtle, but in the debate sketch, one sight gag had Ford with a hypodermic needle stuck in his shoulder. It was, as *SNL* writer Alan Zweibel described, a reference to the swine flu inoculation program instituted by the Ford administration. Zweibel said, "It was a parody of Ford's getting his swine-flu vaccination and Chevy came out and did the whole debate wearing a suit with this hypodermic just sticking in his arm. Nobody even mentioned it."[25]

The vaccination program became a problem for Ford because the vaccinations were quickly portrayed as more potentially hazardous than swine flu. In an attempt to calm public concern about the vaccine, and to support the government's "Roll up your sleeve" campaign, Gerald Ford, members of his family, as well as Ron Nessen and White House photographer David Kennerly, all received the injection from the White House physician, William Lukash. Ford did so in front of a group of reporters and photographers in the Oval Office. This was a day before the second debate sketch aired on *SNL*.

With jokes about many current topics, the second debate sketch was truly a mirror that parodied the latter stages of the 1976 campaign. By far, the subject most frequently joked about was Ford's position on Eastern Europe. In one exchange, Jane Curtin said that there was a lot of pressure during debates and that anyone could make a really stupid mistake. She asked if he would be willing to clear things up by talking about his observations from his last trip to Poland. Ford responded by telling her that Milwaukee was a beautiful city and that the people of Milwaukee have a strong independent spirit. Then, in a reference to an old Polish joke, told a story about a burned out light bulb in his hotel room, which he changed with the help of his Secret Service agents, who turned the desk he was standing on while he held on to the light bulb.[26]

In the political arena, Ford's gaffe was a much-needed diversion for Carter, shifting negative media attention away from him. Carter had recently given a controversial interview in *Playboy*. It was controversial both because of what he said and because it was in *Playboy*. For that and other reasons, Carter had been suffering in the polls. The interview was published in the November issue of *Playboy*, but it was big news far earlier, due to the fact that *Playboy* made the text of the interview available to other media outlets in late September—just a shade too late for the first debate sketch on *SNL* on September 18. The interview was very long and the majority of it is focused squarely on the campaign and questions about policy. The first story about the interview appeared in the *New York Times*, for instance, on September 21 and it led with the line, "Jimmy Carter has said in an interview that he has 'looked on a lot of women with lust' and that he has 'committed adultery in my heart many times,' but that 'God forgives me for it.'"[27]

Carter delivered the lines in the context of talking about faith and made into headline material, including comments about sex and Lyndon Johnson. Concluding the interview, Carter said that he didn't sin on purpose, but that it was impossible not to sin. He then said, as an example, that he had never committed the sin of adultery by having an affair with another woman. But, he admitted, he had had lustful thoughts about other women, and that was also a sin. It was important for him, he said, not to think of himself as better than other people, perhaps some who had actually cheated on their wives, just because he hadn't done it. Thinking about it, he argued, was just as bad, and he was guilty of that.

Ford and his campaign team did their best to take advantage of the negative coverage of Carter's interview. Ford condemned Carter's decision to do the interview, especially at a press conference on October 20, in which he offered criticism of Carter on many issues. When Ford was asked about the *Playboy* interview, he repeated a statement that he made before—that he had turned down an invitation to do an interview for the magazine and denied that he had even seen the issue in which Carter's interview was published. A reporter later asked, "Mr. President, if I could go back to that *Playboy* interview for a moment, sir. If you haven't read it or seen *Playboy*, why do you think it is fair to criticize Mr. Carter about it?"[28] Ford replied, "I have read the article. I haven't read it in the magazine."[29] The reporter then challenged Ford with a direct question about campaign strategy, asking, "Well, if I could follow up on that, when you criticize him, is it because you specifically disagree with some things that he said in that, or is it because of the political benefit that a person might be expected to get in criticizing *Playboy* magazine?"[30] Ford responded, "I don't know why Mr. Carter agreed to the interview. That is not for me to judge. That was a decision made by him. I don't think a president of the United States ought to have an interview in a magazine that has that format. It's a personal conviction."[31]

It is reasonable to ask why he did the interview at all. It couldn't really have been surprising to the campaign that evangelicals would be offended by *Playboy*. Just as Nessen and Ford decided to go on *SNL* to show that Ford "got it" and that he was hip, Carter decided to speak to *Playboy* to send a signal about his image to people who were wary of his oft-discussed deep religious faith, as Robert Scheer explored to the point of irritating Carter in the interview. By talking about lust and using salty language, Carter clearly felt that it would help him with voters who were worried about his religiosity. He said as much in comments to the press in Houston after the contents of the *Playboy* interview began to emerge in late September. Carter said, "I think this frankness might very well not be a good, safe thing to do in a political campaign," but added that he thought that it might "have alleviated the concerns that people might have felt because of my Southern Baptist religion."[32]

The *Playboy* interview undoubtedly seemed like a good idea at the time Carter and his team consented to do it. At *Playboy*, they hoped for a chance to get away from campaign hype, as editor Barry Golson wrote in his introduction to the interview: "What will be less available and less familiar is what kind of person Carter is. To many Americans, the old charge that he was 'fuzzy' on the issues may be less accurate than the persistent feeling that he is fuzzy as a personality. Even this late in the campaign, Carter remains for many an unknown quantity." Reporter Robert Scheer also wrote about why the Carter campaign had decided to do the interview, relating a conversation between Golson and Carter's aide, Hamilton Jordan: "Golson had bumped into Jordan at a party in New York. Neither of them was entirely sober, and they discussed the interview. Golson said something about all the time Carter had spent with me. Jordan replied, 'We wouldn't do it if it weren't in our interest. It's your readers who are probably predisposed toward Jimmy—but they may not vote at all if they feel uneasy about him.'"[33]

The concept of Carter lusting after other women provided a goldmine of material for comedians the world over, including the *SNL* team. On the Saturday after the contents of Carter's *Playboy* interview became public, *SNL* aired a faux campaign commercial in which Aykroyd-as-Carter spoke from the back of a train about his lust for the American people, saying that he was going to be a "lusty" president and flirting with women in the audience. He promised that he would follow the example of other lusty presidents, such as Kennedy, Johnson, and FDR. He then listed some of the women who he'd lusted after and promised the country that he looked forward to, "satisfying each and every last one of you!"[34]

SNL writer Rosie Shuster discussed the problems that the sketch gave them with NBC's censors. Shuster said, that it was tricky to have Jimmy Carter telling the country that he wanted to have sex with everyone. Carter's line about satisfying everyone originally included the word "sexually," which was cut by the censors. She also explained that she had originally included a line about the sex life of Harry and Bess Truman that the censors also cut. She was not allowed to have Carter say that he guessed that "Bess Truman was one satisfied customer."[35]

Although the *Playboy* interview was Carter's cross to bear, *SNL* also found a way to make a Ford joke out of it on "Weekend Update." During the September 25, 1976, "Weekend Edition," anchor Jane Curtin told this joke: "Our top story tonight: in a *Playboy* interview to be published next month, President Ford reveals that, in his heart, he committed celibacy."[36]

The *Playboy* interview also came up in the second *SNL* debate. Jane

Curtin asked Carter if it was possible to be too honest and wondered if he was still lusting for other women. Carter told her that he didn't think it was possible to be too honest and told her in rather graphic terms how he was lusting after her right there. In his imagination, he told her, he was "wearing a leather mask" and blowing in her ear.[37] The effect of the *Playboy* interview on Carter's lead in the polls—which had already been shrinking—was immediate.

As Carter's pollster, Pat Caddell, said, "*Playboy* killed us. The story broke on Monday. On Tuesday night, our polling showed that we were falling. We went from nine or ten points ahead to about even. And by Wednesday night, we had fallen behind! We were trailing Ford for one night. I don't think there was ever any decline that was so rapid, except perhaps for what happened to McGovern because of the Eagleton thing."[38] Caddell's polling for the campaign was not the only indication that the interview had a negative impact on Carter's standing in the campaign. A very large percentage of registered voters polled about the interview were aware of it. One Gallup Poll, for instance, found that 72 percent of those surveyed knew about the interview. Those who were aware of it were asked if Carter's *Playboy* comments made them more or less favorably inclined toward him and 22 percent of voters responded that they were less favorably inclined.[39] A *Time* magazine poll showed similar results, with 21 percent of respondents fully agreeing and 13 percent of respondents partially agreeing that Carter's interview "raises real questions about his judgment and might affect your vote."[40] A Harris Poll showed that 43 percent of voters asked felt Carter had been "wrong to have talked about sex the way he did to *Playboy*."[41]

Digging Out from the Playboy *Troubles with the Help of Eastern Europe*

Playboy wanted the public to learn something about Carter, and Carter hoped the interview would help him with independents and with liberal Democrats who weren't sure about him. Things certainly worked well for *Playboy*, but not so well for Carter. The truth was that the Carter campaign was badly in need of a subject-changer after the battering they took from the *Playboy* interview. Ford's comments about the Soviet Union and an unfortunate racist joke from one of Ford's cabinet secretaries, made public a week before the second debate, gave Carter two of the best political subject-changers in American political history.

Secretary of Agriculture Earl Butz was on a plane flight from Kansas City, site of the Republican Convention, to California. He was travelling with John Dean, the key witness against Nixon in the Watergate scandal and Nixon's former White House counsel, and singers Pat Boone and Sonny Bono. Butz told the following joke in response to a discussion about why the Republican Party had trouble appealing to African Americans: "Do you know why you can't attract coloreds? Because coloreds only want three things. You know what they want? I'll tell you what coloreds want. It's three things: first, a tight pussy; second, loose shoes; and third, a warm place to shit. That's all!"[42]

The joke became public knowledge after John Dean wrote about it, without naming Butz, referring only to an anonymous Ford cabinet secretary, in an article for *Rolling Stone*. Dean, who had been recently released from prison after serving time for his involvement in Watergate, was hired by the magazine to cover the Republican convention. It was only after an investigation, conducted by the magazine *New Times,* that Butz's name became known publicly on September 30. Butz resigned from office on October 4, after several days of apparent waffling by Ford. There was little political cover for Butz after his name was connected to the joke, although James Edwards, the Republican governor of South Carolina, and Robert Bennett, the Republican governor of Kansas, both argued during an appearance on the ABC program *Issues and Answers* that the comments were no more serious than Carter's comments about sex in *Playboy*.[43]

One of the most outspoken critics of Butz was African American leader and Republican Senator Edward Brooke of Massachusetts. Brooke's anger prompted one of a pair of "Weekend Update" jokes about the Butz situation on the October 2 episode of *SNL*. The jokes, delivered by Jane Curtin, who was substituting for the still-injured Chevy Chase, began with Butz's comments, saying that Ford reprimanded his agriculture secretary, but that Senator Brooke, the African American Republican from Massachusetts was insisting that Butz resign. Butz's response to Brooke, Curtin reported, was to send him hair-straightening tonic and a bale of cotton. A second story, about a boxing match between Muhammad Ali and Ken Norton, which Ali won in a controversial decision, ended with this joke that Ali announced his intention to retire, "Stating that he is old, he's lost his punch, and looks forward to settling down to a life of good sex, comfortable shoes, and a warm place to go to the bathroom."[44]

On the October 16 episode, which is also when the second debate sketch aired, Chevy Chase was back in the anchor's chair for "Weekend Update," fully recuperated from his podium injury. The segment featured this pair of jokes, one about *Playboy* and one about Earl Butz, both at Gerald Ford's expense. The first joke was about *Playboy* (but was aimed at Ford, not Carter. Chase said that Ford was critical of Carter's comments in *Playboy*, making it surprising that Ford had given an interview to the even more sexually graphic magazine, *Hustler*. It happened, Chase explained, because Ford thought the magazine was "for aggressive athletes." Chase continued with a joke about Earl Butz, who resigned during the week. Butz, he said, was reported to be suffering from sickle cell anemia, a condition typically suffered mostly by African Americans. Chase said Butz was believed to have gotten it from either "bad sex, tight shoes, or a chilly bathroom."[45]

The Ford Poland gaffe—and it was a huge gaffe—and the Butz controversy gave Carter's campaign a jolt of badly needed energy, pushing him back ahead of Ford in the polls. After the first debate, a *CBS News/New York Times* poll showed that 46 percent of voters strongly supported or leaned toward Ford, while Carter had 47 percent. In the same poll, 36 percent of those who saw the debate felt Ford won, while 36 percent felt it was a tie, and only 19 percent felt Carter won.[46] After the second debate, however, there were noticeable changes in opinion in the *CBS News/New York Times Poll*. Carter had the support of 45 percent of respondents for president, while Ford had 40 percent. Of those who watched the second debate, 57 percent felt Carter won, while only 19 percent felt Ford won, and only 15 percent felt it was a tie.[47]

Carter didn't miss any opportunities to remind people of exactly what Ford had said at the debate. In the days following it, Carter frequently said things such as, "I think Mr. Ford showed confusion about our people, about the aspirations of human beings, about human rights, about liberty, about simple justice. For anyone to state that the people of Hungary, Czechoslovakia, Romania, and East Germany are free of Soviet domination is ridiculous."[48] For Carter, Ford's missteps were a great boon. Not only were there no questions about the *Playboy* interview in the second debate because the subject was foreign policy, but Ford gave Carter the opportunity to change the topic of public discussion for days to come.

9

The Final Days
(of Campaign '76) Through
the Looking Glass of *SNL*

*Earlier this week, Democratic vice presidential candidate Walter F.
Mondale said he does not think Gerald Ford is intelligent enough to
be a good president. At a press conference, Mr. Ford retorted that he
does not understand what Mr. Mondale means. Later, the chief executive swam briefly on the White House lawn and signed his hand for
some Olympic athletes.*—"Weekend Update"[1]

The 1976 general election campaign was waged on television, and
SNL was part of the campaign from start to finish. The combination of
live performance and comedic expression on television spurred audiences
of the campaign to think of the candidates as characters in a number of
ways. The show played the part of the trickster, the instigator, and the
not-so-innocent bystander. The organizers of Ford's campaign believed
that using television was the only way to win, regardless of what *entertainment* television had to say about the president. As Ford advisor Mike
Duval summarized in a campaign strategy report written in August, "The
President's campaign must be television oriented. We must change the
perception of literally millions ... of voters, and this can only be done
through the mass media with the principal emphasis on television."[2]

The challenge they had was significant, because they needed to convince voters that the president was actually presidential material. In his
report, Duval wrote: "In general, the voters do not have a firm perception
of any specific positive trait of the President. There are, however, some
general 'feelings' which contribute to the President's approval rating: He
is basically non-arrogant and honest. He is safe—will not make major
errors as President. However, many of our target voters have the following
negative perceptions of the President: He is weak—not decisive or in control.

He is not thought of as being bright. He is somewhat identified with the status quo of big, unresponsive government."[3] The same public opinion data told the Ford team about Carter: "In general, many voters have the following positive perceptions of Carter, based almost entirely on a very soft 'awareness' factor: He is new—represents a fresh approach and change. He is honest and religious. He is a conservative Democrat—just to the right of center. In general, the voters do *not* have a negative impression of Carter, but he has the following weaknesses which could result in a negative opinion by the voters: He is vague—almost arrogant. This raises questions about his honesty and openness. He is almost mystical, evangelical. He may be joining the Democratic establishment."[4]

Ford's campaign team figured they had two major tasks: to define Carter as an arrogant, inexperienced, and uninformed flip-flopper; and to redefine Ford as presidential, as opposed to not very bright, indecisive, and too easily controlled by powerful figures in his administration. The key to this was to focus on issues: "Issues can be a potent weapon in this year's Presidential campaign. Indeed, a fundamental element of the recommended strategy will be to break with traditional campaign wisdom and attempt to rely heavily on issues as a fundamental element in our attack."[5] Focus on issues, such as the economy and taxes, national defense, education, and crime would allow Ford to seem informed, proactive, and presidential, while highlighting the fact that Carter had not been very specific about anything during the campaign.

Another critical part of redefining Ford, his advisors felt, was to get people to take Ford more seriously as a leader in charge of his administration, and that included no longer doing something some of his advisors, such as Bob Orben and Ron Nessen, in different ways, felt was helpful: using self-deprecation. One section of the August campaign strategy document was dedicated to this subject: "Establish leadership qualities: Avoid self-deprecating remarks (Ford not a Lincoln) and acts (being photographed with a cowboy hat)."[6] The campaign's attempt to characterize Ford as just "one of you" to audiences had been too strong of a performance. The importance of this was explained further in another section of the report: "President Ford has overcome one of the most serious challenges any 1976 Presidential candidate must deal with, which is, the perception of arrogance. We believe that many people equate perceptional arrogance with deviousness (probably a 'lesson' of Vietnam and Watergate). There is probably nothing President Ford can do between now and the election which would result in the voters perceiving him as arrogant. Of course, the difficulty is that, in striving to appear the opposite of arrogant, the

President has also managed to appear undignified, uninspired, and mediocre. This 'price' which has been paid to avoid the 'imperial Presidency' charge has been enormous and, tragically, probably totally unnecessary. There is no way that President Ford (especially in comparison with Nixon or, for that matter, Carter) will ever appear arrogant. Therefore, self-deprecating comments, such as 'I am a Ford, not a Lincoln,' rather than having any beneficial impact, have, in fact, resulted in a substantial negative result."[7] In other words, engaging in activities such as playing along with Chevy Chase and the gang at *SNL* was no longer acceptable. Unfortunately for the campaign, however, the gang at *SNL* didn't read the memo.

On October 23, two weeks before the election, the show was hosted by Steve Martin. One of the highlights of the episode was a futuristic version of the game show *Jeopardy!*, which was entitled "Jeopardy 1999." Steve Martin was the host, "Art F-114," modeled after the show's first host, Art Fleming. The contestants were "Danny M-125," played by Dan Aykroyd, "Laraine A-270," played by Laraine Newman, and "Lee P-413," played by Chevy Chase. In true *Jeopardy!* style, the first answer presented to the contestant was "First president to accidentally kill himself in office." Laraine A-270 buzzes in and guesses Ford. But she is wrong, Art F-114 tells her. The answer is about a president who died while still in office. Lee P-413, buzzes in and guesses the correct answer, Walter Mondale.[8]

Rather than simply sticking with the by then obvious joke of Ford having an accident in which he finally kills himself, they made a more substantial political joke, in which Ford can't kill himself in office because he isn't *in* office. Further, they pushed their comedic license to create a script that assumed a Carter administration successful enough to allow Walter Mondale to subsequently be elected.

The election-related scripts continued on "Weekend Update," which began with a series of jokes told by Chevy Chase, starting with a story about the candidates' standing in the polls following the third debate, which was held the night before. Playing on the still hot topic of the Ali-Norton fight, Chase reported that Carter was leading in one poll, Ford was leading in another, and that a group of experts had declared Norton to be the winner of the fight. He then said that when Carter was asked about the polls he said he didn't pay attention to them. But when Ford was asked, he said, "The Poles are and independent and autonomous people, and I don't believe they consider themselves to be under Soviet domination." Chase ended this news about the third debate by revealing that the biggest surprise of the debate came when Carter said he occasionally enjoyed dressing up as Eleanor Roosevelt.[9]

The first joke, about poll numbers, reads to public opinion polling skeptics as a lesson on the meaning of an important statistic in polling: the margin of error. The poll by Burns-Roper, conducted for PBS immediately after the debate, had a margin of error of plus or minus 6 percentage points. The Associated Press poll, on the other hand, had a margin of error of just plus or minus 2.9 percentage points.[10] This means that both polls found essentially the same thing: statistically, the "winner" of the third debate was too close to call. The findings of both polls are within their margins of error. Thus, it really was just as arbitrary to call Carter the winner of the debate as Chase implies was the decision in the September 28 Norton-Ali fight that ended in a very close decision for Ali.

A combination of elements—some good work by the Ford campaign, some missteps by the Carter campaign, and good luck—helped Ford's efforts tremendously. Over the month of October, building up to the third and final debate on October 22, Jimmy Carter's lead slowly shrank, and it shrank even more after that third debate. By the time Election Day arrived, Carter's lead was a statistically insignificant 1 percentage point, making the contest a dead heat. This was, from the perspective of Carter pollster Pat Caddell, Carter's own fault. Caddell said, "Jimmy had hit his stride by the last week of September, but then after the second debate he got strident. Ford was a major casualty of the debate, but so was Jimmy— he knocked himself off his stride and changed his tone."[11]

The problem, reported by Caddell and summarized by Martin Schram, was: "The public was just not going to believe Ford was dishonest.... The President's reputation for being an honest guy was that strong."[12] In other words, Carter thought he had Ford by the neck and he moved to put him down for good. To an electorate that was both only mildly interested in this race *and* turned off by politics in general, it was the wrong strategic decision. There was something about Carter that made some people uncertain and that uncertainty made it almost possible for Ford to pull a last-second, Truman-like victory out of the air. Ron Nessen addressed the fact that Ford was able to make the race so close, saying, "The debate in San Francisco where Ford seems to say the Soviet Union doesn't dominate Eastern Europe. Why did that make such a big fuss? Because it fed into the image that Ford was dumb, that Ford was a bumbler and he can't say what he means and he still came within one and a half percent of winning."[13] Why? Because people didn't quite trust Carter and one of the reasons was because the Ford campaign did a pretty good job of making people doubt him.

Emphasizing Ford's experience, his positions on the issues, and

Carter's untrustworthiness was the Ford campaign strategy, as Ford aide Mike Duval wrote in a campaign memo: "Our recommendation is to use this sequence: Force Carter to take positions (don't worry too much *how* he comes out on a particular issue); Give high visibility to his positions and target on the groups offended; Assume he will react to the inevitable erosion in the polls by 'softening' his positions. Then begin to make the 'flip-flop' case. Point out that he goes from a conservative-moderate position to liberal. Stress that this is a fundamental character flaw—it's deceitful."[14] Strategy always looks great on paper and, in the real, dynamic, ever-changing world of a campaign, it is impossible not to deviate at some point from a strategy. There were errors and unforeseen events that hurt the Ford campaign, and the press and *SNL* were there to pounce on all of them. But *SNL* also pounced on the issue of Carter's untrustworthiness, playing to it in the debate sketches and in "Weekend Update" jokes.

Not all the errors and unforeseen events were attributable to the Ford campaign and, despite the errors and unforeseen events, perhaps because of them, the Ford campaign managed not one, but two, great comebacks, first in September and then again in October, closing the gap with Carter entirely by Election Day. As pressures increased, Carter and his staff showed a different side to the press and the tone of their coverage changed dramatically. Carter's own pollster, Pat Caddell, said that Carter knocked himself off his stride, but it didn't happen entirely by himself—the Ford team knew what buttons to push and they helped Carter show himself in a less flattering light.[15] *SNL* was more than willing to have fun in that vein. But if *SNL* made fun of the flaws and foibles of both candidates, the show's team made their real feelings clear during the October 30 episode, which aired just three days before Election Day.

Saturday, October 30, 1976: SNL's *Parting Shots*

SNL was heavy with political material on the Saturday before the election. The first political sketch was a Barbara Walters parody, with Gilda Radner doing her familiar impersonation of the journalist, exaggerated speech impediment and all. In the sketch, "Not for First Ladies Only," an obviously jealous Walters interviews Jane Curtin as First Lady Betty Ford and Laraine Newman as would-be First Lady Rosalynn Carter. In it, Carter is proud of her husband, while Betty Ford offers several negative assessments of hers, such as when she is asked how she supported her husband during the campaign. She answered that while one good thing about the very straightforward and honest interviews she gives the press is that they show how smart she is, they also help distract from how dumb her husband is, whom she calls a "dim bulb." On the other hand, Rosalynn answered that her husband did all the hard work of winning the Democratic nomination, while she helped. When Walters asks the ladies if they have any nicknames for their husbands, Rosalynn tells him that she calls hers Jimmy. Then, picking up on the joke from "Weekend Update," she adds that she calls him "Ellie" when he dresses up like Eleanor Roosevelt. But when Betty is asked, she says, "Dim Bulb," or "Mr. Dim Bulb."[16]

While Rosalynn makes reference to Carter's lust, she says she and Jimmy lust together. Betty Ford, on the other hand, says that she sleeps with her husband all the time. But she means sleep, and not sex. He is so boring, she implies, that one can't help but sleep when he's around.[17] Once again, Carter was not presented as a flawless man, but Ford was presented as an unbearably dull man with perhaps the worst possible flaw for a person in the presidency—incompetence. And this sketch was just the first of three lengthy political sketches that all portrayed Ford in the standard *SNL* way—as a bumbling fool.

The show's third and final debate sketch aired shortly after the Barbara Walters sketch. This debate was structured differently from the first two, which looked somewhat like the actual presidential debates in their staging. The third debate sketch was made to look like a Miss America–style beauty contest, with a panel of judges instead of journalists asking questions; guest host Buck Henry played the role of Bert Parks, who hosted the Miss America Pageant from 1955 to 1979.[18] Aykroyd, as Carter, and Chase, as Ford, appeared in old-fashioned bathing suits and demonstrated talents for Henry and the audience. Ford's talent was voting. Ford came out in his swimsuit, wearing a flotation ring and swim fins, which made it comically difficult for him to enter the voting booth at the end of the catwalk. He ends up crashing to the ground and off the catwalk. Carter's talent, on the other hand, was dentistry, and he performed oral surgery on a Secret Service agent, played by Garrett Morris. Once again, the audience saw the president as unable to perform the most basic civic duty, and Carter as a man so smart that dentistry was simply a hobby. The sketch ended with questions for each candidate. Carter's question played to the recurring theme that he was really quite ambitious and, perhaps, in the campaign for his own gain. Smiling broadly and making obvious eye contact, he speaks with false modesty as tells Buck Henry that if he wins the election and becomes "the most powerful man in the world," he would simply travel the country meeting the people so he can get to know them as well as possible. As Henry tries to thank him for this answer, he asks if he gets a new car or a convertible if he wins.

For Ford, the question dealt with the international situation he faced. Buck Henry laid out a ridiculous scenario, asking Ford what he would do if he were attending a state dinner in Moscow and things started going wrong when his tie fell into Mrs. Brezhnev's soup bowl. As he tries to fix this, he haplessly sets in motion a series of other disasters occur, making for the possibility of an international incident, with serious injuries to several Soviet officials. Taking this in with a bewildered expression on his face, Ford tells him that the people of Puerto Rico are free and he doesn't believe they are under the domination of the Soviet Union.[19]

In general, the third debate sketch didn't break any new ground. It played on the themes *SNL* had developed all along—Carter was super smart, and Ford was clumsy and ignorant. Also noteworthy in the credits of all three debates, the last line reads, "Special Thanks to F.C.C. for Waiving Equal Time Ruling." The insertion of the line at the end of each of the *SNL* debate sketches points out that without the cooperation of the FCC, there would have been no debates, there might have been no historical moments like Gerald Ford on Poland or Jimmy Carter on *Playboy*, and the nation would likely have been deprived of the comedy gold the crew at *SNL* was able to mine from the verbal sparring of Ford and Carter.

The next segment after the debate sketch was "Weekend Update," which was almost entirely dominated by election-related (and mostly Ford-negative) jokes. Chase joked that the first election returns had been reported and both candidates were tied at zero. He then told the first of the segment's jokes about Watergate, about how Nixon aide John Ehrlichman had reported to prison, pending appeal. His lawyers' advice to him was to avoid other inmates or bending over in the shower. Moving to campaign jokes, Chase reported, while showing a photo of Betty Ford kissing a dog, that the First Lady won a dog-smelling contest in Michigan while campaigning for her husband; and, showing a photo of Jerry Ford kissing Miss America, reported that while visiting Atlantic City, he accidentally swallowed a hypodermic needle and gave Miss America a swine flu shot in the face.[20]

The campaign jokes continued as Chase announced that Robert Dole had suggested World War II was the fault of a Democratic administration. Chase added that, in speaking to a group of Japanese Americans, Dole called World War II an insult to the people of Japan and suggested changing the name of Pearl Harbor to something that would be less offensive to the Japanese. He suggested something like, "Surprise City." Next, Chase reported that a Ford campaign staffer had to be fired when it was discovered that in addition to making campaign ads, he also made adult films. The campaign became aware of this after the staffer made an ad featuring Ford's daughter Susan in bondage gear, "while a masked Nazi tattooed 'Vote for My Dad' all over her body."

This joke, about Ford campaign advertising, was a lead-in to the central joke of the "Weekend Update" segment—two recently discovered campaign ads, one a Carter ad and the other a Ford ad, which had supposedly been suppressed by the campaigns and never used. He notes that the campaigns had agreed not to release them, but that "Weekend Update" had obtained copies and was broadcasting them. The first ad, a Ford campaign spot, shows Jimmy Carter working on his farm but quickly cuts to images of beautiful, scantily-clad women. The voice-over by Akroyd tells viewers that they need a President who not only feels their pain, but who "lusts your lusts." He repeats several lines from the *Playboy* interview and ends, telling voters, that while God has forgiven him, he hopes that the American people and Rosalynn will also forgive him.

Amy Carter hugs her father as the film fades out and a title reads, "Vote for Gerald Ford." A second title reads, "Paid for and Authorized by The Committee to Re-Elect the President." The "Committee to Re-Elect the President" was the name of the official campaign committee of Richard Nixon in 1972, which became widely known by the acronym, "CREEP."

Chase then introduced the never-before-seen Carter ad. It faded in on Ford sitting in the Oval Office, delivering a national address on September 8, 1974. It was Ford's announcement that he was pardoning Richard Nixon for anything related to Watergate. As he reads the speech, the video cuts from him sitting at the desk to the Fords and the Nixons walking down a red carpet, and Ford and Nixon laughing. It ends with Ford finishing the address and signing his official pardon of Nixon. On-screen text and the *SNL* announcer Don Pardo both say, "Four More Years." The video cuts to Nixon waving his arms above his head and waving the "V for victory" sign he was famous for. The film fades and a title card reads, "Paid for and Authorized by the Committee to Elect Jimmy Carter." There is applause and the scene shifts to Chevy Chase dozing at the anchor desk. On screen behind him are photos of wrecked cars. He wakes and delivers yet another line directed at Ford's clumsiness, saying, "Still to come, the presidential motorcade makes a pit stop, after this message."

The notion that an ad about Carter's lust for women and Ford's pardoning of one of the most hated men in American politics are in any way equivalent is ridiculous on its face and Lorne Michaels suggested NBC did not want the fake Carter ad to run. He said, "The weekend before the election, we ran the ads. They were the ones that had been 'suppressed.' I mean, Carter's was from the lust in my heart thing and for Ford we ran the Nixon pardon. At the time NBC news would not give us the footage. So we had to step outside and acquire it."[21] This was the first thought that came to Michaels when he was asked what impact he thought the show had on the outcome of the election. Doug Hill and Jeff Weigand reported: "Lorne is proudest of the time *Saturday Night* replayed, three days before the 1976 election between Ford and Jimmy Carter, the speech in which Ford announced his pardon of Richard Nixon. The feeling on the 17th floor [of 30 Rockefeller Plaza, *SNL*'s offices] was that the pardon had been conveniently forgotten by the press and that a reminder was in order."[22] Indeed, Michaels created his improvisation sketch comedy show to be what a tradition of theater performers have wanted to be for thousands of years: relevant.

It is noteworthy that, according to Michaels, NBC didn't fight to the keep the fake ads out of "Weekend Update," but refused to cooperate with supplying the footage, in the obvious hope that the ads wouldn't be run. It seems clear that network executives were aware of the political punch the segment had. Asked why NBC wouldn't supply the footage, Michaels said only, "It was just a thing that wasn't shown any more."[23] However, it is much more likely that NBC officials didn't want to use that footage in such a highly charged political context. For, at that point, the candidates were tied in the polls. The people above Michaels must have wondered if there could be any negative fall-out from the segment if Ford won the election. The point of the segment is obvious: *SNL* wanted to do what it could to affect the outcome of the race. If there was any doubt about political intent, it was erased by the way Chase closed the newscast, his last as the "Weekend Update" anchor.

After Jane Curtin made a "People in the News" joke about Chase leaving *SNL* to become the new host of *The Tonight Show* (he actually left to pursue a movie career), "Weekend Update" returned to Chase, with photos of Ford and Carter appearing over his shoulder. The photo of Ford was doctored with a large, black, curly mustache. As he begins to speak, the phone rings. Chase answers it to find Francisco Franco on the other end and has a brief conversation with him.

Hanging up, Chase turned to a different camera and delivered a closing statement in which he asserted that throughout the campaign, "Weekend Update" had made a point of remaining neutral and objective in its coverage. They had, he said, presented both sides fairly regardless of how they might feel about the election. Therefore, he said, "Weekend Update" would not endorse a candidate in the election.[24] Of course, the very differently toned fake campaign ads could be seen as having done just that. This part of the script was as much about asserting the point that *SNL* "matters." No matter the election outcome, sketch comedy pronounces itself a winner.

By the time the final public opinion polls of the campaign were taken, the two men were very close, within the margin of error, and many on Ford's team thought they had pulled out an amazing comeback. Ford speechwriter Bob Orben said, "We thought we had won the election. I left the campaign plane in Boston two days before the election and we had been tipped by one of the polling services that we were gonna make it by like a half a percentage point. I somewhere have the victory speech I remember I wrote, I rode down with Jim Baker on the train on the way back to New York, back to Washington."[25] Ron Nessen was similarly optimistic just before the election. He spoke of the fact that, despite several disadvantages, Ford was beating Carter as the campaign drew to a close, saying, "You're in the middle of a war. You're in the middle of the deepest recession since the 1930s and you have Ford ahead on the polls the Saturday before the election."[26]

Ford ended up losing the election by 1,682,970 votes, or about 2.1 percent. He won 240 electoral votes to Carter's 297 electoral votes, and he actually won more states than Carter, beating him by a total of 27 to 23.[27] He did not win the election, coming from behind, as Truman did in 1948, but he came much closer than most people would have thought possible after the second debate. In 1948, the last polls were done well before the election because pollsters, such as George Gallup, felt that voters' preferences were unlikely to change (although when they did their last polls, there were still roughly 14 percent of voters who were undecided). Ford's performance was not the greatest comeback in presidential campaign history, nor was it the closest election in history. The election of 1800 was so close that the House of Representatives had to vote more than 70 times to decide it. The 1960 election was decided by roughly 100,000 votes. The popular vote in the disputed election of 2000 was close in both the popular vote, with a difference between Gore and Bush of about 550,000 votes, and in the Electoral College, which Bush won by a margin of 271 to 266.

However, except for Truman, there has never been an incumbent president who has made up so much ground in a general election campaign, and Ford did it twice in two months. At the beginning of September, Ford trailed Carter by 11 percentage points in a Gallup poll. By the beginning of October, Ford cut the Carter lead to just 2 percentage points, which was within the Gallup poll's margin of error, meaning that the two were, essentially, tied. After the second debate and Ford's Eastern Europe gaffe, Carter once again extended his lead to between 6 and 7 percentage points for much of October in Gallup's polls. After the third debate and by the time of the election, however, Ford had once again closed the lead, this time to just 1 percentage point, according to Gallup.[28] Much of Ford's ability to comeback twice in a month was the "fault" of Carter, who many voters didn't know and didn't trust on Election Day, but much of that credit also goes to the Ford campaign for helping to make sure that many people came to the conclusion that they shouldn't trust Carter. An impossible-to-answer question is this: what role did *SNL* play in the outcome of this election? It is a tantalizing speculation but it is just that—a speculation.

In a piece about the impact of the presidential debates, *Chicago Tribune* Washington correspondent Jim Squires wondered, "Just how many votes, if any, have been swayed by the three 90-minute spectaculars may never be known. Neither man has demonstrated the clear superiority in style or substance that John F. Kennedy displayed in the first televised presidential debates with Richard Nixon in 1960—and historians believe that those meetings affected only about 1 percent."[29] However, he continues, arguing that the 1 percent could have been the decision maker, "As slight as Kennedy's advantage was, it provided his victory margin. And from all indications, the 1976 election could be just as close."[30] It wasn't quite *as* close as 1960, but it was very close. Many factors could have influenced undecided voters on Election Day and one, at least for some, could have been *SNL* and its repetitious message that Ford was a bumbling fool. For others, the portrayal of Carter as a deceptive man who might say anything he needed to say in order to be elected.

10

SNL in Campaign '76— What Was Their Intent and What Difference Did They Make?

What did liveness add to the Saturday Night *aesthetic? It returned sketch comedy to its roots in live stage and broadcast performance...*
—Michelle Hilmes[1]

Performances are always in-process, changing, growing, and moving through time. Though a specific performance event may appear to be fixed and bounded, it is actually part of an ongoing sequence that includes the training of the performers, rehearsals and other forms of preparation, the presentation of the performance to a specific audience in a specific time and place, and the aftermath, in which the performance lives on in recordings, critical responses, and the memories of performers and spectators.—Henry Bial[2]

It is clear that Chevy Chase wanted Jimmy Carter to beat Gerald Ford. This was shown in his October 30th "Weekend Update" commentary, which were the final words he spoke as a regular member of the cast. When Chase was asked just before Nessen's hosting of the show in April 1976 about what actual influence he thought *SNL* had on viewers, he demurred, saying, "We are on the air to make people laugh, and our jokes are basically just physical humor lacking deep meaning or significance."[3] The reporter added her own commentary after this quote, writing, "Though there would be those—even among his fans—who are sure to disagree,"[4] and after the election, Chase himself seemed to disagree. In the 1977 *Playboy* interview Chase was asked if he thought that he had anything to do with Ford's defeat. His response, as noted earlier, was, that he thought, because of the closeness of the race, he and *SNL* had, in fact, played a role in Ford's defeat.[5]

For his part, Dan Aykroyd denies there was a pro–Carter or anti–Ford bias on the show. Decades later, he spoke both of that season and more broadly about *SNL*, saying, "*SNL* never had a political bias when I was there and to the best of my knowledge it does not now. One of the major political writers [Jim Downey] on the best pieces over the last eight years which clearly denigrated Republicans is himself a right-of-center voter. There are mostly Democrats at *SNL* but what's funny and truthful is what counts rather than an agenda attempting to influence politics."[6]

Aykroyd's opinion about bias is shared by many from the show. Lorne Michaels denied that the show has a political bias. He half-jokingly said, "Yeah, we always are, you know, we are non-partisan ... if we were partisan I think we would lose all our power and influence."[7] Garrett Morris agreed:

Well, I don't think anyone had a political agenda, I think the agenda was to make people laugh. Let's face it, there's political implications even if we're trying just to be funny, which is probably never really the case, but the main thing is to be funny and to entertain. So that's really what we're trying to do. Even in a more academically situated theater like you, if the audience comes there and they don't enjoy themselves, they ain't comin' back. So the main thing, you gotta make them enjoy themselves and laugh and whatever when they come there. And quite often it may be not that you have to not say the truth, but revise it and re-form it.[8]

Twenty-first century cast member Kenan Thompson reflected a very similar perspective about how *SNL* decides whom to target:

I don't know if they necessarily lean one way or the other, honestly. Like, we point out the, you know, the ridiculousness in everybody, pretty much. That's kind of like what we do. I don't think we necessarily take sides, especially—Lorne is a Canadian from humble beginnings who happens to be a powerful man, so he's kind of, like, teetering on both sides of different issues. Issues like tax breaks, I'm sure, affect him, but probably not as much as how his fellow man is treated, or if his fellow man can even get a job, and I believe that's more concerning to him, just me knowing him as a person. And it would seem like he would just be hard driven on whatever powerful people are hard driven on, but that's not necessarily the case.[9]

In their book about the early days of *Saturday Night*, Doug Hill and Jeff Weigand wrote of the show's politics:

But *Saturday Night's* principal political goal, as it has been for satirists throughout history, was to reveal the underlying absurdity of the political game, whoever was in power—playing, as Lorne put it, "the loyal opposition." *Saturday Night* simply took its opposition further than other television shows. Theirs wasn't the all-in-good-fun, deep-down-we're-all-patriots humor of Bob Hope, or the more corrosive but still liberal style of Johnny Carson. *Saturday Night* wore its contempt for the political status quo on its sleeve.[10]

There is an interesting almost-but-never-was moment that belies Michaels's assertion that *SNL* didn't intend to impact the 1976 election. In the fall of

1976, *Saturday Night* planned to take the show on the road, touring college campuses. Shows were planned in Boston, at Princeton, and at Georgetown University. The Georgetown show was supposed to have been on October 30, right before Election Day. At the time the show was announced, on September 10, Lorne Michaels said, "That will be our last chance to influence the November 3 election. I desperately wanted to be in Washington that Saturday, and the people at Georgetown have decided to let us use their gym for the program."[11] The plans for all of the college shows were ultimately cancelled, due to what NBC characterized as technical problems that "proved too immense."[12] The intent, however, was clear in Michaels's statement.

There are also events that really did happen which suggest a tendency on the part of the *SNL* cast to support Carter. Although Pat Caddell, Carter's pollster, doesn't remember any contact with anyone from *Saturday Night*,[13] and although everyone agrees that they never actually met Carter, Dan Aykroyd does feel that the Carter team paid attention to what they were doing on *SNL* and he and John Belushi went to hang out at Carter headquarters on Election Night. He said, "I never met or spoke with President Carter. I met his son Chip on the night his father was elected. Belushi and I were in Atlanta, having gained access to the event with *Rolling Stone* press credentials."[14]

Carter media advisor Gerald Rafshoon remembers the Belushi-Aykroyd trip to Atlanta, but suggests that he did not, personally, have any contact with them. He said, "I think I remember when it got up to the general election, I think, John Belushi and Dan Aykroyd and some of the folks came down, they came down to Atlanta or maybe somewhere on the campaign trail. I have a recollection of them following or spending a few days. I think they really spent some time with Hamilton [Jordan] during the time."[15] Regardless of *whom* they met, a visit to Carter campaign headquarters on Election Night suggests more than a passing interest in the outcome of the election. This impression is furthered by the fact that Aykroyd performed at an inaugural event for Carter.

If it is true that the show's creative team did, in fact, want to affect the outcome of the race, it is worth asking if there is really anything wrong with a desire to affect the race. *SNL* wasn't a news show. It was a long sketch comedy-variety show that offered occasional political parody. It had no standard of ideological balance to live up to as journalistic standards demanded NBC's news division did. Denying a political motivation today seems like a defensive response to the highly politically charged environment in which we now live, where everyone, everywhere is accused of having a political bias *by people with a political bias.* The truth is that most people have biases when it comes to politics. In some forums we have an obligation to suppress them. Comedy shows specializing in parody and satire, however, do not seem to be among the forums in which we must suppress our biases.

The live and current sketch-comedy performances on *SNL* contributed to a long-lasting impression of Gerald Ford on the American public as a stumbling, bumbling dolt. Who, upon seeing Chevy Chase's physically comic take on Ford, could take Ford seriously as the leader of the free world? Even with only occasional forays into actual political subjects, the show had real political consequences. This characterization of Ford as doltish remained in viewers' perceptions whether or not they chose to support his candidacy. Similarly, *SNL* went on to reinforce the public's perceptions that George H.W. Bush was a goof; Bill Clinton, a letch; Al Gore, a prig; and George W. Bush, a fool.

Because no data exists to make empirical tests of *SNL's* impact on the race in 1976, it is impossible to precisely determine the effect on voting behavior. The public opinion data did not exist in 1976, nor did the academic interest to ask the questions which would have taken advantage of such data. That began to change, however, during and after the 2000 presidential election, when scholars began to wonder what impact late-night comedy was having on campaigns.

Although there has been academic curiosity about the impact of political satire on politics for a long time (e.g., Annis, 1939, Brinkman, 1968, Gruner, 1972),[16] and even Hubert Humphrey wondered about the opportunity he missed by not appearing on *Laugh-In* as Richard Nixon did,[17] many researchers did not become interested in the impact of late-night TV comedy until the election of 2000. This new interest was driven, it seems, at least in part by the finding of a Pew Poll in February 2000, which found that 9 percent of respondents 18–29 reported that they regularly learned something from comedy shows, while 28 percent reported that they sometimes learned something from comedy shows. Even more, 13 percent and 34 percent reported regularly (or sometimes) learning something from late-night television.[18] Studies examining the impact of late-night and comedy television regularly cited the findings of the Pew survey. Bruce Williams and Michael Delli Carpini argued in 2001 that there were a number of factors in the mid–20th century which reinforced a distinction between news and entertainment in what was a "socially constructed distinction."[19] This artificial distinction, for many reasons they argue, is not a reasonable distinction.

Citing the Pew data as one of their reasons to call for new attention to entertainment media, Delli Carpini and Williams asserted the following in 2002: "We must stop categorizing politically relevant media by genre (for example, news versus drama), content (fact versus fiction), and source (journalist versus actor). Instead, we should categorize by utility. The extent to which any communication is politically relevant depends on what it does—its potential use—rather than on who says it and how it is said. In a democratic polity, politically useful communications are those that shape: (1) the conditions of one's everyday life; (2) the lives of fellow community members; and (3) the norms and structures of power that influence those relationships."[20]

Delli Carpini and Williams base this argument on the premise of the demise of the "Golden Age of Broadcast News." During the mid–20th century, they argue, there grew a tremendous faith in a professional class of journalists to keep the public informed with "trustworthy and sufficient information." They assert that from the early 1980s to the time of their writing in 2002, "cultural, technological, political and economic changes have severely undermined the notion" that we could continue to have faith in such journalists as sources of reliable and adequate information. They cite the growth of other sources of information, such as entertainment television.[21]

The findings of Matthew Baum (2002) support that so-called "soft news," which includes late-night talk shows and entertainment programs such as *The Daily Show*, exposes otherwise uninterested people to political information.[22] Kathleen Hall Jamieson and Paul Waldman (2003) concluded that late-night comedy in 2000 "telegraphed substantive information as it reinforced a limited range of candidate traits, introduced into public discussion some assumptions unwarranted by existing evidence, and invited cynicism about the quality of those who seek public office."[23] Baum (2006) found that viewers of entertainment talk shows who were not politically engaged were "prone to be persuaded by properly tailored candidate appeals," and argues that this is the reason candidates increasingly go on, and should go on, entertainment talk shows.[24]

Other studies of the 2000 election found that two late-night talk shows, *The Late Show with David Letterman* and *The Tonight Show*, and the jokes featured on those shows, had some impact on voters' impressions of George W. Bush and Al Gore. For example, Dannagal Young (2004) found viewers were affected differently by exposure to such jokes, depending on their partisanship and levels of political knowledge.[25] Patricia Moy, et al. (2005), also examined *The Tonight Show* and *The Late Show with David Letterman,* but with an eye to the impact of appearances on those shows by George W. Bush and Al Gore. They found that viewers of these shows were more likely than non-viewers to base their evaluations on George W. Bush, though not of Al Gore, on character traits after his appearance on *The Late Show with David Letterman*.[26]

In a 2005 article, "Presidential Election Campaigns and American Democracy," Pfau, et al., work to answer Delli Carpini's assertion that "the relationship between media use and civic and political behavior is complicated and only partly understood." Pfau et al.'s study reveals that "more reliance on television comedy was negatively associated with likelihood of participating"; the authors also strongly assert that studies should continue to go beyond "broad generalizations about mass media and democracy."[27] These findings extend to the 2004 campaign and beyond. Paul Brewer and Xiaoxia Cao (2006) used data collected by Pew and found that in the 2004 primary campaign, people who watched late-night talk shows and political comedy shows, such as *The Tonight Show, The Late Show with David Letterman, SNL,* and *The Daily Show*, were likely to demonstrate increased knowledge of those candidates. Meanwhile, those who saw candidates on morning talk shows, such as *The Today Show* and *Good Morning America*, or news magazine shows, such as *60 Minutes, 20/20,* and *Dateline NBC*, did not demonstrate the same increased knowledge. It suggests that, at a minimum, "audience members may have been accidentally informed about the primary campaign through their efforts to seek out amusement."[28] Also examining the 2004 campaign, Jody Baumgartner and Jonathan Morris (2006) found that people exposed to jokes about both John Kerry and George W. Bush on *The Daily Show* tended to see both candidates more negatively.[29]

In 2008, a major new political presence burst on the national scene in the form of Sarah Palin. Palin was a well-known entity in her home state of Alaska but before John McCain chose her as his running mate, she was relatively unknown to the rest of the country. She received some attention nationally for the fact that she was pregnant as the governor of Alaska and gave birth to a child with Down syndrome in April 2008, but most Americans knew little else about her, if they knew that. When John McCain chose her as his running mate in late August, her media appearances, especially those which were not highly structured, became fodder for doubts about her readiness for the political big time. Liberals didn't like her conservative positions, but many were also troubled by her seeming lack of knowledge about many important issues. The best-known incident which caused people to doubt Palin's readiness was an interview on the *CBS Evening News* with anchor Katie Couric.

The interview, which aired in late September, provided one of several opportunities for *SNL* to parody Palin. In the interview sketch, where Tina Fey played Palin, and Amy Poehler played Couric, some of the lines were heavily inspired by the interview transcript. For example, one topic in the interview was foreign policy. The actual interview on NBC went like this:

> COURIC: You've cited Alaska's proximity to Russia as part of your foreign-policy experience. What did you mean by that?
>
> PALIN: That Alaska has a very narrow maritime border between a foreign country, Russia, and, on our other side, the land boundary that we have with Canada. It, it's funny that a comment like that was kinda made to.... I don't know, you know.... Reporters...
>
> COURIC: Mocked?
>
> PALIN: Yeah, mocked, I guess that's the word, yeah.
>
> COURIC: Well, explain to me why that enhances your foreign-policy credentials.
>
> PALIN: Well, it certainly does, because our, our next-door neighbors are foreign countries, there in the state that I am the executive of. And there...
>
> COURIC: Have you ever been involved in any negotiations, for example, with the Russians?
>
> PALIN: We have trade missions back and forth, we do. It's very important when you consider even national security issues with Russia. As Putin rears his head and comes into the air space of the United States of America, where do they go? It's Alaska. It's just right over the border. It is from Alaska that we send those out to make sure that an eye is being kept on this very powerful nation, Russia, because they are right there, they are right next to our state.[30]

On *SNL*, the exchange went like this:

> POEHLER: On foreign policy, I want to give you ... one more chance ... to explain your claim that you have foreign policy experience, based on Alaska's proximity to Russia. What did you mean by that?
>
> FEY: Well, Alaska and Russia are only separated by a *narrow* maritime border *(holds up her hands)*. You've got Alaska here, and this right here is water, and then, that up there is Russia. So we keep an eye on them.
>
> POEHLER: And how do you do that, exactly?
>
> FEY: Every morning, when Alaskans wake up, one of the first things they do is look outside and see if there are any Russians hanging around. If there are, you gotta go up to them and ask, "What are ya' doing here?" And if they give you a good reason—they can't—then, it's our responsibility to say, you know, "Shoo! Get back over there!"[31]

Sarah Esralew (2009) found, in an experiment which showed different groups either the Couric interview or the *SNL* parody of the interview, that both pieces influenced viewers' impressions of Palin's abilities, by increasing "the salience of constructs associated with her intelligence, competence, experience...." This finding is supportive of the assertion made by Delli Carpini and Williams, that the solid line once believed to exist between news and entertainment is, in fact, not a very solid boundary. One other finding of Esralew speaks to the particular power of *SNL*'s brand of political parody. Only the *SNL* sketch made viewers more aware of Palin's rural traits. Why? Because Fey really played up that part of Palin's persona, exaggerating the governor's speech patterns and folksy expressions.[32] Although Esralew doesn't discuss the Palin-Biden debate sketch, this kind of exaggeration of Palin's speech is blatantly played upon when Fey says, "I'm, uh—I'm happy to be speaking directly to the American people to let them know if you want an outsider who doesn't like politics as usual or pronouncin' the 'g' and the end of the words she's sayin', I think you know who to vote for."[33]

The Palin interview on CBS received an enormous amount of coverage, and so did *SNL* the following weekend. As Esralew concludes, many people were familiar with the troubling questions the interview raised about Palin whether they saw Tina Fey parody Palin's answers or not. But the particularly folksy way in which Fey played Palin was unique to the *SNL* sketches. Esralew suggests that schema activation was at play in both the *CBS News* and *SNL* interviews. Schema theory has been used in many contexts in psychological and political science research. Schemas are intellectual short cuts that allow us to make conclusions about political parties, politicians, policies, and so forth, without having to have a large amount of detailed information cluttering our heads. The theory comes from research by scholars such as Amos Kahneman and Daniel Tversky on short cuts they called heuristics.[34] Schemas are summaries of information, rather than detailed supplies of information. As one pair of researchers, Susan Fiske and Shelley Taylor (1991), put it, we are "cognitive misers,"[35] who have limited knowledge storage space and we develop mental shorthand to condense a lot of information into a short, easily used impression, such as Palin doesn't know what she's talking about; or, Palin isn't ready for Prime-Time; or, Palin is a hick from the sticks.

Tina Fey appeared as Palin six times during the campaign of 2008. Palin certainly had diehard supporters among the most conservative elements of the Republican Party, the elements which would later begin the Tea Party movement, but moderates in her party, along with Independents and Democrats, were certainly surprised to see a candidate for the vice presidency so unprepared. It is hard to argue that there was ever much of a real chance that any Republican could have won the election in 2008. The economy was in terrible shape, the country was weary of war, and the outgoing Republican president, George W. Bush, was very unpopular, with an approval rating of 25 percent by Election Day 2008.[36] While it would be a long stretch to argue that *SNL* had anything to do with the final outcome of the election in which Obama soundly defeated McCain, it is possible to argue that *SNL* had some role in the size of Obama's victory. Baumgartner, et al., found, for instance, that viewing Tina Fey's impression of Sarah Palin in a faux debate with Democratic nominee Joe Biden (played by Jason Sudeikis) negatively affected viewers' opinions of Palin, opinions that were shared by Republicans, Independents, and Democrats.[37] They found, for instance, that "an individual who saw the spoof had an 8.5 percent probability of approving, and a 75.7 percent probability of disapproving of the Palin choice. Those who did not see the *SNL* debate had a 16.1 percent chance of approving and a 60.1 percent chance of disapproving the choice."[38]

Not only was opinion of Palin harmed, opinion of Biden was helped by the sketch. Baumgartner, et al., found, "Approval of Obama's selection of Biden, on the other hand, was positively associated with viewership of the spoof. Although the *SNL* debate was not especially kind to Biden, it is possible that his image was positively influenced by the simple comparison to Fey's portrayal of Palin."[39] Furthermore, the researchers found that the disapproval of the choice of Palin led to a decreased chance of voting for McCain for president. "When all other variables in the model are held at their mean, those who watched the *SNL* clip had a 45.4 percent probability of saying that Palin's nomination made them less likely to vote for McCain. This same probability drops to 34 percent among those who saw coverage of the debate through the media."[40]

There are reasons to question if the findings from studies of 2004–2008 apply to 1976, of course. Williams and Delli Carpini, writing in 2002, are reviewing the previous twenty years. That would take them back to 1982—just seven years after the start of *SNL*. The argument Delli Carpini and Williams make is not at all unreasonable. As the communications marketplace has grown and splintered, it is no longer reasonable to think of a few broadcast news providers as having a monopoly on political, or any other, information. It is also perfectly reasonable to extend their time window a bit to the creation of *SNL,* along with other developments, such as the 1975 launch of HBO, the first cable television network with the ability to reach the entire United States. The second cable network was Ted Turner's WTCG, which was soon renamed WTBS, in 1976. Pat Robertson followed soon after that, starting CBN in 1977.[41] From this beginning, the country quickly took the first steps in the "cultural, technological, political and economic changes" that undermined the supremacy of broadcast news.

Delli Carpini and Williams also argue that one of the reasons entertainment media matter now is because of changes in the television universe that break down the once-artificial barrier between news and nonnews, or news and entertainment. However, those boundaries can easily be seen to be beginning to collapse as early as 1975, *SNL*'s first season on the air. From this perspective, *SNL* could even be seen as starting the process. Second, the studies considered here all find an effect for various entertainment shows with audiences far smaller than the huge audiences garnered by *SNL* in its first season. If there was a measurable impact in 2000, or 2004, it is not unreasonable to expect there was a measurable impact in 1976.

The work of Esralew suggests that both the news media and *SNL* contributed to the development of intellectual short cuts, heuristics, for voters about Sarah Palin. In this book, we argue that another heuristic existed for at least some voters in 1976: Ford is a bumbling fool, and that *SNL* had some influence on it. Chase played Ford as a clumsy buffoon eleven times on *SNL* between November 8, 1975, and October 30, 1976. There was nothing unique about the notion that Ford was not too smart, as has already been reviewed, but Chase was unrelenting in this take on Ford, much as Fey was unrelenting in her verbal play with Palin's mannerisms. In January of 1975, the Harris Survey asked respondents if they agreed with this statement about Ford: "He does not seem to be very smart about the issues facing the country." An estimated 41 percent of respondents agreed with that statement, while 45 percent disagreed; another 14 percent were unsure.[42] In December of 1975, they asked again and the numbers were up. This time, 50 percent of respondents agreed with the statement, only 35 percent disagreed, and 15 percent were unsure.[43] In the same survey, Harris asked, "Let me read you some statements that have been made about President Ford.... He has the intelligence and qualifications to be a first-rate President." To this statement, 39 percent agreed, while 40 percent disagreed and 19 percent were unsure.[44] It is noteworthy that this survey data was collected between December 20 and 30.

By December 20, Chase had played Ford on *SNL* three times. He played him for the fourth time on January 17. It is frustrating that nothing was asked in that survey about Chase or *SNL*. In June, a *Time* survey asked a somewhat complicated question between June 21 and 24 about Ford's intelligence: "Gerald Ford—will you tell me whether this bothers you, doesn't bother you—or don't you think it's fair? He's not smart enough."

In response, 24 percent said it bothered them, 37 percent said it didn't bother them, and 39 percent said they thought it was not fair.[45] It is hard to know what to make of the 37 percent who said it didn't bother them. Did they mean that it didn't bother them that Ford wasn't very smart, or did they mean that they didn't agree with the statement? It is likely that some agreed that Ford wasn't smart but weren't bothered by it, while others disagreed with the statement. It is still noteworthy that at least 24 percent of the respondents were worried that the president wasn't smart enough and at least some of those 37 percent must have agreed that Ford wasn't smart—it just didn't bother them.

The Harris Survey asked a more straightforward question between August 18 and 22: "Tell me if you tend to agree or disagree: He does not seem to be very smart about the issues the country is facing." Of the respondents, 49 percent agreed, 37 percent disagreed, and 14 percent were not sure.[46] Also in August, a *Time* survey asked voters to respond to a somewhat different statement: "What about some of the things people say about Gerald Ford—will you tell me for each of the following whether you agree with or disagree with this statement: He's not smart enough." In response, 19 percent agreed, 70 percent disagreed, and 11 percent were not sure.[47] The questions are different and must certainly account for the difference in responses. The Harris question asks specifically about Ford's smartness with regard to the issues, while the *Time* question gets more directly at Ford's overall intelligence. Still, two things are noteworthy about the *Time* question: (1) the idea that the people running the survey felt compelled to ask the question at all suggests a low opinion of Ford; and (2) there were still 19 percent of the respondents who felt Ford was not smart enough to be president. Translated to the entire voting eligible population, it amounts to millions of people, in an election decided by fewer than two million.

Time asked the same question roughly a month later in a survey administered September 24–29, just after the first debate with Carter on September 23. The results were nearly identical, with 19 percent in agreement, while 70 percent disagreed and 11 percent were unsure.[48] Despite the fact that the survey followed the first debate, which many voters felt Ford won, the needle didn't move at all on people's assessment of Ford's intelligence. The percentage of voters who felt Ford was not smart enough was unchanged. *Time* asked the same question a third time, in a survey administered October 16–19. Once again, the results were similar, with 22 percent agreeing, 69 percent disagreeing, and 10 percent unsure.[49] It would have been interesting to see responses to this question in closer proximity to the second debate, held on October 6, when Ford made his gaffe about Soviet domination of central Europe. Despite the passage of time, however, there was still an uptick in the percentage of respondents agreeing that Ford was not smart enough.

Did *Saturday Night's* jokes about Ford have a significant impact on forming some people's impression of Ford and reinforcing other people's opinions of him? It seems that the answer to that question must be "Yes." Not only did the weekly Saturday night audience see what the "Not Ready for Prime-Time Players" had to say about Ford, but the show crossed over into the broader popular culture as the press began to report about the show's first breakout star, Chevy Chase, and his impersonation of Gerald Ford.[50]

These data about Ford's intelligence represent a correlation with *SNL's* material, not a causal relationship. But if it can be shown that Tina Fey's portrayal of Sarah Palin reinforced people's impression of McCain's running mate, it is reasonable to suggest the same relationship existed for at least some of *SNL's* viewers in 1975 and 1976. If Chase's Ford didn't create the impression of Ford as not smart enough to be president, he certainly reinforced it.

Ford's intelligence was not the only subject of criticism on *SNL*. The final episode before the election made that point with the two fake ads, one for Carter featuring Ford's pardon of Nixon, and one for Ford featuring Carter lusting. To many, a fake ad in which Jimmy Carter fantasizes about bikini-clad women is quite seriously different from one in which the country is reminded of Ford's pardon of Nixon. The Carter ad featured a woman in a bikini and an actor, Aykroyd, impersonating Carter on a topic that makes many people giggle as they giggled in sixth grade health class. The Ford ad used real footage, which the network tried to prevent them from using because they understood the important symbolism of it, and dealt with the most important political scandal and near-constitutional crisis in U.S. history.

However, public opinion data from the peak of the campaign suggests that, perhaps, the American public was more troubled by the *Playboy* interview than people today might realize. The polling data regarding the *Playboy* interview and Ford's pardoning of Nixon are rather similar. After Ford had the nomination safely in hand, following the close of the Republican National Convention on August 19, 1976, a number of surveys asked voters about the pardon of Nixon.

A Harris survey conducted in August asked respondents, "Let me read you some statements that have been made about President Ford's pardon of Richard Nixon. For each, tell me if you tend to agree or disagree: The whole Watergate mess was brought on by a Republican administration, and to avoid such problems in the future, it would be better to put a new Democratic Administration in the White House." Of the respondents, 58 percent disagreed, 29 percent agreed, and 13 percent were unsure. In another question in the same survey, respondents were asked to agree or disagree with this statement: "Ford was right to issue the pardon because it would have been impossible to govern the country if Nixon were on trial even if he were not still President." A whopping 56 percent of the respondents disagreed with this statement, while 38 percent agreed, and 6 percent were not sure.

The Harris survey also asked respondents to indicate their feelings about this statement: "Gerald Ford is a man of such high integrity, I am sure that he had nothing but the best interests of the country in mind when he pardoned Nixon." A majority, 53 percent, of respondents agreed with this statement, while 34 percent disagreed, and 13 percent were unsure.[51] On the other hand, a *Time* survey, also conducted in August, asked respondents to agree or disagree with essentially the opposite statement from the Harris poll: "President Gerald Ford did not act in the best interests of the country when he pardoned Richard Nixon before he had been impeached or tried." An estimated 46 percent of respondents fully agreed with this statement, while 22 percent partially agreed, and only 32 percent disagreed.[52]

Time surveyed Americans about Ford's pardon of Nixon in both late September and late October. In September, 50 percent of respondents indicated that Ford made a mistake when he pardoned Nixon, 40 percent felt he did not, and 10 percent were unsure.[53] In October, 53 percent said Ford made a mistake, 39 percent said he did not, and 8 percent were unsure.[54] That certainly indicates that, as the campaign drew to a close, there was a negative shift in opinion about Ford's pardon of Nixon. In a race as tight as the 1976 campaign turned out to be, the opinion changes could well have mattered and the bold statements on the pardon made by *SNL* and Chevy Chase may have had an important last-minute influence on some voters.

At the same time, however, several pollsters also asked voters about Carter's *Playboy* interview, and the results are revealing. A large percentage of voters knew about Carter's interview in the men's magazine, as indicated by an October Gallup survey, which found that 72 percent of respondents were aware of the interview, while 28 percent indicated they were not.[55] A *New York Times/CBS News* poll similarly found that 25 percent of registered voters hadn't heard about the interview. A majority, 69 percent, said they had heard about it and that it had no impact on their choice for president. A mere 2 percent, however, indicated that they knew about the interview and had changed from supporting to Carter to supporting Ford, while another 2 percent said they had changed from supporting Carter to not knowing whom they supported.[56]

In a Harris Survey also conducted at the end of September, 43 percent of likely voters indicated that they felt Carter was "wrong to have talked about sex the way he did to *Playboy Magazine*," while 36 percent disagreed with that statement, and a large number, 21 percent, were unsure.[57] In a *Time* poll, 21 percent of registered voters indicated that they "fully agree" with the statement "Jimmy Carter's interview in *Playboy* in which he uses vulgar language raises real questions about his judgment and might affect your vote [for president in 1976]," and 13 percent partially agreed. Far more, 65 percent, disagreed with that statement, but in a race as tight as the election turned out to be, 34 percent of registered voters was a sizeable number of voters.[58]

Another poll that asked about the *Playboy* interview was conducted by Gallup in early October. In that poll of people over eighteen, respondents were asked, "Do his comments make you more favorably inclined toward Carter or less favorably inclined toward him or doesn't it make much difference?" A significant 68 percent of respondents indicated there was no difference, while 8 percent actually said the comments made them more likely to vote for Carter. These are exactly the people Carter and his staff were hoping to reach when they said yes to the interview in the first place. While 22 percent of respondents indicated that Carter's comments made them less favorable toward him.[59] Granted, 22 percent is a relatively small minority of respondents but, again, in a close election, it represents enough voters to have an impact.

What is to be made of these poll numbers? First, it is always important to remember to take poll numbers with a grain of salt. They are far from perfect representations of public opinion. They are, at best, only reasonably accurate reflections of public opinion, within margins of error. With that disclaimer in mind, however, it is notable that the poll numbers on these two issues are reasonably similar, suggesting that similar numbers of people had concerns about Ford's pardon of Nixon as had concerns about Carter's granting an interview to *Playboy*. From this perspective, it is possible that the two ads on *SNL* could have had the same impact on voters.

However, the *SNL* audience was not a representative sample of the

American public. The audience skewed heavily toward a younger, male demographic. During the first season, Dick Ebersol, the NBC executive who worked with Lorne Michaels to create *SNL*, said, "It has the most saleable audience of any show on TV, a high percentage of 18- to 34-year-olds, which is what almost every advertiser outside of Geritol is begging for."[60] Reporter Johanna Steinmetz noted, "According to NBC research, only four programs in Prime-Time attract as high a percentage of that rare tube-viewing species, young men, as does 'Saturday Night.' (They are the 'Sunday Night Movie,' 'Monday Night Football,' 'Starsky and Hutch,' and the 'Six Million Dollar Man.') 'Saturday Night' has become such a desirable advertising commodity that in terms of cost per thousand to the advertiser—the amount it costs to expose a product to a thousand people—it is selling at a higher rate than the 'Tonight Show.'"[61]

What the cast and writers may have wanted to do in terms of influencing the outcome of the election is different from asking whether or not *SNL* had an impact on the race. For Chevy Chase to be something more than "heinously egotistical," it would have to be true that the show had an impact on some crucial percentage of voters' opinions and votes. The lack of data, however, doesn't mean there was no impact. Buck Henry, guest host of the final episode before the election, saw *SNL* having an impact on people's perceptions of politicians. He said, "Well, I don't know how you would measure that. No newsman ever asked someone coming out of a voting booth whether their opinion was shaped by comedians. I helped write that first sketch that had Chevy playing Ford. I'd say that '*SNL*'s focus on politicians helped, in certain cases, to whittle them down a notch."[62]

Carter pollster Pat Caddell says that he never polled voters about *SNL* during the campaign, but he conceded that *SNL* and Chevy Chase could have had some impact, saying of Chase's comments in *Playboy*, "No, I'm not so sure I would go that far to give them credit, but every little bit helps, you know, and I'm not going to criticize him if he wants to think that."[63] Caddell offered an alternate hypothesis about the impact of *SNL* during the 1976 campaign—not that it caused voters to vote for Carter, but that it reinforced its core audience's general lack of interest in politics. Caddell had this to say about young Americans and *SNL* in 1976: "Well, they were complacent in general. I think that we carried them, but after Watergate, it was not the kind of political energy among young voters that there had been. I think they were particularly disillusioned and turned off by it…. And probably *Saturday Night Live* overall, if you really wanted to go that far, there is no specific evidence, but if it's anything like I suspected, only reinforced that sense of cynicism and disillusion with politics in general."[64]

Another Carter aide, media advisor Jerry Rafshoon, saw *SNL* as having a more positive impact on Carter's campaign than Caddell, though he declined to see it as a deliberate effort by the program's writers and stars to push Carter over the top. Rafshoon described *SNL's* effect on the campaign in this way:

> They certainly weren't pushing Carter, as far as that goes. They were having fun at his expense as much as they were at Ford's, but I think that the pop culture at the time in many respects mirrors what goes on in the presidential election, and vice versa. And I think that the unusual aspect of somebody that you've never heard of, a person who was anti-establishment and not from Washington, you know, a bunch of young rebels, coming from Georgia trying to overthrow the status quo also fit in with the atmosphere at the time, the anti-establishment atmosphere that *Saturday Night Live* was espousing. So, to the extent that it helped the general [election], it helped the cultural aspect of *Saturday Night Live,* that was of help to our campaign. We were the anti-establishment, we were the unknowns who were coming along and we were the upstarts and so was *Saturday Night Live.* If you remember, the Academy Award picture that year was *Rocky.* I know Irwin Winkler, who produced it, and he told me he didn't think *Rocky* would have been a success if it hadn't been for the Carter campaign, the underdog, the nobody. And he said he knew when Carter got elected president that they were going to win the Academy Award. So, I think *Saturday Night Live* helped the atmosphere, you know, it helped perpetuate the atmosphere that elected Carter.[65]

Rafshoon's argument that *SNL* wasn't pushing Carter and that the show went after Carter as much as they went after Ford is true in this sense: there were a lot of jokes about Carter. However, when one considers the predominant demographics of the *SNL* audience—young and male—it seems less likely they would be negatively influenced by a young woman in a bathing suit than they would by a replay of Ford's speech pardoning Nixon. It is also highly unlikely that most of the writers at *SNL,* most of whom were male, saw the two "offenses" as equivalent, and there is a fair amount of evidence, in the comments of people such as Lorne Michaels and Chevy Chase, of support for Carter over Ford in Campaign '76. The reality is that during the campaign, there was no theme for Carter on *SNL* as damaging as the theme they used for Ford. Ford was written into the sketches as dumb, quite possibly too dumb to be president, and the writers found every possible opportunity to make that point.

Others who were deeply involved in the intersection of Campaign '76 and *SNL,* such as Dan Aykroyd, are highly skeptical that the show had any influence. He said, "My personal perception is that people do not vote based on satirical television shows.... Most people believe as I do that

Carter was elected because Nixon's political ghost was still haunting America.... Perhaps a poll, if creditably conducted, might say different."[66]

Unlike in his autobiography, in which he suggested *SNL* influenced the election, more recently Ron Nessen argued against the proposition that *SNL* had a significant impact on the outcome:

> Let's talk about the '76 election and what was the framework of the 1976 election. You have the resignation of a Republican Vice-President. I covered that story. Then you had a deep recession going on, right? You had the Vietnam War going on. You had Richard Nixon resigning, and his pardoning, and Ford being elevated. With all that going on, do you think that a Saturday night ½comedy show really had an impact on this election?[67]

He also went on record as saying,

> "It had an effect on the margins at the very best. I might agree that, yeah, it had some small effect on the margins. I think when you put it in that perspective ... is it conceivable that a Republican president who had never run for a national office before would be ahead on the Saturday before the election if there was a huge backlash [from *SNL*]? I don't think so. Then Carter pulled ahead that last weekend and won by what, 1 percent? 1½ percent? That's not all the stuff on Ford's plate, you know? The debate in San Francisco where Ford seems to say the Soviet Union doesn't dominate Eastern Europe. Why did that make such a big fuss? Because it fed into the image that Ford was dumb, that Ford was a bumbler and he can't say what he means, and he still came within 1 1/2 percent of winning."[68]

Nessen returned to the topic a third time during the interview, saying, "The challenges and the outcome of that election—I'm just trying to think of what impact they really did have, and when you think about all the other things that are going on. Particularly this huge financial disaster; Ford with his slip of the tongue in the debate in San Francisco; the fact that he was the one that pardoned Nixon; the fact that we had this war still going on; the fact that it wasn't a good time to be a Republican. And so, it's sort of amazing that he wasn't hurt more by what was going on."[69]

Nessen's answer to the question of *why* Ford was able to close the gap with Carter was, "Well, Carter didn't run a very good campaign, I don't think. I don't know whether the debates helped Ford or hurt Ford, or helped Carter or hurt Carter. It seems to me that, when you get in the voting booth and think about, 'Who do I want to be president of the United States for the next four years?' some people paused and said, 'Jimmy Carter, he's had one term as governor of a small southern state, should we really entrust it to him?' I don't know why it was so close. If it would have been held two days earlier, Ford would have won."[70] But in Nessen's comments, there are contradictions which leave room for an *SNL* impact. On one hand, he argues there were so many large factors in the campaign—

war, economy, Nixon pardon—that *SNL* couldn't possibly have had an impact. However, he also argues that the election ended up being very close because people didn't trust Carter. In a very close race, decided by about two million votes, it is certainly possible that a show which was drawing weekly audiences of more than 20 million viewers had an impact after airing such a blatantly political—and biased—episode the Saturday before the election. Might—for at least a crucial two million people— being reminded of Ford's many flaws in such a pointed way have allowed voters to weigh their distrust of both men and decide to vote for Carter? It is certainly plausible.

When asked if he truly didn't think *SNL* had an impact on creating Ford's image, Nessen said, "I think to the contrary. I think the image was already there and *Saturday Night Live* took advantage of the image.... Do you think that people made up their mind who to vote for in an election based on *Saturday Night Live*? I think common sense would tell you not."[71] Nessen added, "If you were Lorne Michaels, if you were Chevy Chase, or any of the other regulars on the show at the time, wouldn't you like to have the bragging rights that, 'Hey, we're the ones that defeated Gerald Ford'? How much does that discount the notion that they, in fact, did affect the election?"[72] For all his disagreement with the thought that *SNL* could have had an impact on the outcome of the election, Nessen did acknowledge that the show could have had an effect on the margins and it was a very close election in which Carter pulled ahead on the last weekend—a weekend filled with many events, including *SNL*'s re-broadcast of Ford's pardon of Richard Nixon. One can't help but wonder—as Nessen did in his 1978 autobiography—if it hadn't been for *SNL* affecting things at the margins, would Ford have won?

Ron Nessen certainly felt differently about *SNL*'s potential to affect the race back in 1976. If he didn't, then why would he host the show and encourage the president to appear on it with him? As was noted in chapter six in his autobiography, published in 1978, Nessen wrote, in direct response to Chase's comments in *Playboy*, "So, it wasn't all innocent fun and games after all. Looking back, it's obvious that my attempt to smother the ridicule of Ford by joining the laughter on 'Saturday Night' was a failure. Ford's reputation as a bumbler persisted and was a factor in the election outcome, as Chevy Chase claimed."[73] Nearly forty years later, Dan Aykroyd spoke up on behalf of Nessen, saying, "Nessen and Ford made the correct decision to appear on the show. They were fans and it made Jerry Ford seem more human and less stolid. Again, blame Nixon for Ford's defeat, as well as Carter's own appeal, which was fresh at the time."[74]

In analyzing the 1976 election and *SNL*'s role in it, Lorne Michaels waxed philosophical and, ultimately, concluded that the show did not affect the outcome of the race:

> I think coming after the, just complete, day-in, day-out attention on Watergate that riveted the nation, the hearings and its end result, and what was a huge, kind of traumatic thing following the war in Vietnam. And in the sense of a Shakespearian tragedy, you know at the end of, uh, in Shakespeare's tragedies when there is nothing but corpses strewn all over the stage, there is always a character called Albany, or Blunt, who comes in and says that things are going to be all right. We will carry on and order will be restored. And I think Gerald Ford was deemed to be that character. You know, the person, the decent man, who comes in and reestablishes normalcy. And I think that was sort of conveyed in Chevy's portrayal of him and the way we wrote him and it was a contrast to Carter who, later on when we did things like "Ask President Carter," he talked a guy off an acid trip. Seemed to be nothing he didn't know. It was one of—I am not sure anyone could have won that election, but I don't think we particularly hurt Ford. If you know what I mean.[75]

But if Michaels saw Ford as a benevolent Shakespearian character and Carter as an annoying know-it-all, why did the show run footage of Ford pardoning Nixon on the Saturday before the election? If Hill and Weigand are correct in their assertion that showing the Watergate footage was Lorne Michaels's proudest moment—up to that point—then why is that the case? It must certainly be because Michaels believed, at the time, that the show had an impact.

What is the answer? Was *SNL* a factor in the outcome of the election? It certainly was, if only in the role it played in generating popular culture's discussion of the election and in strongly emphasizing a particular image of the candidates, especially Jerry Ford, which people remember for years after broadcast. But, it was just one factor—maybe a small factor—among many other factors: the economy, gaffes like Poland, the handling of Earl Butz, the swine flu vaccination program and, most egregiously, the pardoning of Richard Nixon. No matter how much people liked Ford, they hated Nixon and, as the man who pardoned Nixon, Ford gave many Americans an outlet for their hostility. Still, though, despite the hostility millions of Americans felt about Nixon and Watergate, Ford lost the election by only a narrow margin. A narrow enough margin that it is reasonable to think that at least some of the two million voters who made the difference were part of *SNL*'s weekly audience of 22 million Americans. What is important to remember when considering the impact of *SNL* on the outcome of the election is that the show was more than happy to remind the American public, with great frequency, of all of the real-world factors, such as the economy, Vietnam, and Watergate, especially as the election drew near, and they never stopped making jokes about Ford's intellect. The show both literally and figuratively set up the world as a stage for the election to be played out.

What can ultimately be said about the difference *SNL* made (or didn't make) in 1976? It is a question that is very difficult to answer with the kind of statistical certainty that social scientists like to claim, but the evidence leans toward a real impact, if only a small one. There really are no data available to put the question to the kind of rigorous statistical testing on which modern political science relies. Today, much data exists to test many different questions about the impact of popular culture on politics, such as data collected by the Pew Center for the People and the Press, which indicate that many people, especially those in younger demographics, get much of their political information from entertainment programs. In 1975 and 1976, the notion that such things could make a difference was new territory, and Nessen and Ford were the first politicians of their stature to appear on a show like *SNL*. At the time, many people assumed that the program had an impact on the election and it clearly had an impact on many people's lasting impression of Gerald Ford. Even if they liked him, many also saw him as an amiable dolt, the simpleton of the family who everyone is nice to but from whom no one expects great things. Much of the responsibility for people having that impression can be laid at the feet of *SNL*. It is also undeniable that *SNL* influenced today's media landscape and the behavior of modern politicians, who, in large numbers, feel compelled to appear on late-night entertainment television as a matter of course. If only for that reason, it is impossible to say that the show had no impact in 1976 or beyond.

Conclusion

Ultimately, it is possible to answer the question about what the cast and writers of *SNL* wanted to do in 1976 this way: They were both unbiased and biased at the same time. Here, it is worth considering the arguments made by people like Lorne Michaels and Gerald Rafshoon that what *SNL* was in 1976, and still strives to be today with varying degrees of success, is anti-establishment. In 1976, Jimmy Carter was, or at least campaigned as if he was, anti-establishment. Ultimately, it may not be right to accuse *SNL*, circa 1976, of having a liberal bias. What it may be more accurate to accuse the show of having—and it is almost certainly a bias the show's team would wear as a badge of honor—is a bias against the establishment.

If you're in power, you're a target. If you want to be in power, you *may* be a target, or they may just wait until you're in power. And then, there are no holds barred. Such was the experience of Jimmy Carter.

What can be said with certainty about *SNL* is that it has almost always had an impact on the types of things people talk about around the proverbial water cooler. It is also true that, even if *SNL* may have seemed to be lending support to a candidate such as Jimmy Carter in 1976, or Barack Obama in 2008, they have also been quick to turn their comedic knives on the favored politician when the favored politician becomes the politician in office. After all, in 2014, *SNL* portrayed a smiling President Obama pushing an innocent immigration bill down the Capitol steps in a parody of *Schoolhouse Rock*'s "I'm Just a Bill," seemingly attacking the entire democratic process on which the country was founded, in favor of the use of presidential executive orders.

A little more than a month after the 1976 election, before Carter even took office, *SNL* blatantly demonstrated doubts about Carter's sincerity in a brief speech by Dan Aykroyd as Carter sitting outside a warehouse in Plains, eating from a bag of shelled peanuts. Smiling broadly, he proceeded to tell the audience that it would simply not be possible for him to keep all the promises he made during the campaign. He made those promises without knowing the sort of stuff only a president gets to know. So now, after the election, as he was getting ready to become president, it was becoming clear to him that Ford had been a pretty good president after all. He now knew that it would simply be impossible to cut unemployment *and* reduce unemployment as he'd promised during the campaign. Saving the economy would take a long time. People shouldn't expect to see any improvement until his *second* term. But, ending with a smile and "Merry Christmas," he promised that by 1984, the United States would have full employment and a balanced budget.[76]

The sketch is relatively gentle, but at the same time, it speaks to the concerns that many expressed about Carter during the campaign—that what he was promising to do was too good to be true. *SNL*'s writers had full-out fun with Carter's ego and his know-it-all reputation early in his presidency—less than two months after he took office—satirizing a real Carter media event. The sketch "Ask the President," which Lorne Michaels referred to when comparing *SNL*'s treatment of Ford and Carter, featured Carter and Walter Cronkite doing a radio call-in show. The real Carter tried this once, on March 5, 1977. The call-in show was broadcast on CBS Radio and lasted for two hours, moderated by Cronkite, with Carter answering questions on a dizzying array of topics, including foreign policy, the economy, illegal drugs, cancer research, and the future of the now-closed Frankford Arsenal in Philadelphia, which was a major issue during the 1976 campaign.[77] Carter's media advisor, Gerald Rafshoon, suggested that things simply got away from them as the administration progressed, but he expressed regret that Carter only did the call-in show once, saying, "Yeah, I don't know why we dropped the ball on that. We should have kept doing that."[78]

SNL's version of "Ask President Carter" aired on March 12, with Aykroyd as Carter and Bill Murray as Cronkite. Callers were Jane Curtin as a postal worker, Garrett Morris as an angry man, Tom Davis as "Peter," a kid on a bad acid trip, and Aykroyd as Richard Nixon. The first call was from Curtin, "Mrs. Edward Horbath," asking Carter about the problems she was having with a mail sorting machine, the "Marvex 3000." Aykroyd instantly diagnosed the problem, claiming he was just discussing this machine with Vice President Mondale that morning. When he's done with Mrs. Horbath, he fields an obscene call from a guy calling himself "Dr. Midnight," and then takes a call from a teenager named Peter, played by Tom Davis, who is having a bad acid trip. Aykroyd asks him all kinds of questions about what the pills looked like and concludes, "Okay, right. You did some Orange Sunshine, Peter." He tells Peter how to handle the next few hours and tells him that he's just suffering the effects of a strong drug. He should try to relax and listen to some music, maybe the Allman Brothers and remember that he is safe.[79]

As Tom Davis observed about this sketch, "The handle for Jimmy Carter, for us, was that he was, uh, really smart. That he had been the captain of the nuclear submarine, or whatever. And that, so like in the Carter phone-in piece, these incredibly complex, obscure questions are asked and he answers them perfectly. And the joke is how smart he is."[80] It was certainly better than the handle Davis, et al., had on Ford, which was, in Davis's words, "The joke with Jerry Ford, which is what Chevy commandeered, was that he was a goofball who bumped his head and fell down all the time, and was incoherent."[81]

At this point, Carter and his staff were still apparently on board with *SNL's* take on Carter. As Dan Aykroyd said, "The Carter people definitely knew what we were doing and, in fact, they told us they liked the scene where Jimmy talks a kid down from a bad acid trip."[82] They may have liked that sketch, but they couldn't have liked the biting sketches such as those which aired in episodes hosted by Ralph Nader on January 15, 1977, before Carter even took the oath of office, or by Julian Bond on April 9, 1977.

11

Post '76, *SNL* Marches On

CHASE: *That business about lusting after women in his heart—why didn't he just say, "I've seen a lot of ass in my day and thought about it, but I've been faithful to my wife?" You don't have to lust after women in your mind. Let's drop the rhetoric. I'd like to know what the guy's like.*

AYKROYD: *It's our duty as satirists in America to nail Carter to the wall as much as possible. However, there's the dynamic of the fact that I'm a Canadian citizen and, at any time, he could just give the word and I'd be out of here. One phone call to immigration and I'm gone.*

BELUSHI: *Half the people on the show would be gone.*

AYKROYD: *That's right. You could wipe this whole show right off the map.—Playboy, 1977[1]*

Almost immediately after the election, it was clear that though there was a predisposition among many at *SNL* to favor Carter over Ford, it did not mean they were going to take it easy on him as president. As Carter stopped being a candidate and took the oath of office, the themes that were only lightly suggested, or which were treated with a sort of benevolent fondness—for example, Carter's perceived disingenuousness, and his know-it-all smugness—during the campaign became much more pronounced and were presented with a much harder edge. The transition from one president to the next was new for *SNL* and in almost no time, it was treating Carter with the same irreverence with which it had treated Ford, setting up a model that *SNL* continues to follow today. Although the show can, at times, be identified as having a clear bias for (or against) a specific political figure, as it did for Carter and against Ford in Campaign '76, its clear focus is to parody everyone in power. If one were going to brand *SNL* with a label of bias over the breadth of its life, it would be too simplistic to say it has a liberal or conservative bias. It would be much more accurate to say that it has an anti-authority bias. Carter's presidency presents excellent evidence of that bias.

Even in the very earliest days of the Carter administration, it was quickly clear that the *SNL* team was not going to treat the new president with kid gloves, and before they had serious issues of policy and politics to go after him about, they made jokes about his eccentric family, as is evidenced by the "Weekend Update" segment which aired the Saturday after the inaugural. It was clear that the Carter family, full of southern characters, promised to offer a comedic gold mine to the *SNL* crew. No one made a bigger or, ultimately, more tragic target than Billy Carter. The jokes centered around an interview with Jimmy Carter's mother, Lillian, as portrayed by actress Ruth Gordon.

In response to a question of Carter's honesty, Gordon as Lillian replies that once Carter looked at her and told her he could never tell a lie. She also said that she had never in her life called herself "Miss Lillian," as Jimmy Carter took to calling her during the campaign. She figured that, "if he can sell that crap to his own mother," then he could also be the president. Jane Curtain ended the segment with a story about the Carter family and the rest of the population of Plains staying in the Lincoln bedroom at the White House after the inauguration. They all stayed in Lincoln's bed, she reported, except for Billy Carter, who slept under it. Curtin said that Billy Carter's reaction to the events was a loud burp.[2] And so, this "Weekend Update" report ended with a joke about Billy Carter's drinking, which became much more serious as the Carter administration wore on, as did the problems he caused his presidential brother.

Twelve years his junior, Jimmy's brother Billy was a spectacle from the beginning of the campaign. At first, Billy was an amusing character, with a much different outlook on life than his very serious, pious, and ethical big brother. Billy Carter was a good ol' boy in the classic sense and he was an instant celebrity who hired an agent and was soon making $5,000 an appearance. It seemed innocent enough in 1977, but if one views Carter as the first of a new type of candidate, largely eschewing his party and making use of the new mechanisms of nomination created by both the Republican and Democratic parties in the early 1970s, then Billy Carter's willingness to turn his fame to financial advantage, looks more like a preview of the widespread accusations that members of the Trump family are trying to monetize the presidency. In an analysis of Billy Carter's celebrity, written early in Jimmy Carter's presidency, journalist Joseph Lelyveld wrote:

> Nixon, Ford and Kissinger can be accused of exploiting a public trust. Not Billy Carter, who never claimed any such thing: He's exploiting public curiosity. Having been turned into a stock character on TV in the silly season of a Presidential campaign, he now plays the part for a price. But if a brother can do it, why not a wife, son or

daughter? The temptations and the restraints crumble so rapidly that it's hard to guess where the line will finally be drawn. For now, it's all right for a former President to have an agent to package and merchandise him, but not a sitting President; all right for his brother but not his child.[3]

Read from the perspective of post–Election 2016, Lelyveld's words seem prophetic.

One thing is certain: Billy Carter was more than willing to exploit his connection to the president for personal gain and, as Carter's presidency continued, the problems he caused became more and more significant. In the first month of Carter's presidency, *SNL* ran a Mardi Gras special that featured Aykroyd as Carter astride the statue of Andrew Jackson in Jackson Square. In reference to his brother, Billy, Carter promised that he was ready to fulfill his responsibilities as president. He would start, he said, by carrying out a program of energy conservation. He would carry his own bags when he travelled. And when his brother was too drunk to walk, he would carry him too.[4]

While the drinking was played for laughs here, eventually it became obvious that Billy had a serious drinking problem and he spent time in rehabilitation at a naval hospital in California. He also became embroiled in a scandal that deeply embarrassed his brother when Billy became a paid agent for the Libyan government. The drinking, the pursuit of fame, and the connections to the Libyan government were all fodder for *SNL* over the course of Carter's presidency.

At the beginning of the Carter administration, the relative uniqueness of having a child in the White House also offered an opportunity for humor, especially since Jimmy and Rosalyn Carter had insisted that their daughter, a fourth-grader when they moved into the White House, would attend public school. When they made the announcement that she would, indeed, go to public school as the Thaddeus Stevens School, near the White House, press secretary Jody Powell said that he was "once again merely confirming that they are doing what they said they would do."[5] *SNL* was more than happy to offer a sketch, with Laraine Newman as Amy Carter, Dan Aykroyd and Bill Murray as Secret Service agents, Gilda Radner and Garrett Morris as students, and Jane Curtin as the teacher. It aired nine days into the Carter administration and suggests that although the Carters might have been continuing to try to demonstrate that they were just regular folks, having the president's daughter in a public school fourth grade class would be anything but "regular." The performance includes Secret Service agents who can't help but feed answers to Amy and to stuff a student who accuses her of cheating into a desk.[6]

Questions about race and Carter were apparently not far from the minds of the *SNL* writers as he assumed office and many people loudly questioned Carter's commitment to the promises he made on the campaign trail. One of the strangest politically oriented sketches that ever aired on *SNL* was performed on the March 12, 1977, episode, about Amy Carter and her nanny. Called "Amy's Bedtime Story," it featured Sissy Spacek as Amy Carter, and Garrett Morris as Amy's nanny, a woman named Mary Fitzpatrick. Mary Fitzpatrick was Amy's nanny in real life, taking care of her for the four years Jimmy Carter was the governor of Georgia. She was a prisoner of the state of Georgia, having been convicted of murder in 1970 and when Carter moved to Washington, he got permission for Fitzpatrick to move with the family. In his memoir, Carter wrote about this as a social experiment which turned out well for everyone. But, it clearly got the attention of the folks on *SNL*, who definitely did not treat it as a positive social experiment.

The sketch, which also aired in March 1977, does not take the same upbeat tone of Carter's memoir. Instead, it has a very tough edge to it and suggests that Jimmy Carter has something much less than a progressive attitude about race—both in terms of using Fitzpatrick as a stereotypical black southern nanny, and in terms of using Fitzpatrick, along with his daughter and a gimmicky radio call-in show, for media gain. The portrayal of Fitzpatrick by Garrett Morris is of an unrepentant criminal, speaking in stereotypical black dialect, happily telling a "fairy tale" of criminal exploits that bore no relation to the real Mary Fitzpatrick to an innocent, impressionable, and lily-white Amy Carter. When Amy asks if Mary will tell her a bedtime story, says yes and proceeds to tell her a version of "Goldilocks and the Three Bears" which paralleled her prison and work release experience, including her work at the governor's mansion in Georgia.[7] In classic *SNL* fashion, no one gets the benefit of the doubt in this sketch. Mary Fitzpatrick is depicted with every negative stereotype imaginable and the judgment and motives of Jimmy Carter are fully questioned and played for uncomfortable laughs.

Politics

Carter's family wasn't the only thing *SNL* played for laughs and political commentary in the first few months of his administration. While a majority of the people at *SNL* preferred Jimmy Carter to Gerald Ford in the election, it is certainly true that as Carter's presidency wore on, they grew less and less fond of him. As Aykroyd said, the Carters were never known as "world-class yukkers." Lorne Michaels compared his visits with Ford to his visit with Carter's people, saying, "But Ford couldn't have been more gracious and warm. And then it was a year later and we went down to the Carter White House and I didn't meet the President, but I did meet Jody Powell and Hamilton Jordan, those guys. And all I remember was cowboys boots up on the desk and just a kind of, what seemed to me to be, a kind of smugness and 'we know what we are doing.' But you know, none of us came away with the idea, you know, that these are people we had anything in common with."[8] Michaels added, when asked if he believed Carter's assertion that he had never watched *SNL* until Tina Fey's portrayal of Sarah Palin in 2008, "I would—yeah, I don't think humor was ever his strong suit."[9]

The gang at *SNL* started in on Carter before he even took office, as questions began to quickly arise about his appointments to his new administration. In turns, his actions seemed both unprofessional *and* to be playing to many more Washington insiders and power-brokers than his outsider campaign might have indicated.

The sketch that took place in Carter's peanut warehouse a month after the election, in which he explained that he wouldn't be able to keep all of his campaign promises was merely a prelude for how they would treat *President* Carter. When 1977 began, *SNL* started to go very negative, very quickly, starting with a guest-host appearance by consumer advocate Ralph Nader, who hosted five days before Carter became president. Nader supported Carter's promise to change Washington during his campaign, but he became highly critical of the president-elect as his displeasure grew with the people Carter was choosing for important administration positions.

Nader quickly began to complain about the direction in which Carter was moving with his appointments, accusing Carter of reneging on his pledge to consult with him about his appointments and saying that he worried whether or not Carter would be able to control corporate interests and that the names Carter was mentioning for high-level positions indicated that "the departments that have traditionally been in-house advocates for business interests will remain that way."[10] It sounded very much like complaints made in 2017 that promises to "drain the swamp" were not being kept.

Of Carter's possible nominees for treasury secretary, Nader said, "There is not one who is not an old-line, money, establishment corporate type,"[11] and that the Treasury Department would become "a plantation for bankers, the old-line establishment, money-centered people."[12] Nader made similar complaints about Carter's proposed nominees for other important positions, and he was not alone in doing so. As the transition wore on, more observers noted how many familiar names were being considered for administration posts. Reporter Leslie Gelb observed in a column, "The Carter organization found that even its long list of realistic candidates for Cabinet appointments was relatively short.... In almost all cases where the lists have been revealed, they have been short on women, blacks, dissidents and the like—short, in other words, on people who have not previously held positions of responsibility in the Federal Government."[13]

On January 15, 1977, Nader made a major statement critical of Carter. In reference to Carter's choices for the Council of Economic Advisors, Nader said that Carter had failed a litmus test to appoint "a strongly liberal and unorthodox thinker" to the Council.[14] January 15, 1977, was a noteworthy day in the Nader-Carter relationship for another reason. It was the day Nader hosted *SNL*, in an episode that was heavy with criticism of the president-elect. Nader was political throughout the episode. In a "Weekend Update" segment, he played a "Texxon" oil company executive, "Mr. Rigg," speaking his role in crafting a new solar energy bill. The bill was crafted with three concessions to Texxon, according to Mr. Rigg: "Texxon thinks it, first, should own the sun. We also need a Solar Depletion Tax Allowance—since the sun depreciates over time ... and Texxon must have the right to order its prices raised whenever there is an eclipse."[15]

The critical commentary about Carter came in a sketch which played directly off his very public criticism of Carter's appointments for his administration. In it, Nader falls asleep and has a nightmare about Carter's plans to restore the Confederacy. In the dream, Carter tells Nader that he shouldn't worry about his cabinet appointments—they were only to placate the conservatives. Once he's taken the oath, he'll roll out the changes Nader wants. Nader lists several liberal proposals and Carter says yes to them all. And then, he unveils his plan for the southern takeover of America, in the form of his plans for the inauguration. As "Dixie" plays in the background, Carter tells Nader that he is finally going to be able to set things right for the South after 110 years of mistreatment by the Yankees. And, he wants Nader to know, Carter is counting on his help. As Carter tells him it's time for him to go to the office he's had set up for him in Plains, Nader wakes up to find he's been having a nightmare, sleeping on his desk, which is covered in peanut shells.[16]

The Confederacy sketch both allowed Nader to continue to criticize

Carter's choices for his top-level positions, with Nader uttering lines such as, "Ah, Carter. What a cabinet. I wonder if he really cares what I think—now that the election is over," and plays on the notion that Carter, a southerner, might not be as forward-thinking about race relations as he professed to be during the campaign, with references to things such as the "George Wallace Tactical Air Wing of the Confederate Air Force." Finally, at the end of the episode, as the cast and Nader gathered onstage with musical guest George Benson to wish the audience goodnight, Nader grabbed a box of peanuts and started throwing them to the audience, shouting, "Have some peanuts. Peanuts! Peanuts!"

Ralph Nader was not the only Carter supporter who was disappointed by his choices for appointments in the administration. Following the election, many advocates of women's and African American causes, quickly became impatient for Carter to fulfill his promises of creating a diverse administration. Just as Nader was frustrated by the high volume of political insiders getting top spots in the administration, others quickly became frustrated with the small number of women and people of color getting high-ranking positions. As journalist Joseph Lelyveld observed, there was a sense of disappointment in African American circles about Carter's choices: "In black political circles, there was a sense of letdown when it became evident that the overwhelming black vote for Jimmy Carter was not to be repaid with numerous black appointments to top-level Administration jobs."[17] There was much criticism for a relative lack of appointments of African Americans to top positions, and for the appointment of Georgian Griffin Bell to be attorney general, because of concerns about his record on civil rights. There was also criticism for the appointment of Andrew Young, who during the campaign was Carter's top black campaign strategist and tie to the black community, both for an eventual appointment that was deemed too lowly—ambassador to the United Nations—and for the fact that he wouldn't be in direct contact with Carter on a daily basis and, thereby, be able to serve as a link for the black community directly to Carter. Critics came from the Congressional Black Caucus, from the National Urban League's Vernon Jordan, and one of his most outspoken African American critics was Georgia state senator Julian Bond.

On April 9, 1977, about a month after the biting Amy Carter–Mary Fitzpatrick sketch, Julian Bond guest-hosted *SNL* in what was the second episode of the show devoted largely to matters of civil rights and race relations. Bond's opening monologue touched on a wide variety of issues, but it was framed around him wondering why *SNL* asked him to host. He reviewed the reasons that went through his mind, thinking maybe it was because of his reputation as a civil rights activist; or perhaps it was because he was the first African American to be nominated for vice president; or because of his work helping the poor and unfortunate. But, he said, when he got to New York to work on putting the show together, he realized none of these were the reason they'd asked him to host the show. He concluded, saying, "These people had me come all the way up here from Atlanta to ... to be their Chocolate Easter Bunny. And I am."[18]

Civil rights and ethnic matters were inevitably going to come up during the campaign of '76, not the least of which ended up being Carter's strange "ethnic purity" comments. Another strange matter of ethnicity came up right before the election when an African American minister and civil rights activists from Albany, Georgia, the Rev. Clenon King, announced his intention to join Carter's church in Plains, the Plains Baptist Church. King, who was no relation to the Rev. Martin Luther King, Jr., was denied membership because of a church policy, dating back to 1965, which explicitly barred African Americans from membership. The issue had come up during the campaign and Jimmy Carter repeatedly insisted that he and his family voted against the ban when it was adopted by the congregation in a 54 to 6 vote.

The Rev. Clenon King was a Republican and the Carter campaign portrayed the incident as politically motivated and got many African American leaders from around the nation to make public statements to that effect. But the controversy extended past the election, continuing the embarrassment for Carter, now the president-elect. Complicating the situation was the fact that when the church's pastor, the Rev. Bruce Edwards, opposed the church's deacons' decision to enforce the ban on African Americans in the church and keep Clenon King from joining, the church's board of deacons voted to remove him from the church.[19]

Less than a week after the election, on the November 13th episode of *SNL*, during "Weekend Update," Jane Curtin reported that the members of Carter's church would be voting the next day on the question of whether or not to allow black congregants. She said that people in Plains must think the vote would be yes, because they were having alligators shipped up from Florida to put in the church baptismal basin.[20] The next day, Sunday, November 14, the church congregation voted to (1) allow African Americans to attend services at the church; (2) create a committee to screen applications for membership; and (3) to keep the Rev. Bruce Edwards as their pastor. President Carter was reported to be involved in persuading the congregation to approve these moves while members of the Ku Klux Klan marched outside the church and the Rev. Clenon King waited on the church's doorstep. After the vote, Carter said, "I am proud of my church." He was certainly relieved that his church had taken a step to get the embarrassing dispute off the front pages of America's newspapers, but it is hard to imagine, if he was as dedicated to racial harmony as he claimed, that he could have been proud of the way the members of his church had behaved since 1965.

During Julian Bond's episode, there were many sketches which touched on the idea of being black in America, in addition to his opening monologue. He and Garrett Morris, the only black cast member, debated which was better, being light- or dark-skinned. There was a fake ad for a product called "Afro Lustre," with a jingle based on the Virginia Slims cigarette campaign aimed at women ("You've come a long way, baby," with "negro" taking the place of "baby"). Another sketch featured Garrett Morris and *SNL* writer Mike O'Donoghue, in which "Mr. Mike" shares one of his "least loved bedtime stories," telling the story of B'rer Rabbit to Uncle Remus. If this sketch were to be shown on television today, it is hard to imagine any scenario in which people wouldn't be fired, as Garrett Morris spoke in stereotypical black dialect and was patronized by Mr. Mike. When Mr. Mike loftily tells Uncle Remus that he's stopped by to tell him a story about B'rer Rabbit. Uncle Remus responds, "B'rer Rabbit? Why, ah loves dat floppy-eared rascal, Mr. Mike! An' if ah knows B'rer Rabbit, he's a-cookin' up some devilment, ain't he?"[21]

Bond's episode of *SNL* is noteworthy for many reasons, including the fact that it was the only episode in which someone—John Belushi—did an impersonation of one of the civil rights era's most controversial figures, Alabama Governor George Wallace. In the sketch, the former presidential candidate talks about how much the South, and Alabama, have changed. He concludes that Carter's election should cause people to stop thinking of the South as such a backwards place where blacks had to ride in the back of the bus. Progress was being made. Blacks, he said, now also ride in the back of all sorts of modern forms of transportation, like jets and maybe even "rockets to the moon."[22] No doubt, had he seen the episode— and again, Carter claims never to have watched the show before 2008— Carter would not have been happy with any of the sketches, this one included. Julian Bond, however, was not troubled by the material in his episode because he felt it was intelligently written, raising important topics in a humorous way.

Much as when Ron Nessen hosted, it contained a lot of material that posed the risk of generating controversy for the president, the Julian Bond episode was loaded with sketches that could have gotten him in trouble with his core constituency, his fellow African Americans. However, when Bond was asked about these "civil-rights–related" sketches, he said, "I wouldn't call them 'civil rights-related' but rather 'black-related.' I think well of them in retrospect—the show was what it was, a path-breaking humorous look at American society where anything (for the times) went. I got some grief about the Garrett Morris light-skin, dark-skin sketch from one or two people, but it didn't bother me. I liked the character Mr. Mike. I believed then—and now—that you can make jokes about almost anything."[23]

The most politically charged moment of the show came in a sketch entitled "An Oval Office." It featured Jimmy Carter at his worst, both in terms of slipperiness and possibly racist tendencies. It also featured Andrew Young at his most servile and Julian Bond at his most skeptical. It is quite negative in its portrayal of both Carter and Young. The sketch begins with Carter kicking Amy out of the Oval Office. Angry, she accuses him of making "hundreds" of promises but not keeping any of them. Bond and Young enter and Bond tells Carter he thinks it's time Carter stop worrying so much about human rights around the world and worry about human rights in the United States. This prompts Carter to ask Bond if he's seen the home Carter grew up in and shows him a model made of Lincoln Logs. Bond points out that Carter promised to have more Blacks on his cabinet than Ford but, like Ford, he has only one. He then tells Carter that he also promised to have more women than Ford but, like Ford, he has only one. And the same person, Patricia Harris, filled both slots at the time this episode was broadcast. Harris served in Carter's administration first as the secretary of Housing and Urban Development, and then as the secretary of Health, Education, and Welfare.[24]

In the sketch, as the conversation becomes more uncomfortable, Carter is saved by a meeting. He tells Bond and Young that he's going to call for a meeting of the National Security Council to address a human rights violation. It is not, we see, anything to do with issues of concerns to African Americans but, rather, has to do with a Turkish sailor being held prisoner in Paraguay. He tells them that with his help, the help of the American government, and the Coca-Cola company, they should be able to do something to help this poor man. He leaves and Andrew Young turns to Bond, excitedly telling him, "You see that? You see, Julian? I TOLD you! The man really cares!" In a tone reminiscent of the characters from *Amos 'n' Andy*, Bond replies, "He sure do, Andy!"[25]

Asked about the nomination of Griffin Bell to the attorney general position and whether it influenced Bond's performance in the sketch,

Bond said, "It didn't touch my attitude toward the sketch—but it did touch and reinforce my attitude toward Carter. I testified against Bell's appointment. Afterward, he came out into the hallway and apologized."[26]

The episode is noteworthy for many reasons. First, it was historic in that it was only the second time an African American had hosted the show. Second, it gave Julian Bond a chance to speak, in a joking way, with an audience that was almost certainly largely unaware of who he was, as was reflected in his opening monologue. Third, it was the second episode since Jimmy Carter's inauguration—the Nader episode being the first—that took real, seriously negative comedic shots at the young Carter administration.

The Other Headaches of Being President for Jimmy Carter (especially in the age of SNL)

As Carter's presidency wore on, the material for jokes on *SNL* came from many areas: scandal in the administration, in the form of an ethics charge against his Office of Management and Budget director, Bert Lance; seemingly endless sketches about the Carter Administration energy policy, starting in May 1977 and going through the Three Mile Island accident in 1979; inflation and the poor economy; his poor relations with his own party in Congress; a recurrent problem with hemorrhoids; and foreign policy, including the treaty to turn control of the Panama Canal over to Panama, negotiations between the Israelis and the Egyptians, negotiations between the Israelis and the Palestinians, and the unrest in Cypress. All of these were the source of many *SNL*–Carter sketches.

Trump—A Carter for the 21st Century?

From a political standpoint, there are reasons to think historians may one day compare Carter and Trump as similar presidents. It remains to be seen, of course, if Trump will be a more successful president than Carter. What is true in 2017 is that Trump is even more of a political amateur than was Carter. While Carter served one term as a Georgia state senator and one term as governor of Georgia, he had no Washington experience. Trump had no political experience at all before becoming president of the United States. They both made many missteps in their early days as president. Carter continued to make many missteps throughout his presidency. Whether Trump will continue to do so is an open question.

One dimension on which they are similar is the change in tone with which *SNL* treated them from campaign season to president-elect and governing. The tone for both candidates was similar—skeptical, but not without affection. Trump was portrayed during the campaign by two actors, Taran Killam and Darrell Hammond. When Trump hosted the program, he appeared on stage with Hammond playing Trump.

For Carter, the portrayals were done by Dan Akyroyd, both before and after the election, but the tone changed, no so much because Akyroyd made big changes in his portrayal of Carter but because there was no longer the clownish figure of Chase's Gerald Ford to make Carter look better. With Ford out of the picture (Chevy Chase didn't appear as Ford again until February 1978, in a response to Carter's decision to negotiate turning control of the Panama Canal over to the nation of Panama), the writers as *SNL* had one main political target: Carter. And the way they treated him was very different after the election than it was before.

The same is true of how the portrayal of Trump changed during and after the election of 2016. Early in the primary campaign, Trump and Bernie Sanders were treated as almost merry troublemakers, as rascals. They were portrayed as people who were shaking things up, but they were also portrayed as people who didn't possibly have a chance to win the election, so there was no need to be too harsh with them. As the primary campaign wore on, the commentary about Trump changed somewhat, but still, he was not the subject of the same tone that he was subject to during the fall campaign and after the election. Early in the primary campaign, *SNL* was solicitous of Trump and the high ratings he brought to every show on which he appeared.

The 2015 season, *SNL*'s 41st, began with a cold open that paired Kate McKinnon as Hillary Clinton with the real Hillary Clinton, along with Darrell Hammond reprising his impersonation of Bill Clinton. As the sketch begins, a couple sits at a table talking enthusiastically about the Republican field. The man says, "Did you see Trump on *O'Reilly* this week?" The woman he's with replies, "I love that guy. He just says whatever he wants." Her date responds, "Yeah, my tops are Trump and then black doctor." The woman responds that she likes Carly Fiorina and discusses the idea that she would make a great first female president.

The scene pans to the bar, where McKinnon sits with Cecily Strong, who is playing Clinton's closest advisor, Huma Abedin. Clinton fumes to Abedin about why the people won't just let her lead. Huma leaves and

Clinton vents to the bartender, Val, who is played by the real Hillary Clinton, who tells Clinton she's a regular person who thinks the Keystone pipeline is a terrible idea. The sketch is full of inside jokes that play on the many perceived weaknesses of Clinton's campaign—such as her slowness to opposing Keystone, to supporting gay marriage. The discussion then circles around to Trump. McKinnon laments that all anyone wants to do is talk about Donald Trump. Clinton says, sarcastically? "Donald Trump? Isn't he the one that's like, 'Uuuh, you're all losers?'" She delivered the last part of the line in the manner of Trump. Clinton then asks McKinnon if she thinks Trump will win the primaries. She responds, "He must. I want to be the one to take him down. I will destroy him and I will mount his hair in the Oval Office!" Clinton, sensing McKinnon's Clinton's stress, suggests she should take a vacation, and Darrell Hammond appears as Bill Clinton, saying, "Somebody say 'vacation'?"[27] The sketch is lighthearted. It doesn't take Trump seriously, but it doesn't urge people not to vote for him. It doesn't suggest he's a danger. To those who see *SNL* as liberally biased, they seem to be hoping for a Trump victory in the primary because he'd be such an easy target in the general election. It is a sketch that assumes much about Clinton and is dismissive, but playfully so, of Trump.

In a parody of a Democratic candidates debate on October 17, Alec Baldwin appeared, not as Donald Trump, but as Jim Webb, a former senator from Virginia and part of a field that included Webb, Lincoln Chaffee, Martin O'Malley, Bernie Sanders, and Clinton. In this sketch, it is again assumed that not only will Clinton win the nomination, she will win the presidency. The sketch ends with Larry David as Bernie Sanders announcing, "I'm Bernie Sanders and come next November, I will be Hillary Clinton's vice president!"[28]

The next episode, broadcast on November 7, a year and a day before Election Day, was hosted by Donald Trump himself. The episode begins with a Democratic Forum. It is dismissive of Martin O'Malley, has Hillary Clinton smugly announcing that she crushed the Benghazi hearings, saying they "couldn't break me and they never will." Last up is Larry David who, in a game that involves picking an envelope to reveal a question for him to answer, picks the envelope on the left, "So far left it can never be elected."[29]

During the opening monologue, Trump reminds the audience that many greats have hosted *SNL*, including himself in 2004. He slams Rosie O'Donnell and then banters with two actors who played him on the show, Taran Killam and Darrell Hammond, saying, "They don't have my talent, my money, or especially my good looks." At the end of the monologue, Larry David, standing in the wings, yells, "Trump's a racist!" When Trump confronts him, David shrugs and says, "I heard if I yelled that they'd give me $5,000."[30] And with that, a major issue of contention—protests by Latino groups against Trump hosting because of his derisive comments—was defused, not to be addressed again during the show.

The main sketch which refers to Trump's campaign for the presidency in this episode is called "White House 2018." In it, Trump sits in the Oval Office with Melania and a group of advisors, reflecting on their first two, triumphant, years in office. He is told by an unnamed aide that prosperity is at an all-time high, the United States is killing China on trade. The aide says the American people are tired of winning and he just doesn't know how Trump does it. Trump responds, "I don't really have to get into specifics. With me, it just magically happens." He's told by a general that the situation in Syria is under control and ISIS has been eliminated. His secretary of state, Omarosa, tells him that the situation with Russia has never been better. She says that Putin has withdrawn from the Ukraine and, "Believe me, he doesn't want to be called a loser again." His secretary of the Interior, daughter Ivanka, played by the real Ivanka, tells him that the White House renovation is nearly done and they are going ahead with plans to cover the Washington Monument in gold mirrored glass. He is visited by Mexican President Enrique Peña Nieto, who presents him with a check for $10 billion to pay for the wall and promises to make sure Univision only broadcasts in English from now on. Trump then speaks directly to the camera and says, "If you think that's how it's going to be, you're wrong. Even better."[31] The sketch is uncritical of any of these Trump campaign issues and while it may seem absurd to imagine him succeeding in getting them done, there is no real question raised about the possibility in this sketch.

In this episode, *SNL* fell victim to the same impact so many in the media fell victim to during the campaign, especially in its early phases: Trump was ratings gold. And the fact that he was ratings gold led him to appearance after appearance, which gave his campaign the momentum it needed to keep going. Speculation about why Trump ran for president entertains many theories, including nothing beyond a desire to promote his own businesses and to advertise the Trump brand. Whatever actually motivated him, however, the Trump brand was certainly promoted by *SNL* and others, especially early in the campaign.

The tone of *SNL*'s treatment of Trump changed a bit in the 2015–16 season, as it became more and more apparent he was going to receive the

Republican nomination. In a cold open from January 23, 2016, Darrell Hammond appears as Trump at a rally with Tina Fey's Sarah Palin. Palin is endorsing Trump and after every few lines of her speech, Trump speaks directly to the camera, saying things such as, "I hope nobody's allergic to nuts, 'cause we got a big one here. She's two Corinthians short of a Bible. And is it just me or does everything she's saying sound kind of dirty?"[32] The sketch is full of these cut-ins by Trump and it appears that the show's writers are using his comments about Palin to say what they think of Trump. The problem, however, is that the point is lost to most, who are only thinking about Fey's Palin and the election from eight years before. If they are trying to subtly pan Trump, they are too subtle by half.

The references to his personality, his positions, and the ugly incidents at Trump rallies became more pointed, but still, *SNL* never seemed to acknowledge he had a chance of winning the presidency, and that prevented the parody from becoming genuine biting satire. At the same time, the jokes about Clinton's stiffness continued, along with jokes about her stilted attempts to appear relatable. There were many positive references to Bernie Sanders and a clear notion that the show was partial to him but that, in the end, they were going to end up with Clinton and that would be okay. One sketch, in an episode aired on February 13, 2016, involved a discussion at a table in a restaurant. A ghost-like Clinton appears and hears the discussion at the table. She sings the Bonnie Rait song, "I Can't Make You Love Me," and someone says, "Did everybody just get cold?" The response is, "I felt cold but safe."[33] And that was the general take on Clinton: she was cold, but safe, and she would absolutely wipe the floor with Trump.

In the final episode of original material of the season, broadcast on April 6, 2016, the show began with a cold open that involves Darrell Hammond as Trump, appearing in video clips during a CNN segment between anchor Kate Bouldan and Trump supporter Scottie Nell Hughes, who is portrayed by Cecily Strong.[34] The crux of the sketch is for Hughes to do what she did in real life: dismiss every crackpot statement made by Trump, incident of violence at his rallies, and to, in general, promote the Trump campaign. The sketch shows Hammond parodying various outrageous events from the real Trump campaign. It could have been damaging, but it is really Hughes who is made to look ridiculous and, in the final words of the sketch, any damage that might have been done to Trump is greatly mitigated by this exchange: Hughes says, "I know you can agree on three things: (1) He is drop dead gorgeous." Bouldan disagrees. "(2) He is bringing trade back so we can make American grapes again." Bouldan is dismissive.

"and (3) He is way better than Ted Cruz." To which Bouldan agrees, "Okay, yes, that I do agree on." And then they shout together, "And Live from New York, it's *Saturday Night!*"[35] It is hard to take this as any kind of serious anti–Trump commentary because it is not. They truly do seem to think that Trump, whom they've portrayed as a buffoon, not as a real threat, is preferable as the Republican nominee to an ideologue like Cruz.

When the show returned to the airwaves on October 1, 2016, much of the political landscape had changed. Not only had Trump won the nomination of the Republican Party, but he was doing quite well in the polls and it no longer seemed crazy that he might win the presidency. The tone at *SNL* was suddenly quite different and it has remained that way since the season premiere. The first, and most noteworthy, change was the replacement of Darrell Hammond by Alec Baldwin as the show's Trump, with a much more biting portrayal that focused on Trump's hair, his appearance, and his facial and hand gestures, to the point that they seem grotesque.

The season's first cold open includes a parody of the first debate between Clinton and Trump. Clinton is treated to the same jokes she was given throughout the campaign—she's stiff, she's too scripted, she works too hard to land one-liners. Baldwin's Trump is rude, shouting "Wrong!" into the microphone frequently. When he's given the opportunity to keep talking by Clinton, he delivers lines such as, "The thing about the Blacks is that they're killing each other." These lines are greeted by wide-eyed stares and joyous looks by Clinton. At one point, the moderator, Lester Holt, played by Michael Che, asks her why she's crying, and she says, "This is going so well!" At other times, when asked to respond to a statement by Trump, she says things such as, "Can America vote right now?" and "I think I'm gonna be president."[36] Trump no longer looks just like a buffoon, he looks like a malevolent idiot. Whether it resonated with anyone intending to vote for a candidate other than Clinton, however, is doubtful.

The portrayals of both Trump and those who supported him continued in this vein. The following week, the cold open dealt with both the vice-presidential debate and the newly breaking story of Trump from 2005 on an *Access Hollywood* bus with Billy Bush. The debate begins only to be interrupted by a breaking-news alert on CNN. Trump appears to explain the incident to Kate Bouldan and offers a strangely worded apology, mispronouncing "apologize" as "appleigize." He then jokes about how funny it is that the only Bush relevant in this election is Billy Bush. When Bouldan confronts him with statements from Republicans condemning this behavior, Trump trashes them. Of McCain, he says, "Coward." Of Carly

Fiorina, he says, "A four." Of Congressman Mike Crepo, he says, "More like Crap-o." He says, "I'll always have Mike Pence. I love Mike Pence." But when McKinnon informs him that Pence has also criticized him, Baldwin says, "He's a loser. I call him 'Puny Pence.'" He closes with this line to women: "If you give me a chance, I promise I can do a whole lot more than just grab it."[37] In this same episode, Kate McKinnon appeared as Trump advisor Kellyanne Conway. The show's treatment of Conway has changed a great deal over the past few months. In a musical montage in this episode, she was portrayed mostly as a long-suffering aide, being forced, even on her day off, to come on the air repeatedly to explain away Trump's behavior. At one point, in exasperation, she says, "He's the worst person I've ever known. What do you want me to say?" The host interviewing her says, in exasperation, "That!"[38]

The next week, October 15, the show once again opens with a debate sketch. The hosts of the debate introduce the candidates and ask, "Can we say this yet? President Hillary Clinton." In it, Baldwin moves around menacingly behind Kate McKinnon, says women accusing him of sexual assault need to "shut the hell up," and says Hillary Clinton has committed so many crimes that "she's basically black." At the end of the sketch, when she is asked for something nice to say about her opponent, McKinnon says that what she likes about him most is how generous he is because, last Friday, in reference to the *Access Hollywood* tape, "He gave me this election."[39] This episode also features a parody of the Beyoncé music video, "Lemonade," called "Melanianade." In it, several women in Trump's life announce they are finished with him: his wife, Melania, Omarosa, his daughters Ivanka and Tiffany, and Kellyanne Conway.

On October 22nd, *SNL* broadcast a parody of the final debate. It ends with the argument that Trump is going to lose the election. He shouts, "Wrong!" when McKinnon talks about Mexico; "Liar!" when she mentions Russia; and "Not true!" when she critiques his plan to deal with ISIS. Tom Hanks, as the debate's host Chris Wallace, says, "It has become clear you're probably going to lose," to which Baldwin replies, "Correct!" Watched with the retrospect of knowing how the election turned out, one can't help but feel this was the crew at *SNL* trying to say how they hoped things would turn out. But, in a very real sense, they were as tone deaf to the electorate as many pollsters and journalists. One of the things said by Baldwin in his concluding statement was that he was "winning in every poll taken outside a Cracker Barrel."[40] This joke was demeaning and dismissive of Trump supporters and almost certainly no help if there was an underlying intention of persuading people not to vote for him.

The next episode did not air until November 5th, just three days before Election Day. The show's cold open was an interview on CNN, with Hillary appearing from Florida and Trump from Colorado. They trade insults and then Alec Baldwin broaches the recent revelation by FBI director James Comey that they were once again looking into Clinton's e-mail scandal. Baldwin says that he never uses e-mail, he uses a very secure thing no one can see called Twitter. He's told everyone can see Twitter. "Really? And I'm winning? America, you must *really* hate her!" They have him, at various points throughout the sketch, kiss an FBI agent, kiss a member of the KKK, and kiss Vladimir Putin, all while Kate McKinnon, as Clinton, watches with growing indignation. But then, Baldwin breaks the fourth wall, speaks to McKinnon as McKinnon, and they run out of the studio to lead an everybody-should-love-each-other kind of rally in Times Square. They run back into the studio and say, "Now it's time to vote," and that this will all have been a waste if people don't do so. McKinnon says, "We can't tell you who to vote for, but on Tuesday we all get to choose what kind of country we live in." It seems they are imploring people to vote for Clinton. Certainly nothing they've done before then would indicate anything else. But it has an air of panic and desperation to it.

If there was any doubt about the seeming tone of the November 5th episode, the November 12th episode begins with a funereal tone, with Kate McKinnon, dressed as Clinton in a white pantsuit, sitting at a piano on a darkened stage, singing the Leonard Cohen song "Hallelujah." The host for the episode, Dave Chapelle, then delivered a biting monologue with jokes about what is funny, and what is not, about the state of the country in the wake of the election. The show also features a sketch about a group of Clinton supporters at an election returns party, growing more despondent as the night wears on.

After the election, the show has grown increasingly critical in its treatment of Trump, both during the transition period and after Trump took office. In a parody of Trump's pre-inaugural press conference, broadcast on January 14, Baldwin begins with the line, "Yes, this is real life, this is really happening." During the press conference, a hapless Trump says he's going to replace Obamacare with the Affordable Care Act. When a reporter says that if Trump just scraps Obamacare without a new plan, 20 million people could die, Trump responds, "Listen, sweetheart, I'm about to be president. We're all going to die."[41]

One theme that became increasingly prominent after the election was the use of Beck Bennett as a shirtless Vladimir Putin, a man with ever-growing influence over a Trump, played by Baldwin, who is both sinister and hapless. He appeared almost weekly, suggesting Russia did, in fact, hack the election and that he had an inordinate level of control over Trump. During the press conference sketch, he threatens Trump with a video cassette labeled "Pee Pee Tape," in reference to a story that alleged Trump engaged in several unusual sexual acts with prostitutes on a trip to Russia. In the following week's episode, the day after the inauguration and the day of the international women's march, Bennett handles the cold open as Putin, telling Trump, "Donald, let's talk as friends—you're not off to that great a start." At the end, he offers these calming words: "Listen America, it's going to be fine. Remember, we're in this together."[42]

Another consistent theme following the election was a focus on Kellyanne Conway as Trump's advisor and spokesperson. But as the season wore on, and as the real Conway made increasingly outrageous statements in defense of Trump, two things happened. First, news outlets stopped inviting her to appear on their shows. Second, Kate McKinnon's portrayal of her on *SNL* became more and more deprecating. The most outrageous of these was a filmed parody of the movie *Fatal Attraction*, in which Kate McKinnon plays Kellyanne Conway as a dangerous woman scorned, trying to kill CNN's Jake Tapper for ignoring her. The cold open of the March 4th episode was a parody of *Forrest Gump*, with Kate McKinnon as Attorney General Jeff Sessions playing the Forrest Gump role. McKinnon shows the person sitting next to him on a bus bench a photo of Kellyanne Conway. This was a widely circulated photo of Conway sitting with her legs folded under her on a couch in the Oval Office, apparently ignoring the leaders of the nation's historically Black colleges and universities. McKinnon says, "She ain't got no legs.... She could sell stink to a skunk, but they don't let her talk anymore."[43]

Another theme in the post-election milieu on *SNL* was the role of Trump's advisor, the former head of Breitbart Media, Steve Bannon. In one episode, broadcast on February 4th, he was introduced as the Grim Reaper and then continued to appear in that form. In the first Grim Reaper appearance, at the end of the sketch, he tells Trump he wants his desk back. He moves to the big desk in the Oval Office and Trump moves over to a little desk beside it. In that same episode, they also introduced an impersonation of Trump's press secretary, Sean Spicer, by Melissa McCarthy, telling the press that she had come there to punch them and that she expected an "apology on behalf of *you* to *me*. Not accepted!"[44]

Nearly every major decision, whether concerning policy, an appointment to office, a late-night Tweet, or a Trump confidant became fodder for *SNL* in the second half of its forty-second season. Evidently, Trump continues to be good for ratings. What is striking from the perspective of the election of 1976 and the inauguration of a new, outsider president in 1977, Jimmy Carter, is the similarity of *SNL*'s treatment of Carter and Trump. It is important not to take the comparison too far, but the following is definitely true: In 1976, during the campaign, *SNL* treated Carter with deference in comparison to how they treated Ford. They made fun of him, but it was always positive in a way. They made fun of him as a know-it-all. They made fun of him for his *Playboy* interview, but it was humor that was likely to make *SNL*'s audience like Carter more, not less. But then, after the election, they turned on him almost immediately. *SNL* turned on Trump faster than they turned on Carter, but they had also begun by treating Trump positively. They allowed him to host the show, as they had once offered to both Ford and Carter in 1976. They made fun of him, but it was never suggested, in the forty-first season, that he was dangerous to America. But after a summer of Trump's campaign behavior and, especially after his presidency became a reality, *SNL* became a leading critical voice, much as they were an early critical pop-culture voice where Carter was concerned.

The 1976 campaign was the first presidential battle using television as a weapon. If four hundred years earlier William Shakespeare was right that "all the world's a stage," then an audience engages even more when that world stage is in the living room ... and "Live from New York, it's *Saturday Night!*" And the humor on *SNL* has often been sharply critical over the decades. The show's solid base of improvisational sketch comedy as trickster to all matters of tradition, convention, and/or mainstream thought, has remained steadfast despite numerous changes in writers, cast, and network producers.

Chapter Notes

Preface

1. Burke, as cited in Amber Day and Ethan Thompson, "Live from New York. It's the Fake News! Saturday Night Live and the (Non)Politics of Parody," *Popular Communication* 10, nos. 1–2 (2012): 170–182.
2. The program began airing as *NBC's Saturday Night*. Toward the summer of 1976, it became *Saturday Night*. It wasn't known as *Saturday Night Live* until a couple of years into its existence. This was due to a prime-time variety show hosted by Howard Cosell on ABC that was called *Saturday Night Live with Howard Cosell*. For a discussion of this, see Doug Hill and Jeff Weingrad, *Saturday Night* (New York: Vintage, 1986), 74–75.
3. Amber Day and Ethan Thompson, "Live from New York. It's the Fake News! Saturday Night Live and the (Non)Politics of Parody," *Popular Communication* 10, nos. 1–2 (2012).
4. Lorne Michaels interview with the author, October 2010.
5. *Ibid.*

Chapter 1

1. Lorne Michaels interview with the author, October 2010.
2. *Ibid.*
3. Lorne Michaels interview with the author, October 2010.
4. Lorne Michaels interview with the author, October 2010.
5. Doris Graber, "Conclusion: Why Humor is Serious Business," in *Laughing Matters: Humor and American Politics in the Media Age*, ed. Jody Baumgartner and Jonathan Morris (New York: Routledge, 2007), 337.
6. Gerald R. Ford, *Humor and the Presidency* (New York: Arbor House, 1987), 15.

7. Lorne Michaels interview with the author, October 2010.
8. *Ibid.*
9. Howard Kurtz, "The SNL Effect," *Washington Post*, March 14, 2008.
10. Ron Nessen interview with the author, March 2009.
11. Bob Orben interview with the author, July 2009.
12. Fred Ferretti, "TV News Chiefs Find Gloomy Economic Picture of Their Industry All Too Clear as They Cut Back," *New York Times*, February 1, 1971, 62.
13. Philip Auslander, *Liveness: Performance in a Mediatized Culture* (London: Routledge, 2008), 61.
14. Graber, 338
15. *Ibid.*

Chapter 2

1. Ford, *Humor and the Presidency*, 15–16.
2. Geoffrey Baym, "Serious Comedy: The Expanding Boundaries of Political Discourse," in *Laughing Matters: Humor and Politics in the Media Age*, ed. Jody Baumgartner and Jonathan Morris (New York: Routledge, 2007), 27.
3. Gerald R. Ford, *A Time to Heal* (New York: Harper and Row, 1979), 41.
4. Robert Hartmann, *Palace Politics* (New York: McGraw-Hill), 159–60.
5. Bob Orben interview with the author, July 2009.
6. John Robert Greene, *The Presidency of Gerald R. Ford* (Lawrence: University of Kansas Press, 1995), 31–32.
7. Barry Werth, *31 Days: The Crisis That Gave Us the Government We Have Today* (New York: Doubleday, 2006), 17–18.
8. "The Pardon That Brought No Peace," *Time*, September 16, 1974, 11.

9. Werth, 328.

10. Jerald terHorst, *Gerald Ford and the Future of the Presidency* (New York: The Third Press, 1974), 237.

11. Ford, 198

12. Ford, *A Time to Heal*, 199.

13. Philip Shabefoff, "Aides Say Ford Ignores Skepticism about Ability: Staff Members Bitter as They Assail View That the President Is Ineffectual," *New York Times*, December 29, 1975, 53.

14. *Ibid.*

15. *Ibid.*

16. *Ibid.*

17. *Ibid.*

18. See William T Horner, *Ohio's Kingmaker* (Athens: Ohio University Press, 2010).

19. Nicholas Van Hoffman, "On the Abortion Amendment," *The Washington Post*, September 20, 1976, B1. The pet rock was a fad, marketed by a Californian named Gary Dahl in the mid–1970s. It consisted of a small rock in a box, complete with air holes, resting on a bed of shredded newspaper. It sold in the millions at two dollars a rock and giving one as a gag gift represented the ultimate in non-substance.

20. "Weekend Update," *NBC's Saturday Night*, September 25, 1976, transcript at http://snltranscripts.jt.org/76/76bupdate.phtml.

21. Gerald Ford, "Inauguration Remarks, December 6, 1973," 1973, Box 127, Gerald R. Ford Vice Presidential Papers.

22. Richard Reeves, *A Ford, Not a Lincoln* (New York: Harcourt Brace Jovanovich, 1999), 107.

23. Reeves interview with the author, April 1, 2010.

24. Orben interview with the author, March, 2010.

25. Robert Sigel, "Writer Changed His Tune on Ford's Place in History," *National Public Radio*, December 2006. www.npr.org/templates/story/story.php?storyId=6687043.

26. Richard Reeves, "I'm Sorry, Mr. President," *American Heritage*, Vol. 47, December 1996, #8, http://www.americanheritage.com/articles/magazine/ah/1996/8/1996_8_52.shtml.

27. Ford, *A Time to Heal*, 368–9.

28. Reeves interview with the author, April 1, 2010.

29. *Ibid.*

30. Reeves, *A Ford, Not a Lincoln*, 102.

31. "The Ridicule Problem," *Time*, January 5, 1975, http://www.time.com/time/magazine/article/0,9171,947602–2,00.html.

32. "Chevy Chase," *Playboy*, June 1988.

33. Rena Fruchter, *I'm Chevy Chase and You're Not* (London: Virgin Books, 2007), 157.

34. Ford, *Humor and the Presidency*, 48.

35. "The Ridicule Problem," *Time*, January 5, 1975, http://www.time.com/time/magazine/article/0,9171,947602-2,00.html.

36. *Ibid.*

37. *Ibid.*

38. Ron Nessen, *It Sure Looks Different from the Inside* (Chicago: Playboy Press, 1978), 164–165.

39. *Ibid.*, 165.

40. Nessen interview with the author, March 19, 2009.

Chapter 3

1. Dan Aykroyd interview with the author, April 2010.

2. John Blumenthal and Lindsay Maracottam, "Playboy Interview: NBC's 'Saturday Night,'" *Playboy*, 1977, 63.

3. "Weekend Update"

4. Blumenthal and Maracotta, 65.

5. *Ibid.*

6. Timothy White, "Saturday Night Quarterback," *Rolling Stone*, December 27, 1979, 33.

7. *Ibid.*, 43.

8. Blumenthal and Maracotta, 88.

9. *Ibid.*

10. Blumenthal and Maracotta, 223.

11. White, 34.

12. *Ibid.*

13. White, 43.

14. Tom Shales, "The Crew of 'Saturday Night': Alive and Crazy in the Capital," *Washington Post*, April 17, 1976, B1.

15. Blumenthal and Maracotta, 63.

16. White, 34.

17. Tom Shales, 1975, "Zingers on 'Saturday Night,'" *Washington Post*, November 8, 1975, A19.

18. Jeff Hill and Doug Weingrad, *Saturday Night: A Backstage History of Saturday Night Live* (New York: Vintage Books, 1987), 184.

19. "Weekend Update," *Saturday Night Live*, January 17, 1976, transcript at http://snltranscripts.jt.org/75/75jupdate.phtml.

20. "Weekend Update," *Saturday Night Live*, February 21, 1976, transcript at http://snltranscripts.jt.org/75/75nupdate.phtml.

21. "Weekend Update," *Saturday Night Live*, April 17, 1976, transcript at http://snltranscripts.jt.org/75/75qupdate.phtml.

22. Matthew Fotis, *Long Form Improvisation and American Comedy* (New York: Palgrave MacMillan, 2014).

23. "Trials: Double Indemnity," *Time*, December 29, 1975. http://www.time.com/time/magazine/article/0,9171,945442,00.html.
24. *Ibid.*
25. Ford, p. 311.
26. Richard B Cheney, in *Ford Presidency: Twenty-Two Intimate Perspectives of Gerald R. Ford*, ed. Kenneth W. Thompson (New York: University Press of America, 1988), 77.
27. In September, 1975, Ford made trips to Sacramento and San Francisco, California. During the visit in Sacramento, Lynette "Squeaky" Fromme, a follower of Charles Manson, pointed a gun at Ford from a distance of less than two feet. She was disarmed without firing a shot. A couple of weeks later, another woman, Sara Jane Moore fired a shot at Ford from the opposite side of the street.
28. "Weekend Update," *Saturday Night Live*, October 18, 1975, transcript at http://snltranscripts.jt.org/75/75bupdate.phtml.
29. "Weekend Update," *Saturday Night Live*, November 15, 1975, transcript at http://snltranscripts.jt.org/75/75eupdate.phtml.
30. "Weekend Update." *NBC's Saturday Night*, November 22, 1975, transcript at http://snltranscripts.jt.org/75/75fupdate.phtml.

Chapter 4

1. Nick Marx, Matt Sienkiwicz and Ron Becker, *Saturday Night Live and American TV* (Bloomington: Indiana University Press, 2013), p. 3.
2. Jeffrey P. Jones, *Saturday Night and American TV*, p. 79.
3. Ford, *A Time to Heal*, 287.
4. Robert Hartmann, *Palace Politics* (New York: McGraw-Hill, 1980), 411.
5. Nessen, 167
6. Ford, *A Time to Heal*, 289.
7. Reeves, 25. According to Richard Reeves, what Johnson actually said was that Ford was so dumb he couldn't fart and chew gum at the same time.
8. Cheney, 76.
9. Ford and other House Republicans became highly critical of Johnson's handling of the Vietnam War, challenging whether he was doing enough to win. Following the midterm election of 1966, when the Republicans picked up 47 seats, Ford, as Minority Leader, was able to be an obstacle to much of Johnson's Great Society legislation. See Roger H. Davidson, Susan Webb Hammond and Raymond Smock, *Masters of the House: Congressional Leadership Over Two Centuries* (Boulder, CO: Westview Press, 1988), 267–75.

10. Bob Orben interview with the author, July 2009.
11. *Ibid.*
12. Ford, *Humor and the Presidency*, 160.
13. Ford, *Humor and the Presidency*, 16.
14. Ford, *Humor and the Presidency*, 48–49.
15. John T. Woolley and Gerhard Peters, *The American Presidency Project* (online). Santa Barbara, CA. Available from World Wide Web: http://www.presidency.ucsb.edu/ws/?pid=5343.
16. Hartmann, 279.
17. "Ford, in Slip of Tongue, Hails Sadat as Israeli," *New York Times*, October 30, 1975, 16.
18. "Weekend Update," *Saturday Night Live*, November 8, 1975, transcribed by the author.
19. This story is chronicled in most biographies of Ford and can be found online in various sites dedicated to the history of the Ford administration, such as this entry on the Miller Center website: http://millercenter.org/president/ford/essays/vicepresident/1830.
20. Gerald Ford, "Transcript of President's Talk on City Crisis, Questions Asked and His Responses," *New York Times*, October 30, 1975, 46.
21. "Weekend Update," *Saturday Night Live*, November 8, 1975, transcribed by the author.
22. *Ibid.*
23. Roper Report 75-8, Aug, 1975. Retrieved May 28, 2011, from the iPOLL Databank, The Roper Center for Public Opinion Research, University of Connecticut.
24. Roper Report 75-9, Sep, 1975. Retrieved May 28, 2011, from the iPOLL Databank, The Roper Center for Public Opinion Research, University of Connecticut.
25. Roper Report 75-10, Oct, 1975. Retrieved May 28, 2011, from the iPOLL Databank, The Roper Center for Public Opinion Research, University of Connecticut.
26. Gallup Poll (AIPO), Oct, 1975. Retrieved May 28, 2011, from the iPOLL Databank, The Roper Center for Public Opinion Research, University of Connecticut.
27. Roper Report 75-10, Oct, 1975. Retrieved May 28, 2011, from the iPOLL Databank, The Roper Center for Public Opinion Research, University of Connecticut.
28. "New York: Some Cheers for an Underdog," *Time*, November 17, 1975, http://www.time.com/time/magazine/article/0,9171,917918,00.html.
29. *Ibid.*

30. "New York: Last-Minute Bailout of a City on the Brink," *Time*, December 8, 1975, http://www.time.com/time/magazine/article/0,9171,947546,00.html.

31. Thomas P Ronan, "G.O.P. in New York Limits Contests," *New York Times*, March 26, 1976, 17; "The New York Primary," *New York Times*, April 4, 1976, E14.

32. Ron Nessen interview with the author.

33. "Weekend Update," *NBC's Saturday Night*, January 24, 1976, transcript at http://snltranscripts.jt.org/75/75kupdate.phtml.

34. Tom Burke, "The First Season," in *Rolling Stone Visits Saturday Night Live*, ed. Marianne Partridge (New York: Dolphin Books, 1979), 28.

35. This was also an inside joke with the reference to Howard Cosell, who was the host of the ABC variety show which originally owned the name *Saturday Night Live* and prompted NBC to name its show *NBC's Saturday Night*.

36. "The President of the United States," *Saturday Night Live*, November 8, 1975, transcript at http://snltranscripts.jt.org/75/75dford.phtml.

37. "Weekend Update," *NBC's Saturday Night*, January 10, 1976, transcript at http://snltranscripts.jt.org/75/75iupdate.phtml.

38. "Weekend Update," *NBC's Saturday Night*, February 21, 1976, transcript at http://snltranscripts.jt.org/75/75nupdate.phtml.

39. Associated Press, "Freudian Ford Flub Fired," *Lakeland Ledger*, March 11, 1976, 7a.

40. "Weekend Update," *NBC's Saturday Night*, October 25, 1975, transcript at http://snltranscripts.jt.org/75/75cupdate.phtml.

41. "Weekend Update," *NBC's Saturday Night*, November 15, 1975, transcript at http://snltranscripts.jt.org/75/75eupdate.phtml.

42. "Weekend Update," *NBC's Saturday Night*, November 22, 1975, transcript at http://snltranscripts.jt.org/75/75fupdate.phtml.

43. "Ford Delegate," *Saturday Night Live*, July 31, 1976, transcribed by the author.

Chapter 5

1. Nessen, 167.

2. "Weekend Update," *NBC's Saturday Night*, February 14, 1976, transcript at http://snltranscripts.jt.org/75/75mupdate.phtml.

3. Jerry terHorst, "The last laugh on Ford will hurt," *Chicago Tribune*, December 19, 1975, A4.

4. Lou Cannon and David S. Broder, "Ford Hopes for Last Laugh," *Washington Post*, January 5, 1976, A1.

5. Nessen, 168.

6. Philip Shabefoff, "Aides Say Ford Ignores Skepticism About Ability...," 1975.

7. Ron Nessen interview with the author, March 2009.

8. David Gelman, "Nessen's Report Card," *Newsweek*, January 12, 1976.

9. "Weekend Update," *NBC's Saturday Night*, January 24, 1976, transcript at http://snltranscripts.jt.org/75/75kupdate.phtml.

10. Hill and Weingrad, 179–180.

11. Tom Shales, "Saturday Night, With Ron Nessen," *Washington Post*, February 25, 1976.

12. *Ibid.*

13. *Ibid.*

14. Bob Orben, interview with the author, July 2009.

15. Shales, "The Crew of 'Saturday Night'"

16. Nessen, 173–174.

17. Nessen interview with the author at the Brookings Institution, March 19, 2009.

18. Nessen, 173.

19. Bob Orben interview with the author, July 2009.

20. Jack Gould, "TV: The Razor's Edge," *New York Times*, February 1, 1964, 49.

21. Bob Orben interview with the author, July 2009.

22. Ford, *Humor and the Presidency*, 39.

23. Quoted in Ford, *Humor and the Presidency*, 40–1.

24. Written interview with the author, August 2009.

25. Hill and Weingrad, 180.

26. Tom Shales and James Andrew Miller, *Live From New York: An Uncensored History of Saturday Night Live* (New York: Little, Brown and Company, 2002), 75

27. Ron Nessen interview with the author, March 2009.

28. Ford, *Humor and the Presidency*, 33.

29. *Ibid.*

30. Richard Reeves, "The High Art and Low Estate of Political Humor," *Washington Post*, February 16, 1975, 10.

31. Ford, *Humor and the Presidency*, 33.

32. *Ibid.*

33. Reeves, "The High Art and Low Estate of Political Humor," 18.

34. *Ibid.*

35. Gerald Ford, "Address at the Yale University Law School Sesquicentennial Convocation Dinner," April 25, 1975. http://www.presidency.ucsb.edu/ws/index.php?pid=4869#axzz1S4w6VCVo.

36. Bob Orben interview with the author, July 2009.

37. *Ibid.*

38. Shales, "Saturday Night, With Ron Nessen."

39. *Ibid.*

40. Written interview with the author, August, 2009.

41. Bob Orben interview with the author, July 2009.

42. *Ibid.*

Chapter 6

1. *Ibid.*

2. Ron Nessen interview with the author, March 2009.

3. "...Nervous reaction," *Chicago Tribune,* April 22, 1976, B1.

4. Nessen, 174.

5. "Can't beat 'em, Ford joins 'em," *Chicago Tribune,* April 18, 1976, 12.

6. Nessen, 176.

7. Hill and Weingrad, 182–183.

8. *Ibid.*

9. Gary Weis interview with the author, February 2010.

10. Ron Nessen e-mail interview with the author, February 10, 2010.

11. Shales and Miller, *Live from New York,* 75–76.

12. Lorne Michaels interview with the author, October 2010.

13. "Opening Monologue," *NBC's Saturday Night,* April 17, 1976, transcribed by author.

14. Nessen interview with the author, March 2009.

15. Johanna Steinmetz, "A Funny Thing Happened to Nessen at NBC," *Chicago Tribune,* April 22, 1976, B1.

16. Hill and Weigand, 185.

17. Davis interview with the author, October 2009.

18. Interview with the author, 3-17-2009.

19. Shales, "Saturday Night, With Ron Nessen."

20. *Ibid.*

21. Shales, "The Crew of 'Saturday Night.'"

22. Burke, 26–7.

23. "...Nervous reaction." *Chicago Tribune,* April 22, 1976, B1.

24. Telegram from Arthur Kent to Nessen, April 15, 1976. Ron Nessen Papers, Gerald Ford Presidential Library.

25. Letter from Nessen to Arthur Kent, April 19, 1976. Ron Nessen Papers, Gerald Ford Presidential Library.

26. Johnna Steinmetz, "A funny thing happened to Nessen at NBC," *Chicago Tribune,* April 22, 1976, B1.

27. Nessen, 177.

28. Hill and Weigand, 184.

29. Blumenthal and Maracotta, 69.

30. Hill and Weingrad, 185.

31. For an excellent account of the life and death of *The Smothers Brothers Comedy Hour,* see: David Bianculli, *Dangerously Funny: The Uncensored Story of "The Smothers Brothers Comedy Hour"* (New York: Simon and Schuster, 2009).

32. "Pryor Restraint," *Washington Post,* December 18, 1975, C14.

33. Johanna Steinmetz, "From New York! Smart Alecks!," *Chicago Tribune,* July 25, 1976, G12.

34. Tom Shales, "Chevy's Gone, But 'Saturday Night' Lives," *Washington Post,* November 17, 1976, C1.

35. *Ibid.*

36. *Ibid.*

37. Tom Shales, "Zingers on Saturday Night," *Washington Post,* November 8, 1975, A19.

38. Steinmetz, "From New York!" G29.

39. Hill and Weingrad, 180.

40. Shales, "The Crew of 'Saturday Night.'"

41. *Ibid.*

42. Bob Orben interview with the author, July 2010.

43. "Super Bass-o-Matic '76," *NBC's Saturday Night,* April 17, 1976, transcribed by the author.

44. Tom Davis interview with the author, October 2009.

45. *Ibid.*

46. Steinmetz, "From New York!" G28.

47. *Ibid.*

48. "Press Secretaries through History," *NBC's Saturday Night,* April 17, 1976, transcript at http://snltranscripts.jt.org/75/75qpress.phtml.

49. "The New Army," *NBC's Saturday Night,* April 14, 1976, transcript at http://snltranscripts.jt.org/75/75qnewarmy.phtml.

50. "Betty Ford Would Accept 'An Affair' by Daughter," *New York Times,* August 11, 1975, 1.

51. "Ford's Son, 23, Says He Smoked Marijuana," *New York Times,* October 5, 1975, 59.

52. "President Disapproved Marijuana, Praises Son," *New York Times,* October 10, 1975, 20.

53. "Weekend Update," *NBC's Saturday Night,* April 17, 1976, transcript at http://snltranscripts.jt.org/75/75qupdate.phtml.

54. *Ibid.*

55. Blumenthal and Maracotta, 214–15.

56. Ibid. 69–70.

57. "Tomorrow," *NBC's Saturday Night*, April 17, 1976, transcribed by the author.

58. "Press Secretaries through History," *Saturday Night Live*, April 17, 1976, transcribed by the author.

59. "Supreme Court Spot Check," *Saturday Night Live*, April 17, 1976, transcribed by the author.

60. Steinmentz, "From New York!" G28.

61. "Press Secretaries through History," *NBC's Saturday Night*, April 17, 1976, transcribed by the author.

62. "Ron and Chevy Yock it up," *Newsweek*, May 3, 1976, 17.

63. *Ibid.*

64. Tom Shales, "What the President Meant Was...," *Washington Post*, April 19, 1976.

65. "It wasn't funny, Mr. Nessen," *Chicago Tribune*, April 24, 1976.

66. Jerald terHorst, "Nessen's Saturday Nightmare," *Chicago Tribune*, April 23, 1976.

67. John J. O'Connor, "NBC 'Saturday Night' Meets Ford People," April 19, 1976.

68. *Ibid.*

69. "...Nervous reaction," *Chicago Tribune*, April 22, 1976, B1.

70. *Ibid.* Walter Mitty was a character in a James Thurber story, "The Secret Life of Walter Mitty," about an average guy with big fantasies.

71. "...Nervous reaction," *Chicago Tribune*, April 22, 1976, B1.

72. Gary Weis interview with the author, February 8, 2010.

73. Letter from Nessen to Gary Weis, May 6, 1976. Ron Nessen Files, Gerald Ford Presidential Library.

74. Ron Nessen interview with the author, February 9, 2010.

75. Ron Nessen interview with the author, March 2009.

76. "Ford Irked at TV Spook," *The Milwaukee Journal*, April 20, 1976, 3.

77. Associated Press, "Did Nessen TV skit irk Ford?," *Miami News*, April 21, 1976, 2A.

78. Nessen, 175.

79. *New York Times*, April 4, 1976; Associated Press, 1976. "'Saturday Night' Show Distasteful to Fords," *The Lewiston Daily Sun*, April 22, 1976, p. 4, associated press.

80. *Ibid.*

81. Nessen, 175.

82. Ford, *Humor and the Presidency*, 19.

83. Bob Orben interview with the author, July 2009.

84. *Ibid.*

85. *Ibid.*

86. Jay Sharbutt, "I'm Gerald Ford nd

You're Not," *Lakeland Ledger*, April 19, 1976, 7.

87. Nessen, 176.

88. For all of these quotes, see the transcript of the Daily Press Briefing, 4-19-76, Ron Nessen Files, Gerald R. Ford Presidential Library.

89. Judy Backrach, "Personalities," *Washington Post*, April 22, 1976, C3.

90. "Weekend Update," *NBC's Saturday Night*, April 24, 1976, transcribed by the author.

91. Hill and Weingrad, 184.

92. Blumenthal and Maracotta, 221.

93. Hill and Weigand, 184.

94. Fruchter, 43.

95. Tom Shales, "The Crew of 'Saturday Night'"

96. Blumenthal and Maracotta, 77–8.

97. Letter from Ron Nessen to Lorne Michaels, April 20, 1976. Ron Nessen Files, Gerald R. Ford Presidential Library.

98. Hill and Weingrad, 184.

99. Blumenthal and Maracotta, 69.

100. Bob Orben interview with the author, July 2009.

101. Ron Nessen interview with the author, March 2009.

102. Nessen, 177.

103. Blumenthal and Maracotta, 77.

104. O'Connor

105. *Ibid.*

106. *Ibid.*

107. Ron Nessen interview with the author, March 2009.

108. Lorne Michaels interview with the author, October 2010.

109. Burke, 36.

110. Tom Davis interview with the author, August 2009.

Chapter 7

1. This was a common Carter phrase during the campaign. He began speeches, including his acceptance speech at the Democratic Convention with it, and it was emblazoned on his campaign posters.

2. "Weekend Update," *NBC's Saturday Night*, May 15, 1976, transcript at http://snltranscripts.jt.org/75/75tupdate.phtml.

3. Jerry Rafshoon interview with the author, November 2009.

4. *Ibid.*

5. Pat Caddell interview with the author, July 2009.

6. Robert S. Lichter, Jody C. Baumgartner, and Jonathan S. Morris, *Politics is a Joke!*:

How TV Comedians Are Remaking Political Life (Boulder, CO: Westview Press, 2015), 45–6.

7. Caddell interview with the author, July 2009.

8. Jimmy Carter, *Why Not the Best?* (New York: Bantam Books, 1976), 63–4.

9. Aykroyd interview with the author, April 2010.

10. Tom Shales, "Chevy's Gone, But 'Saturday Night' Lives," *Washington Post*, November 17, 1976, C2.

11. Davis interview with the author, April 2010.

12. "Awards Sketch," *Saturday Night Live*, April 24, 1976, transcript at http://snltranscripts.jt.org/75/75rawards.phtml.

13. Aykroyd interview with the author, April 2010.

14. Davis interview with the author, September 2009.

15. Aykroyd interview with the author, April 2010.

16. Davis interview with the author, September 2009.

17. Aykroyd interview with the author, April 2010.

18. Marilyn Beck, "NBC 'Live' won't pull punches for Nessen," *Chicago Tribune*, April 15, 1976, B4.

19. "Weekend Update," *NBC's Saturday Night*, February 21, 1976, transcript at http://snltranscripts.jt.org/75/75oupdate.phtml.

20. Lichter, et al., *Politics is a Joke!*, 21.

21. Lee Lescaze, "TV's Bland Political Humor," *Washington Post*, October 17, 1976, A1.

22. Morris K Udall, *Too Funny To Be President* (Tucson: University of Arizona Press, 1988) 38–9.

23. "Carter's Campaign," *Saturday Night Live*, July 24, 1976, transcribed by the author.

24. Betty Glad, *Jimmy Carter: In Search of the Great White House* (New York: W.W. Norton & Company, 1980), 350.

25. *Ibid.*

26. Carter, *Why Not the Best?*, 4.

27. Jimmy Carter, "Acceptance Speech: Our Nation's Past and Future," 1976, http://www.4president.org/speeches/carter1976acceptance.htm.

28. Bob Dylan, "It's Alright, Ma (I'm Only Bleeding)," 1965, http://www.bobdylan.com/songs/its-alright-ma-im-only-bleeding.

29. "Carter's Campaign."

30. Written interview with the author, November 2009.

31. Interview with the author, August 2009.

32. Martin Schram, *Running for President:*

A Journal of the Carter Campaign (New York: Pocket Books, 1977), 135.

33. *Ibid.*

34. *Ibid.*

35. Christopher Lydon, "Carter Defends All-White Areas," *New York Times*, April 7, 1976, 85.

36. Christopher Lydon, "Carter Issues an Apology on 'Ethnic Purity' Phrase," *New York Times*, April 8, 1976, 15.

37. *Ibid.*

38. James M. Naughton, "Ford Says Nation Should Preserve 'Ethnic Heritage,'" *New York Times*, April 14, 1976, 81.

39. "Weekend Update," *Saturday Night Live*, April 17, 1976. Transcribed by the author.

40. "Awards Sketch," *Saturday Night Live*, April 24, 1976, transcript at http://snltranscripts.jt.org/75/75rawards.phtml.

41. Johanna Steinmetz, "From New York! Smart Alecks!," *Chicago Tribune*, July 25, 1976, G28.

42. Julian Bond interview with the author, January 2010.

Chapter 8

1. Doris Graber, "Conclusion: Why Political Humor is Serious Business," in *Laughing Matters: Humor and American Politics in the Media Age*, eds. Jody Baumgartner and Jonathan Morris (New York: Routledge, 2008).

2. An excellent scholarly examination of this argument is made in: James Druckman, "The Power of Television Images: The First Kennedy-Nixon Debate Revisited," *Journal of Politics*, Vol. 65, #2, 2003, 559–571.

3. Christopher Lydon, "Equal-Time Rule on Political News Reversed by F.C.C," *New York Times*, September 26, 1975, 77.

4. Campaign Strategy Plan, August 1976; folder "Presidential Campaign—Campaign Strategy Program (1)-(3)," Box 1, Dorothy E. Downton Files, Gerald R. Ford Library.

5. Schram, 326–7.

6. *Ibid.*

7. Schram, 326.

8. *Ibid.*

9. Schram, 331.

10. *Ibid.*

11. Bob Orben interview with the author, July 2009.

12. Sidney Kraus, *The Great Debates: Carter vs. Ford, 1976* (Bloomington: Indiana University Press, 1979), 474.

13. Reasoner's remarks and video of part of the audio loss can be heard and seen at

the following website: http://www.youtube.com/watch?v=DrP5ZM0otP8.

14. *Ibid.*

15. "Weekend Update," *NBC's Saturday Night*, September 25, 1976, transcript at http://snltranscripts.jt.org/76/76bupdate.phtml.

16. E-mail interview with Davis by the author, 11-16-09.

17. Alan L. Otten, "Politics & People: Speaking Ill," *Wall Street Journal*, February 5, 1976, 18.

18. From SNL Transcripts website: http://snltranscripts.jt.org/76/76adebate.phtml.

19. Lorne Michaels interview with the author, October 2010.

20. Tom Davis interview with the author, August 2009.

21. Blumenthal and Maracotta, 220.

22. Tom Davis interview with the author, October 2009.

23. "Cold Open," *NBC's Saturday Night*, September 25, 1976, transcript at http://snltranscripts.jt.org/76/76bgildafall.phtml.

24. Schram, 353.

25. Blumenthal and Maracotta, 222.

26. "Debate '76," *NBC's Saturday Night*, October 16, 1976, transcribed by the author.

27. Charles Mohr, "Carter, on Morals, Talks With Candor," *New York Times*, September 21, 1976, 1.

28. Gerald R. Ford, "The President's News Conference," October 20, 1976, http://www.presidency.ucsb.edu/ws/index.php?pid=6493#axzz1UoIuv5RM.

29. *Ibid.*

30. *Ibid.*

31. *Ibid.*

32. Charles Mohr, "Carter, in Texas, Says He's Sorry about His Criticism of Johnson," *New York Times*, September 25, 1976, 1.

33. Scheer, 64.

34. Lainie Kazan is an actor and singer who, in 1970, appeared nude in *Playboy* and owned a couple of *Playboy* nightclubs. Phyllis Newman is a Broadway and television actress. As the creator of several children's television shows and the famous puppet "Lambchop," Shari Lewis is the most deliberately shocking inclusion in Carter's list in this sketch.

35. "Paid Political Announcement," *NBC's Saturday Night*, September 25, 1976, transcript at http://snltranscripts.jt.org/76/76bcarter.phtml.

36. Blumenthal and Maracotta, 78.

37. *Ibid.*

38. "Weekend Update," *NBC's Saturday Night*, September 25, 1976, transcript at http://snltranscripts.jt.org/76/76bupdate.phtml.

39. "Debate '76," *NBC's Saturday Night*, October 16, 1976, transcribed by the author.

40. Schram, 337. The Eagleton reference was to the revelation, during the 1972 presidential campaign, that Democrat George McGovern's running mate, Missouri Senator Thomas Eagleton, had been given shock treatments as part of his treatment for depression. Eagleton was subsequently dropped from the ticket and replaced by Sargent Shriver.

41. Gallup Poll (AIPO), Oct, 1976. Retrieved Oct. 22, 2014, from the iPOLL Databank, The Roper Center for Public Opinion Research, University of Connecticut. http://www.ropercenter.uconn.edu.proxy.mul.missouri.edu/data_access/ipoll/ipoll.html

42. Time/Yankelovich, Skelly & White Poll, Sep, 1976. Retrieved Oct. 22, 2014, from the iPOLL Databank, The Roper Center for Public Opinion Research, University of Connecticut. http://www.ropercenter.uconn.edu.proxy.mul.missouri.edu/data_access/ipoll/ipoll.html

43. Harris Survey, Sep, 1976. Retrieved Oct. 22, 2014, from the iPOLL Databank, The Roper Center for Public Opinion Research, University of Connecticut. http://www.ropercenter.uconn.edu.proxy.mul.missouri.edu/data_access/ipoll/ipoll.html

44. Jules Witcover, *Marathon: The Pursuit of the Presidency, 1972–1976* (New York: The Viking Press, 1977), 590.

45. David E. Rosenbaum, "Criticism of Butz Continues to Grow," *New York Times*, October 4, 1976, 1.

46. CBS News/New York Times Poll, Sep, 1976. Retrieved Oct. 22, 2014, from the iPOLL Databank, The Roper Center for Public Opinion Research, University of Connecticut. http://www.ropercenter.uconn.edu.proxy.mul.missouri.edu/data_access/ipoll/ipoll.html

47. CBS News/New York Times Poll, Oct, 1976. Retrieved Oct. 22, 2014, from the iPOLL Databank, The Roper Center for Public Opinion Research, University of Connecticut. http://www.ropercenter.uconn.edu.proxy.mul.missouri.edu/data_access/ipoll/ipoll.html

48. James M. Naughton, "Carter Assails Ford on 'Serious Blunder,'" *New York Times*, October 8, 1976, 18.

Chapter 9

1. "Weekend Update," *NBC's Saturday Night*, July 24, 1976, transcribed by the author.

2. Campaign Strategy Plan, August 1976; folder "Presidential Campaign—Campaign Strategy Program (1)-(3)," Box 1, Dorothy E. Downton Files, Gerald R. Ford Library.

3. *Ibid.*

4. *Ibid.*

5. *Ibid.*

6. *Ibid.*

7. *Ibid.*

8. "Jeopardy 1999," *NBC's Saturday Night*, October 23, 1976, transcript at http://snl transcripts.jt.org/76/76ejeopardy.phtml.

9. "Weekend Update," *NBC's Saturday Night*, October 23, 1976, transcribed by the author.

10. Jim Squires, "Last of Great Debates leaves story unchanged," *Chicago Tribune*, October 24, 1976, 10; Morton Mintz, "Win or Lose, Debates Viewed as a Worthwhile Exercise," *Washington Post*, October 24, 1976, A14.

11. Schram, *Running for President*, 360.

12. *Ibid.*

13. Nessen interview with the author, March 2009.

14. Campaign Strategy Plan, August 1976; folder "Presidential Campaign—Campaign Strategy Program (1)-(3)," Box 1, Dorothy E. Downton Files, Gerald R. Ford Library.

15. *Ibid.*

16. "Not for First Ladies Only," *NBC's Saturday Night*, October 30, 1976, transcribed by the author.

17. *Ibid.*

18. Henry has a bandage on his forehead because he was injured when John Belushi, playing his Samurai character, "Futaba," hit Henry with his sword in the "Samurai Stockbroker" sketch. Throughout the rest of the show, cast members appeared with bandages on their foreheads.

19. "Debate '76," *NBC's Saturday Night*, October 30, 1976, transcribed by the author.

20. Weekend Update," *NBC's Saturday Night*, October 30, 1976, transcript at http://snltranscripts.jt.org/76/76fupdate.phtml.

21. Lorne Michaels interview with the author, October 2010.

22. Hill and Weigand, 183.

23. *Ibid.*

24. Weekend Update," *NBC's Saturday Night*, October 30, 1976, transcript at http://snltranscripts.jt.org/76/76fupdate.phtml.

25. Bob Orben interview with the author, July 2009.

26. Ron Nessen interview with the author, March 2009.

27. Election statistics are available in many places. These data come from The UCSB

Presidency Project, at http://www.presidency.ucsb.edu/showelection.php?year=1976.

28. Jeffrey M. Jones, "Gerald Ford Retrospective," *Gallup*, December 29, 2006. www.gallup.com/poll/23995/Gerald-Ford-Retrospective.aspx.

29. "Last of the Great Debates leaves story unchanged."

30. *Ibid.*

Chapter 10

1. Michelle Hilmes, "The Evolution of Saturday Night," in *Saturday Night Live and American TV*, eds. Nick Marx, Matt Sienkiewicz, and Ron Becker (Bloomington: Indiana University Press, 2013).

2. Henry Bial, *The Performance Studies Reader, Second Edition* (London: Routledge, 2007), 263.

3. Beck, "NBC 'Live' won't pull punches for Nessen."

4. *Ibid.*

5. Blumenthal and Maracotta, 77.

6. Aykroyd interview with the author, April 2010.

7. Lorne Michaels interview with the author, October 2010.

8. Garrett Morris interview with the author, January 2010.

9. Kenan Thompson interview with the author, December 2010.

10. Hill and Weigand, 183.

11. Tom Zito, "'Saturday Night' at Georgetown," *Washington Post*, September 10, 1976, B9.

12. "No 'Saturday Night' on Campus," *Washington Post*, September 23, 1976, D4.

13. Caddell interview with the author, July 2009.

14. Aykroyd interview with the author, April 2010.

15. Rafshoon interview with the author, November 2009.

16. A.D. Annis, "The Relative Effectiveness of Cartoons and Editorials as Propaganda Media," *Psychological Bulletin*, 1939, 36, 328; D. Brinkman, "Do Editorial Cartoons and Editorials Change Opinions?," *Journalism Quarterly*, 1968, 45, 724–726; C.R. Gruner, "Ad hominem Satire as Persuader: An Experiment," *Journalism Quarterly*, 1971, 41, 128–131.

17. Elizabeth Kolbert, "Stooping to Conquer," *The New Yorker*, April 19, 2004, 2. www.newyorker.com/archive.2004/04/19/040419fa_fact1?currentpage=1.

18. "Sources for Campaign News," *Pew Research Center for the People & the Press*,

February 5, 2000, http://www.people-press. org/2000/02/05/sources-for-campaign-news/.

19. Michael X. Delli Carpini and Bruce A. Williams, "Let us Infotain You: Politics in the New Media Environment," in W. Lance Bennett and Robert M. Entman, eds., *Mediated Politics: Communication in The Future of Democracy* (New York: Cambridge University Press, 2010), 163.

20. Michael X. Delli Carpini and Bruce A. Williams, "Heeeeeeeeeeeere's Democracy!," *Chronicle of Higher Education*, April 19, 2002, 48:32, B14–15.

21. *Ibid.*

22. Matthew A. Baum, "Sex, Lies, and War: How Soft News Brings foreign Policy to the Inattentive Public," *American Political Science Review*, 2002, 96:1, 91–108.

23. Kathleen Hall Jamieson and Paul Waldman, *The Press Effect* (Oxford University Press, 2003), 68.

24. Matthew A. Baum, "Talking the Vote: Why Presidential Candidates Hit the Talk Show Circuit," *American Journal of Political Science*, 2006, 49:2. 213–234, 231.

25. Dannagal Goldthwaite Young, "Late-Night Comedy in Election 2000: Its Influence on Candidate Trait Ratings and the Moderating Effects of Political Knowledge and Partisanship," *Journal of Broadcasting and Electronic Media*, 2004, 48: 1–22.

26. Patricia Moy, Michael A. Xenos, and Verena K. Hess, "Priming Effects of Late-Night Comedy," *International Journal of Public Opinion Research*, 2005, 18:2, 198–210.

27. Michael J. Pfau, Brian Houston, and Shane M. Semmler, "Presidential Election Campaigns and American Democracy: The Relationship Between Communication Use and Normative Outcomes," *American Behavioral Scientists*, Vol. 49, Sept. 2005: 48–62.

28. Paul R. Brewer and Xiaoxia Cao, "Candidate Appearances on Soft News Shows and Public Knowledge about Primary Campaigns," *Journal of Broadcasting and Electronic Media*, 2006, 50:1, 18–35, 31.

29. Jody Baumgartner and Jonathan S. Morris, "The Daily Show Effect: Candidate Evaluations, Efficacy, and American Youth," *American Politics Research*, May 2006, 34, 341–367.

30. *CBS Evening News*, September 25, 2008, transcript at http://www.cbsnews.com/ news/exclusive-palin-on-foreign-policy/.

31. "CBS Evening News," *Saturday Night Live*, September 27, 2014, transcript at http://snltranscripts.jt.org/08/08cpalin.phtml.

32. Sarah E. Esralew, *The Influence of Parodies on Political Schemas: Exploring the Tina Fey–Sarah Palin Phenomenon*, Master's Thesis, University of Delaware, 2009.

33. "Vice Presidential Debate," *Saturday Night Live*, October 4, 2008, transcript at http://snltranscripts.jt.org/08/08ddebate.phtml.

34. For example, see Amos Tversky and Daniel Kahneman, "Judgment Under Uncertainty: Heuristics and Biases," *Science*, 1974, 185: 4157, 1124–31.

35. Susan T. Fiske and Shelley E. Taylor, *Social Cognition (2nd ed.)* (New York: McGraw-Hill, 1991).

36. http://www.gallup.com/poll/116500/ presidential-approval-ratings-george-bush. aspx.

37. Jody C. Baumgartner, Jonathan S. Morris, and Natsha L. Walth, "The Fey Effect: Young Adults, Political Humor, and Perceptions of Sarah Palin in the 2008 Presidential Election Campaign," *Public Opinion Quarterly*, 2012, 102.

38. Baumgartner, et al., "The Fey Effect," 98–99.

39. *Ibid.*

40. Baumgartner, et al., "The Fey Effect," 100.

41. Megan Mullen, *The Rise of Cable Programming in the United States* (Austin: University of Texas Press, 2003), 7.

42. Harris Survey, Dec. 1975. Retrieved Nov. 4, 2004, from the iPOLL Databank, The Roper Center for Public Opinion Research, University of Connecticut. http://www.roper center.uconn.edu.proxy.mul.missouri.edu/ data_access/ipoll/ipoll.html.

43. Harris Survey, Jan. 1975. Retrieved Nov. 4, 2004, from the iPOLL Databank, The Roper Center for Public Opinion Research, University of Connecticut. http://www.roper center.uconn.edu.proxy.mul.missouri.edu/ data_access/ipoll/ipoll.html.

44. *Ibid.*

45. Time/Yankelovich, Skelly & White Poll, June 1976. Retrieved Nov. 4, 2004, from the iPOLL Databank, The Roper Center for Public Opinion Research, University of Connecticut. http://www.ropercenter.uconn.edu.proxy. mul.missouri.edu/data_access/ipoll/ipoll. html.

46. Harris Survey, Aug. 1976. Retrieved Nov. 4, 2004, from the iPOLL Databank, The Roper Center for Public Opinion Research, University of Connecticut. http://www.roper center.uconn.edu.proxy.mul.missouri.edu/ data_access/ipoll/ipoll.html.

47. Time/Yankelovich, Skelly & White Poll, Aug. 1976. Retrieved Nov. 4, 2004, from the iPOLL Databank, The Roper Center for Public Opinion Research, University of Con-

necticut. http://www.ropercenter.uconn.edu. proxy.mul.missouri.edu/data_access/ipoll/ ipoll.html.

48. Time/Yankelovich, Skelly & White Poll, Sep. 1976. Retrieved Nov. 4, 2004, from the iPOLL Databank, The Roper Center for Public Opinion Research, University of Connecticut. http://www.ropercenter.uconn.edu. proxy.mul.missouri.edu/data_access/ipoll/ ipoll.html.

49. Time/Yankelovich, Skelly & White Poll, Oct. 1976. Retrieved Nov. 4, 2004, from the iPOLL Databank, The Roper Center for Public Opinion Research, University of Connecticut. http://www.ropercenter.uconn.edu. proxy.mul.missouri.edu/data_access/ipoll/ ipoll.html.

50. See the reporting of Tom Shales, etcetera, cited throughout this book.

51. Harris Survey, Aug. 1976. Retrieved Oct. 27, 2014, from the iPOLL Databank, The Roper Center for Public Opinion Research, University of Connecticut. http://www.roper center.uconn.edu.proxy.mul.missouri.edu/ data_access/ipoll/ipoll.html.

52. Time/Yankelovich, Skelly & White Poll, Aug. 1976. Retrieved Oct, 27, 2014, from the iPOLL Databank, The Roper Center for Public Opinion Research, University of Connecticut. http://www.ropercenter.uconn.edu. proxy.mul.missouri.edu/data_access/ipoll/ ipoll.html.

53. Time/Yankelovich, Skelly & White Poll, Sep. 1976. Retrieved Oct. 27, 2014, from the iPOLL Databank, The Roper Center for Public Opinion Research, University of Connecticut. http://www.ropercenter.uconn.edu. proxy.mul.missouri.edu/data_access/ipoll/ ipoll.html.

54. Time/Yankelovich, Skelly & White Poll, Oct. 1976. Retrieved Oct. 27, 2014, from the iPOLL Databank, The Roper Center for Public Opinion Research, University of Connecticut. http://www.ropercenter.uconn.edu. proxy.mul.missouri.edu/data_access/ipoll/ ipoll.html.

55. Gallup Poll (AIPO), Oct. 1976. Retrieved Oct. 27, 2014, from the iPOLL Databank, The Roper Center for Public Opinion Research, University of Connecticut. http:// www.ropercenter.uconn.edu.proxy.mul. missouri.edu/data_access/ipoll/ipoll.html.

56. CBS News/New York Times Poll, Sep. 1976. Retrieved Oct. 27, 2014, from the iPOLL Databank, The Roper Center for Public Opinion Research, University of Connecticut. http://www.ropercenter.uconn.edu. proxy.mul.missouri.edu/data_access/ipoll/ ipoll.html.

57. Harris Survey, Sep. 1976. Retrieved Oct. 27, 2014, from the iPOLL Databank, The Roper Center for Public Opinion Research, University of Connecticut. http://www.roper center.uconn.edu.proxy.mul.missouri.edu/ data_access/ipoll/ipoll.html.

58. Time/Yankelovich, Skelly & White Poll, Sep. 1976. Retrieved Oct. 27, 2014, from the iPOLL Databank, The Roper Center for Public Opinion Research, University of Connecticut. http://www.ropercenter.uconn.edu. proxy.mul.missouri.edu/data_access/ipoll/ ipoll.html.

59. Gallup Poll (AIPO), Oct. 1976. Retrieved Oct. 27, 2014, from the iPOLL Databank, The Roper Center for Public Opinion Research, University of Connecticut. http:// www.ropercenter.uconn.edu.proxy.mul. missouri.edu/data_access/ipoll/ipoll.html.

60. Steinmetz, "From New York! Smart Alecks!"

61. *Ibid.*

62. Marshall Fine, "The Comedy of Politics," *Cigar Aficionado*, 2011, 54.

63. Pat Caddell interview with the author, June 2009.

64. *Ibid.*

65. Jerry Rafshoon interview with the author, November 2009.

66. Dan Aykroyd interview with the author, April 2010.

67. Ron Nessen interview with the author, March 2009.

68. *Ibid.*

69. *Ibid.*

70. *Ibid.*

71. *Ibid.*

72. *Ibid.*

73. Nessen, 177.

74. Dan Aykroyd interview with the author, April 2010.

75. Michaels interview with the author, October 2010.

76. "Carter's Promises," *NBC's Saturday Night*, December 11, 1976, transcript at http:// snltranscripts.jt.org/76/76jcarter.phtml.

77. "Ask President Carter," *CBS Radio*, March 5, 1977, http://www.presidency.ucsb. edu/ws/?pid=7119.

78. Gerald Rafshoon interview with the author, June 2009.

79. "Ask President Carter," *Saturday Night Live*, March 12, 1977, transcript at http://snl-transcripts.jt.org/76/76ocarter.phtml.

80. Davis interview with the author, September 2009.

81. *Ibid.*

82. Dan Aykroyd interview with the author, April 2010.

Chapter 11

1. Blumenthal and Maracotta, 78.

2. "Weekend Update," *NBC's Saturday Night*, January 22, 1977, transcript at http://snltranscripts.jt.org/76/76lupdate.phtml.

3. Joseph Lelyveld, "The Prince of Plains," *New York Times*, June 26, 1977, 192.

4. "President Carter at Mardis Gras," *Saturday Night Live*, February 20, 1977, transcript at http://snltranscripts.jt.org/76/mgrascarter.phtml.

5. James T. Wooten, "Amy Carter Will Go To A Public School Near White House," *New York Times*, November 29, 1976, 1.

6. "Amy Carter in School," *NBC's Saturday Night*, January 29, 1977, transcript at http://snltranscripts.jt.org/76/76mamycarter.phtml.

7. "Amy's Bedtime Story," *Saturday Night Live*, March 12, 1977, transcript at http://snltranscripts.jt.org/76/76ocarter2.phtml

8. Lorne Michaels interview with the author, October 2010.

9. *Ibid.*

10. Frances Cerra, "Nader Says Carter Seems Ready to Pick Aides With Business Ties," *New York Times*, December 8, 1976, 22.

11. *Ibid.*

12. Hedrick Smith, "Strains in Carter Transition," *New York Times*, December 10, 1976, 53.

13. Leslie H. Gelb, "Carter Finding Few Outsiders," *New York Times*, December 16, 1976, 21.

14. *Ibid.*

15. "Weekend Update," *NBC's Saturday Night*, January 15, 1977, transcript at http://snltranscripts.jt.org/76/76kupdate.phtml.

16. "Carter's Confederate Takeover," *Saturday Night Live*, January 15, 1977, transcript at http://snltranscripts.jt.org/76/76kcarter.phtml.

17. Joseph Lelyveld, "Blacks & Young," *New York Times Magazine,* February 6, 1977, SM19.

18. Julian Bond, "Opening Monologue," *Saturday Night Live*, April 10, 1977, transcript at http://snltranscripts.jt.org/76/76rmono.phtml.

19. Wayne King, "Carter's Church May Dismiss Pastor For His Role in Dispute Over Blacks," *New York Times*, November 2, 1976,

19; "Carter Pastor Asks Meeting to Discuss Possible Resignation," *New York Times*, November 4, 1976, 28.

20. "Weekend Update," *Saturday Night Live*, November 13, 1976, transcript at http://snltranscripts.jt.org/76/76gupdate.phtml.

21. "Mr. Mike Meets Uncle Remus," *Saturday Night Live*, April 9, 1977, transcript at http://snltranscripts.jt.org/76/76rmrmike.phtml.

22. "Alabama Improvements," *NBC's Saturday Night*, April 9, 1977, transcript at http://snltranscripts.jt.org/76/76rwallace.phtml.

23. Julian Bond, interview with the author, January 9, 2010.

24. Carter later had two other women, Juanita Kreps, Secretary of Commerce, and Shirley Hufstedler, Secretary of Education, in his administration, but no other African Americans.

25. "An Oval Office," *Saturday Night Live*, 1977, transcript at http://snltranscripts.jt.org/76/76rcarter.phtml.

26. Julian Bond interview with the author, January 9, 2010.

27. "Cold Open," *SNL*, October 3, 2015. Transcribed by the author.

28. "Cold Open," *SNL*, October 17, 2015. Transcribed by the author.

29. "Cold Open," *SNL*, November 7, 2015. Transcribed by the author.

30. "Opening Monologue," *SNL*, November 7, 2015. Transcribed by the author.

31. "White House 2018," *SNL*, November 7, 2015. Transcribed by the author.

32. "Cold Open," *SNL*, January 23, 2016. Transcribed by the author.

33. "Cold Open," *SNL*, February 13, 2016. Transcribed by the author.

34. There was one more episode, broadcast on April 23, which was a tribute to Prince and featured previously broadcast material.

35. "Cold Open," *SNL*, February 13, 2016.

36. "Cold Open," *SNL*, October 1, 2016.

37. "Cold Open," *SNL*, October 8, 2016.

38. "Day Off," *SNL*, October 8, 2016.

39. "Cold Open," *SNL*, October 15, 2016.

40. "Cold Open," *SNL*, October 22, 2016.

41. "Cold Open," *SNL*, January 14, 2017.

42. "Cold Open," *SNL*, January 21, 2017.

43. "Cold Open," *SNL*, March 4, 2017.

44. "Press Conference," *SNL*, February 4, 2017.

Selected References

Interviews

Dan Aykroyd
Julian Bond
Pat Caddell
Jimmy Carter

Tom Davis
Lorne Michaels
Ron Nessen
Bob Orben

Jerry Rafshoon
Richard Reeves
Kenan Thompson
Gary Weis

Periodicals and Newspapers

Associated Press
Boston Globe
Chicago Tribune
Cigar Aficionado
Contemporary
Contemporary Politics
Harper's

Journal of Politics
Los Angeles Times
New York Magazine
New York Times
The New Yorker
Playboy
Rolling Stone

Time
TV Guide
United Press International
Variety
The Village Voice
Wall St. Journal
Washington Post

Archives

Gerald R. Ford Presidential Papers, the Gerald R. Ford Presidential Library, Ann Arbor, MI.

Websites

The American Presidency Project, http://www.presidency.ucsb.edu/
The Center for Media and Public Affairs, www.cmpa.com
iPoll, Roper Center Public Opinion Archives, www.ropercenter.uconn.edu/data_access/
    ipoll/ipoll.html
The Miller Center, http://millercenter.org
The Project for Excellence in Journalism, www.journalism.org
Saturday Night Live Transcripts, www.snltranscripts.jt.org
The SNL Archives, www.snl.jt.org

Books

Auslander, Philip. *Liveness: Performance in a Mediatized Culture.* London: Routledge, 2008.
Baumgartner, Jody C., and Jonathan S. Morris. *Laughing Matters: Humor and American Politics in the Media Age.* London: Routledge, 2008.

Baym, Geoffrey, and Jeffrey P. Jones. *News Parody and Political Satire Across the Globe*. London: Routledge, 2013.

Bial, Henry, ed. *The Performance Studies Reader*. London: Routledge, 2004.

Bianculli, David. *Dangerously Funny: The Uncensored Story of The Smothers Brothers Comedy Hour*. New York: Simon & Schuster, 2009.

Caesar, Sid, and Bill Davidson. *Where Have I Been? Sid Casear: An Autobiography*. New York: Crown, 1982.

Carpenter, Humphrey. *A Great, Silly Grin: The British Satire Boom of the 1960s*. New York: Public Affairs, 2000.

Carter, Jimmy. *Keeping Faith*. New York: Bantam Books, 1982.

Carter, Jimmy. *Why Not the Best?* New York: Bantam Books, 1976.

Dallek, Robert. *Flawed Giant: Lyndon Johnson and His Times, 1961–1973*. Oxford: Oxford University Press, 1998.

Davis, Tom. *39 Years of Short-Term Memory Loss*. New York: Grove Press, 2009.

Denton, Robert E., Jr., ed. *The 2008 Presidential Campaign: A Communication Perspective*. Lanham, MD: Rowman & Littlefield, 2009.

DeRoche, Andrew. *Andrew Young: Civil Rights Ambassador*. Wilmington, DE: SR Books, 2002.

Fey, Tina. *Bossypants*. New York: Little, Brown, 2011.

Fiske, Susan T., and Shelley E. Taylor. *Social Cognition*, 2d ed. New York: McGraw-Hill, 1991.

Ford, Gerald R. *Humor and the Presidency*. New York: Arbor House, 1987.

Ford, Gerald R. *A Time to Heal*. New York: Harper and Row, 1979.

Fortier, Mark. *Theory/Theatre: An Introduction*. London: Routledge, 2002.

Fotis, Matthew. *Long Form Improvisation and American Comedy: The Harold*. New York: Palgrave, 2014.

Frankel, Max. *The Times of My Life*. New York: Random House, 1999.

Frost, David. *David Frost: An Autobiography: Part One From Congregations to Audiences*. New York: HarperCollins, 1993.

Fruchter, Rena. *I'm Chevy Chase and You're Not*. London: Virgin Books, 2007.

Gardner, Carl. *Andrew Young: A Biography*. New York: Drake, 1978.

Gardner, Gerald. *All the Presidents' Wits*. New York: William Morrow, 1986.

Gardner, Gerald. *Campaign Comedy: Political Humor from Clinton to Kennedy*. Detroit: Wayne State Press, 1994.

Gelbart, Larry. *Laughing Matters*. New York: Random House, 1988.

Gerould, Daniel. *Theatre/Theory/Theatre: The Major Critical Texts from Aristotle and Zeami to Soyinka and Havel*. New York: Applause, 2003.

Glad, Betty. *Jimmy Carter: In Search of the Great White House*. New York: W.W. Norton, 1980.

Greene, Doyle. *Politics and the American Television Comedy: A Critical Survey from I Love Lucy Through South Park*. Jefferson, NC: McFarland, 2008.

Greene, John Robert. *The Presidency of Gerald R. Ford*. Lawrence: University of Kansas Press, 1995.

Hartmann, Robert. *Palace Politics*. New York: McGraw-Hill, 1980.

Heim, Caroline. *Audience as Performer*. London: Routledge, 2016.

Hill, Doug, and Jeff Weingrad. *Saturday Night*. New York: Vintage, 1986.

Inman, David. *Television Variety Shows*. Jefferson, NC: McFarland, 2006.

Jamieson, Kathleen Hall, and Paul Waldman. *The Press Effect*. Oxford: Oxford University Press, 2003.

Karnow, Stanley. *Vietnam: A History*. New York: Penguin Books, 1983.

Kercher, Stephen E. *Revel with a Cause: Liberal Satire in Postwar America*. Chicago: University of Chicago, 2006.

Kraus, Sidney, ed. *The Great Debates: Carter vs. Ford, 1976*. Bloomington: Indiana University Press, 1979.

Lichter, S. Robert, Jody C. Baumgartner, and Jonathon S. Morris. *Politics Is a Joke: How TV Comedians Are Remaking Political Life.* Boulder: Westview Press, 2015.

MacDonald, John D., ed. *A Friendship: The Letters of Dan Rowan and John D. MacDonald 1967–1974.* New York: Alfred A. Knopf, 1986.

Malarcher, Jay. *The Classically American Comedy of Larry Gelbart.* Lanham, MD: Scarecrow Press, 2003.

Martin, Justin. *Nader: Crusader, Spoiler, Icon.* Cambridge, MA: Perseus, 2002.

Marx, Nick, Matt Sienkiewicz, and Ron Becker. *Saturday Night Live & American TV.* Bloomington: Indiana University Press, 2013.

McCarry, Charles. 1972. *Citizen Nader.* New York: Saturday Review Press.

McClennen, Sophia. *Colbert's America: Satire and Democracy.* New York: Palgrave, 2011.

McGinniss, Joe. *The Selling of the President 1968.* New York: Trident Press, 1969.

McLuhan, Marshall. *Understanding Media.* New York: McGraw-Hill, 1964.

Mullen, Megan. *The Rise of Cable Programming in the United States.* Austin: University of Texas Press, 2003.

Nachman, Gerald. *Seriously Funny.* New York: Random House, 2003.

Nessen, Ron. *It Sure Looks Different from the Inside.* Chicago: Playboy Press, 1978.

Nixon, Richard. *RN: The Memoirs of Richard Nixon.* New York: Grosset & Dunlap, 1978.

O'Connor, John E., ed. *American History, American Television: Interpreting the Video Past.* New York: Frederick Ungar, 1983.

Partridge, Marianne, ed. *Rolling Stone Visits Saturday Night Live.* New York: Dolphin Books, 1979.

Patterson, Thomas. *Out of Order.* New York: Vintage Books, 1994.

Patterson, Thomas E., and Robert D. McClure. *The Unseeing Eye: The Myth of Television Power in National Politics.* New York: G.P. Putnam's Sons, 1977.

The Presidential Campaign 1976, Volume One, Part One. Washington, D.C.: United States Government Printing Office, 1978.

Reeves, Richard. *A Ford, Not a Lincoln.* New York: Harcourt Brace Jovanovich, 1975.

Reeves, Richard. *What the People Know: Freedom and the Press.* Cambridge: Harvard University Press, 1999.

Reinelt, Janice, and Joseph Roach, eds. *Critical Theory and Performance.* Ann Arbor: University of Michigan Press, 2007.

Rico, Diana. *Kovacsland: A Biography of Ernie Kovacs.* New York: Harcourt, Brace, and Jovanovich, 1990.

Robinson, Peter M. *The Dance of the Comedians: The People, the President, and the Performance of Political Standup Comedy in America.* Amherst: University of Massachusetts Press, 2012.

Rowan, Ford. *Broadcast Fairness: Doctrine, Practice, Prospects.* New York: Longman, 1985.

Schlesinger, Robert. *White House Ghosts: Presidents and Their Speechwriters.* New York: Simon & Schuster, 2008.

Schram, Martin. *Running for President: A Journal of the Carter Campaign.* New York: Pocket Books, 1977.

Shales, Tom, and James Andrew Miller. *Live From New York: An Uncensored History of Saturday Night Live.* New York: Little, Brown, 2002.

Sherman, Jon Foley. *A Strange Proximity: Stage Presence, Failure and the Ethics of Attention.* London: Routledge, 2016.

Spolin, Viola. *Improvisation for the Theater: A Handbook of Teaching and Directing Techniques.* Evanston, IL: Northwestern University Press, 1963.

Strinati, Dominic, and Stephen Wagg, eds. *Come On Down? Popular Media Culture in Post-War Britain.* New York: Routledge, 1992.

TerHorst, Jerald. *Gerald Ford and the Future of the Presidency.* New York: The Third Press, 1974.

Thompson, Hunter S. *Gonzo Papers, Vol. 1: The Great Shark Hunt, Strange Tales from a Strange Time.* New York: Simon & Schuster, 2014.

Thompson, Kenneth W., ed. *Ford Presidency: Twenty-Two Intimate Perspectives of Gerald R. Ford.* New York: University Press of America, 1998.

Udall, Morris K. *Too Funny To Be President.* Tucson: University of Arizona Press, 1988.

Werth, Barry. *31 Days: The Crisis That Gave Us the Government We Have Today.* New York: Doubleday, 2006.

Witcover, Jules. *Marathon: The Pursuit of the Presidency, 1972–1976.* New York: The Viking Press, 1977.

Scholarly Articles and Book Chapters

Baum, Matthew A. "Sex, Lies, and War: How Soft News Brings Foreign Policy to the Inattentive Public." *American Political Science Review* 96, no. 1 (2002): 91–108.

Baum, Matthew A. "Talking the Vote: Why Presidential Candidates Hit the Talk Show Circuit." *American Journal of Political Science* 49, no. 2 (2006).

Baumgartner, Jody, and Jonathan S. Morris. "The Daily Show Effect: Candidate Evaluations, Efficacy, and American Youth." *American Politics Research* 34, no. 3 (2006).

Baumgartner, Jody, Jonathan S. Morris, and Natsha L. Walth. "The Fey Effect: Young Adults, Political Humor, and Perceptions of Sarah Palin in the 2008 Presidential Election Campaign." *Public Opinion Quarterly* 102 (2012).

Baym, Geoffrey. "Representation and the Politics of Play: Stephen Colbert's Better Know a District." *Political Communication* 24, no. 4(2007): 359–376.

Baym, Geoffrey. "Serious Comedy: The Expanding Boundaries of Political Discourse." In *Laughing Matters: Humor and American Politics in the Media Age,* ed. Jody Baumgartner and Jonathan Morris. London: Routledge, 2007. 21–37.

Blumenthal, John and Lindsay Maracotta. "Playboy Interview: 'NBC's Saturday Night.'" *Playboy* (May, 1977): 63–228.

Brewer, Paul R., and Xiaoxia Cao. "Candidate Appearances on Soft News Shows and Public Knowledge About Primary Campaigns." *Journal of Broadcasting and Electronic Media* 50, no. 1 (2006): 18–35.

Day, Amber, and Ethan Thompson. "Live from New York. It's the Fake News! Saturday Night Live and the (Non)Politics of Parody." *Popular Communication* 10, nos. 1–2 (2012): 170–182.

Delli Carpini, Michael X., and Bruce A. Williams. 2001. "Let us Infotain You: Politics in the New Media Environment." In *Mediated Politics: Communication in The Future of Democracy,* ed. W. Lance Bennett and Robert M. Entman. Cambridge: Cambridge University Press, 2000.

Esralew, Sarah E. *The Influence of Parodies on Political Schemas: Exploring the Tina Fey-Sarah Palin Phenomenon.* Master's Thesis, University of Delaware, 2009.

Graber, Doris. "Conclusion: Why Humor is Serious Business." *Laughing Matters: Humor and American Politics in the Media Age,* ed. Jody Baumgartner and Jonathan Morris. London: Routledge, 2007.

Jones, Jeffrey P. *Entertaining Politics: Satiric Television and Political Engagement,* 2d ed. Lanham, MD: Rowman and Littlefield, 2010.

Jones, Jeffrey P. "Politics and the Brand: Saturday Night Live's Campaign Season Humor." In *Saturday Night Live and American TV,* ed. Nick Marx, Matt Sienkiewicz and Ron Becker. Bloomington: Indiana University Press, 2013.

Jones, Jeffrey P. "Pop Goes the Campaign: The Repopularization of Politics in Election 2008." In *The 2008 Presidential Campaign: A Communication Perspective,* ed. Robert E. Denton, Jr. Lanham, MD: Rowman & Littlefield, 2009. 170–90.

Jones, Jeffrey P. "With All Due Respect: Satirizing Presidents from Saturday Night Live to Lil' Bush." In *Satire TV: Politics and Comedy in the Post-Network Era*, ed. Jonathan Gray, Jeffrey P. Jones and Ethan Thompson. New York: New York University Press, 2009. 37–63.

Jones, Jeffrey P., Geoffrey Baym, and Amber Day. 2012. "Mr. Stewart and Mr. Colbert Go to Washington: Television Satirists Outside the Box." *Social Research* 79, no. 1 (2012): 33–60.

Jones, Jeffrey P., Jonathan Gray, and Ethan Thompson. "The State of Satire, the Satire of State." In *Satire TV: Politics and Comedy in the Post-Network Era*, ed. Jonathan Gray, Jeffrey P. Jones and Ethan Thompson. New York: New York University Press, 2009. 3–36.

Moy, Patricia, Michael A. Xenos, and Verena K. Hess. "Priming Effects of Late-Night Comedy." *International Journal of Public Opinion Research* 18, no. 2 (2005): 198–210.

Osborne-Thompson, Heather. "Tracing the 'Fake' Candidate in American Television Comedy." In *Satire TV: Politics and Comedy in the Post-Network Era*, ed. Jonathan Gray, Jeffrey P. Jones and Ethan Thompson. New York: New York University Press, 2009. 3–36.

Pfau, Michael, J. Brian Houston, and Shane M. Semmler, "Presidential Election Campaigns and American Democracy: The Relationship Between Communication Use and Normative Outcomes," *American Behavioral Scientist* 49, no. 1 (September 2005): 48–62.

Shaker, Lee. "Dead Newspapers and Citizens' Civic Engagement." *Political Communication* 31, no. 1 (2014): 131–148.

Tversky, Amos, and Daniel Kahneman. "Judgment Under Uncertainty: Heuristics and Biases." *Science*. 185, no. 4157 (1974): 1124–31.

Voth, Ben. "Saturday Night Live and Presidential Elections." In *Humor and American Politics in the Media Age*, ed. Jody C. Baumgartner and Jonathan S. Morris. London: Routledge, 2008.

Weber, Christopher. "Emotions, Campaigns and Political Participation." *Political Research Quarterly* 66, no. 2 (2012): 414–428.

Williams, Bruce A., and Michael X. Delli Carpini. "Heeeeeeeeeeeere's Democracy!" *Chronicle of Higher Education* 48, no. 32 (April 19, 2002).

Young, Dannagal Goldthwaite. "Late-Night Comedy in Election 2000: Its Influence on Candidate Trait Ratings and the Moderating Effects of Political Knowledge and Partisanship." *Broadcasting and Electronic Media* 48, no. 1 (2004).

Index